The Therapeutic Tu

CW00348910

'9
⌐ ⌐7
37

In what ways has psychology become more influential in Western society? In this book author Ole Jacob Madsen considers the notion of a 'therapeutic turn' in Western culture – the tendency for psychology to permeate ever new spheres within society.

The Therapeutic Turn evaluates the increasing prevalence of psychology in several areas of Western society: Western consumer culture, contemporary Christianity, self-help, sport and politics. Madsen proposes that there are problematic aspects to this development which are seldom recognised owing to a widely held assumption that 'the more psychology, the better for everyone'. A recurring concern with psychological solutions is that they often provide individual solutions to structural problems. As a result, psychologists may be inadvertently increasing the burden on the shoulders of the people they are meant to help and, at the same time, our capacity to understand individual suffering in the light of major historical and political changes in society is becoming increasingly clouded.

The Therapeutic Turn presents an accessible and engaging critique of the influence of psychology within Western society. It will appeal to a broad audience of students, academics and general readers interested in this aspect of modernity and contemporary society, and it will also be of great interest to practitioners and therapists.

Ole Jacob Madsen is Associate Professor at the Department of Psychology at the University of Oslo, Norway. His primary field of research interest is the unfolding of 'the therapeutic culture' in Scandinavia and the consequent new societal ethical dilemmas facing professional psychologists.

Concepts for critical psychology: disciplinary boundaries re-thought
Series editor: Ian Parker

Developments inside psychology that question the history of the discipline and the way it functions in society have led many psychologists to look outside the discipline for new ideas. This series draws on cutting edge critiques from just outside psychology in order to complement and question critical arguments emerging inside. The authors provide new perspectives on subjectivity from disciplinary debates and cultural phenomena adjacent to traditional studies of the individual.

The books in the series are useful for advanced level undergraduate and postgraduate students, researchers and lecturers in psychology and other related disciplines such as cultural studies, geography, literary theory, philosophy, psychotherapy, social work and sociology.

Published Titles:

Surviving Identity
Vulnerability and the psychology
  of recognition
Kenneth McLaughlin

**Psychologisation in Times of
  Globalisation**
Jan De Vos

Social Identity in Question
Construction, subjectivity and
  critique
Parisa Dashtipour

Cultural Ecstasies
Drugs, gender and the social
  imaginary
Ilana Mountian

**Decolonizing Global Mental
  Health**
The psychiatrization of the
  majority world
China Mills

Self Research
The intersection of therapy and
  research
Ian Law

The Therapeutic Turn
How psychology altered Western
  culture
Ole Jacob Madsen

The Therapeutic Turn

How psychology altered
Western culture

Ole Jacob Madsen

Routledge
Taylor & Francis Group

LONDON AND NEW YORK

First published 2014
by Routledge
27 Church Road, Hove, East Sussex BN3 2FA

and by Routledge
711 Third Avenue, New York, NY 10017

Routledge is an imprint of the Taylor & Francis Group, an informa business

This work is an adaptation and translation of a previously published
work in Norwegian: Ole Jacob Madsen. *Den terapeutiske kultur* (2010)
Universitetsforlaget. Translation to English by Diane Oatley.

British Library Cataloguing in Publication Data
A catalogue record for this book is available from the British Library

Library of Congress Cataloging in Publication Data
Madsen, Ole Jacob,1978-
The therapeutic turn: how psychology altered Western culture/
Ole Jacob Madsen.
Pages cm
Includes bibliographical references and index.
1. Psychology — History. 2. Civilization, Western. 3. Psychoanalysis
and culture. I. Title.
BF81.M33 2014
150.9—dc23
2013050065

ISBN: 978-1-138-01868-6 (hbk)
ISBN: 978-1-138-01869-3 (pbk)
ISBN: 978-1-315-77958-4 (ebk)

Typeset in Times New Roman
by Swales & Willis Ltd, Exeter, Devon, UK

MIX
Paper from
responsible sources
FSC
www.fsc.org   FSC® C013056

Printed and bound in Great Britain by
TJ International Ltd, Padstow, Cornwall

Contents

Foreword   vii
Preface   ix

1   Introduction   1

2   The consumer self   11

3   Crisis of authority: Philip Rieff's critique of
    Freud's worldview   29

4   Psychology and religion   45

    Interlude: psychology in crisis?   65

5   The self-help culture   69

6   Psychology and sports   93

7   Psychology and neoliberalism   109

8   The ethos of the psychology profession   135

9   Conclusion   155

References   173
Index   189

Foreword

This book is about therapy, but it takes a step back from what we think we know about therapy to show us something quite different. Far from therapy being a side-show of psychology, one of the places where psychological knowledge is put to work, therapeutic ideas saturate the discipline of psychology today. Psychology, as something turned therapeutic, together with psychotherapy as such pervade contemporary culture. Ole Jacob Madsen's concern with the way that psychology 'altered' Western culture should therefore be understood in its most extreme exaggerated sense; he will show you that it is not at all far-fetched to claim that the 'psychologisation' we are being subjected to today is a thoroughly therapeutic psychologisation that invites you, incites you, even requires you to speak, to speak about how you feel. If you can speak like that, speak about your feelings as if you were in therapy, then at the very least the psychologists who have been deeply altered by the therapeutic turn will understand what you are saying and will see you as one of their own.

A crucial part of the argument, a point that is driven home time and again in this book explicitly and surreptitiously, is that this therapeutic psychologisation is a global phenomenon. We find this argument at work in the apparently innocent detailed accounts of the way therapeutic discourse frames scientific debate, discussions of psychoanalytic theory, spirituality, self-help media projects, sport and politics in Norway. Does this mean that all of this only applies to Norway, and that if we were to strip out the Norwegian examples we would be left with the good old psychology that we already know so well? In fact, each separate domain testifies not only to the degree to which a therapeutic way of being a human subject has implanted itself; whatever our particular interests, a shock of recognition will disturb the reader wherever they are on the planet. Norway is a fairly small and privileged country, and we are forced to ask ourselves how, if the therapeutic turn has been felt in such an intense way there, we can resist it anywhere else. And, given that Norway is such a powerful influence in human rights work, how would it be possible for the countries of the developing world given aid by it to say no to the therapeutic discourse that accompanies its well-meaning helping hand?

Psychology specialises in the reduction of phenomena to the level of the individual, and it treats as unvarying 'essence' the phenomena that it describes, attempting to find these essential components of human psychology inside every individual everywhere in the world. The discipline of psychology has, in that sense, been ahead of the game in terms of individualisation of experience and in terms of globalisation. The 'therapeutic turn' described in this book thus brings to fruition exactly the kinds of problems that we 'critical psychologists' have been concerned with as problems to be solved. In this book, *The Therapeutic Turn: How Psychology Altered Western Culture*, we see how the problems that critical psychology identified are given even more import than they ever had, and then they are exported around the world. The book traverses the borders of the discipline and shows how psychology crosses national borders in attempts to make itself relevant to those outside the discipline. The book itself moves backwards and forwards from the inside of psychology to its place in popular culture, speaking in this way 'outwith' the discipline and giving us new ways of understanding what psychology does as it attempts to understand us.

Ian Parker
University of Leicester

Preface

Being part of a privileged generation with a range of opportunities, I wondered for a long time about what education I should choose. Sometime in the mid-1990s I flicked through a prospectus from the University of Bergen. It contained ads that would entice young inquisitive students to the various degree programmes, and one of these was psychology. I no longer remember the description, but the illustration made a lasting impression on me: a curious young scientist wearing a white lab coat occupied in examining the skull of a human being. The picture must have been taken before the fMRI machine was introduced in psychology, for the man in the picture kept the skull in his hand. The scientist and Hamlet combined into one sounded alluring, so psychology became my choice. Later, I was disappointed. Hamlet had long ago been forced out of the picture. I got a feeling that modern psychology no longer had anything to say about the human condition. In line with the growth of the scientific reputation of psychology, the questions asked seemed increasingly microscopic. The underlying positivism or scientism in this approach is not the most deplorable aspect of it all, in my opinion. It is rather the fact there is only something sterile left behind. It is of little consolation that this presumably is 'the universal'. The outcome is a discipline and a profession that is poorly equipped to understand the present, while it simultaneously exercises a great influence on it. Thus, the problem of psychology's lack of reflexivity becomes society's problem. Its ethical shortcomings are no longer only of limited interest. Thus, the aim of this book is to introduce both professional psychologists and readers concerned with social issues to the consequences following on from psychology's march into Western culture.

I would like to thank Ian Parker and Senior Editor Michael Strang at Routledge for their interest and support, which has made this book possible.

Ole Jacob Madsen

Moss, 15 October 2013

1   Introduction

All the great problems of our age are becoming more and more psychological the better we understand them. The world needs a new psychology larger in all its dimensions more than it needs anything else.

(Granville Stanley Hall, 1923, p. 437)

Granville Stanley Hall (1844–1924) was the first president of the American Psychological Association (APA) and one of the founders of modern psychology. Like most of the pioneers within the profession, Hall had an unshakeable belief in the idea that the more psychological our understanding of ourselves and society is, the better. With this book my intention is (1) to demonstrate that psychology today continues to operate in accordance with Hall's basic assumption that 'the more psychology, the better', and (2) to present some critical objections to the widespread perception that most of the problems of society should be viewed and handled psychologically.

Although psychology has only been in existence as an independent science and discipline for approximately 135 years, it has nonetheless had an enormous impact on Western culture. The latter for its own part has been assigned contemporary diagnoses such as 'the age of psychology' (Havemann, 1957), 'the triumph of the therapeutic' (Rieff, 1987), 'the psychological society' (Gross, 1978), 'the therapeutic state' (Nolan, 1998; Polsky, 1991) and 'therapy culture' (Furedi, 2004; Imber, 2004). The French sociologist Alain Ehrenberg (2007) has therefore maintained that psychology can no longer be understood in purely scientific terms, but must also be viewed against the background of a cultural climate in which the individual personality has been made the subject of an enormous social and medical interest. In contrast to psychiatry, which is a relatively peripheral institution with a limited range of impact, psychology and the emotional life must be considered the key juncture between the private and political spheres, where the most important contradictions of modern society now find expression. Cultural sociologist Eva Illouz (2008) makes the argument that *a therapeutic ethos* now transcends all national borders and regional differences, hereby providing the basis for a global psychological mentality and discourse about individuality. She claims that no other cultural framework, with the exception of political liberalism and market liberalism's economic logic of profit, has exercised as much influence on the twentieth century's ideas about the individual. The Danish psychologist Svend Brinkmann (2008) has stated that modern psychology has become so predominant in our understanding of ourselves and the surrounding world that it constitutes what the philosopher Charles Taylor (2004) has called a social imaginary, which is not only a specific theory espoused by many about the nature of the world, but the very framework comprising our theories about ourselves and the world.

Modern psychology underwent a rapid development following its establishment as an autonomous, small and experimental science in 1879 in Leipzig, Germany, expanding into a broadly applied science and professional expertise in increasingly more areas of society throughout the course of the twentieth century. As a profession, psychology experienced its first breakthrough in the USA and this geographical 'power shift' from Europe to the USA occurred after Hall invited the leading psychoanalysts of the time to the States in 1909. During the crossing from Europe, in transit to what the historians view as the great inauguration journey and breakthrough of psychoanalysis in the USA – the Clarke lectures of 1909 – Sigmund Freud is alleged to have said to his crown prince Carl Jung: 'they do not know that we bring them the plague' (as cited in Strong, 1984, p. 65). Freud and psychoanalysis were to enjoy a unique penetration of American society throughout the course of the twentieth century. Most of the critical studies of the therapeutic ethos – which often address the issue of psychology's impact on culture – have therefore been written by American sociologists and historians about the USA. There are, however, many signs from the period indicating that the 'cultural plague', Freud's tongue-in-cheek characterisation of psychological ethics, returned to Europe with unmitigated force just a few years later (Rieff, 1987). In today's postmodern, globalised media reality, psychology is propagated along the same lines as other cultural impulses from the USA, such as the entertainment industry. Illouz (2008) maintains that the transmission of psychology is taking place on a scale comparable to that of Hollywood films. Nonetheless, if the descriptions of the therapeutic culture seem somewhat exaggerated from a Norwegian perspective, we should perhaps understand them as a crystal ball providing a vision of the future, rather than reject them out of hand as having little relevance for us (Vetlesen, 2009b).

Implicit in a contemporary diagnosis such as 'the therapeutic society' is the perception that as a phenomenon it extends beyond the incidence of psychological disorders in the population and the clinical expertise employed to treat them. The term is testimony to the fact that therapeutic solutions have overstepped the bounds of the therapist's office. Historian T. J. Jackson Lears (1983) has described the transition from the nineteenth to the twentieth century as an important moral shift in the West, from the Protestant ethic, rooted in the belief in salvation through ascetic self-denial, to a therapeutic ethos offering self-realisation in this life, where the objective is no longer salvation, but attainment of the best physical and psychological health possible. Lears is quick to emphasise that there is nothing historically new about people having an interest in emotional or physical well-being. All cultures, from antiquity to the present day, have probably contained a therapeutic dimension (Ekeland, 1999). What is new is that the therapeutic ethos is introduced as a promise of liberation that does not depend on God or other transcendent, eternal entity, but for the first time in history is based exclusively on the self (Lears, 1983). Freud's psychoanalysis and the subsequent, general psychological movement have therefore unfolded in a situation that is new, historically speaking – involving the cultivation of an individualised and therapeutic culture of rights, in which psychology and the self, respectively, replace religion and God(s), and the role of authority or duty in establishing the position of the individual in society.

Psychology has today become a central part of the social reality and mass culture. A number of historians now claim that psychology and psychotherapy have become commonplace and demystified, so it is in particular through popular culture genres such as self-help literature, health tips and therapeutic reality TV that the therapeutic message is being spread. The popular American monthly magazine *Psychology Today* (1967–) communicates well the split personality of today's psychology, containing everything from self-help advice to the latest scientific research. Here you will find answers to how you can find the most suitable therapist for your needs, and where you can study to become a psychologist. The magazine advertises anti-depressants and weight-loss drinks side by side. The entire message is packaged in a glossy, appealing format, reflecting that psychology has become or is well on its way to becoming something attractive and positive and is no longer in any sense shameful or mysterious. 'Mental life' has quite simply assumed its rightful place within the enormous focus health has come to receive in the daily lives of ordinary people and the media in Western culture. Thus *Psychology Today* provides a precise image of the state of psychology at a time when psychology, much like health in general, has become a boundless and never-ending project, a point which is substantiated by the definition of health presented by the World Health Organization (2006, p. 1) in 1948: 'Health is a state of complete physical, mental and social well-being and not merely the absence of disease or infirmity.'

Over the course of recent decades psychology has also appeared in areas of society that one would not automatically expect, such as in the worlds of finance and sports, which one would assume were first and foremost about monetary and physical values, respectively. The financial crisis of 2007–2010 summoned a steady stream of economic experts who told us that the crisis was about 'the psychology in the market'. Traditional economic theory was even criticised for not taking into account the psychology of consumers to a sufficient extent (Akerlof and Shiller, 2009). By contrast a popular reality TV concept like the *Luxury Trap* now logically features psychologists alongside economic experts, in order to best aid couples troubled with unpaid bills and credit card debts.

This book was largely written in the period between two Olympic Games during which psychology came to receive a great deal of attention in the media coverage. Norwegian athletes in the Summer Olympics in Beijing 2008, such as the speed walker Kjersti Tysse Plätzer, received emotional training with a psychologist throughout, while the handball player Tonje Larsen needed psychological help for insomnia. For the Norwegian women's football team in Beijing, their psychologist was an important weapon, in that nobody was as well prepared in terms of the 'mental part' as they were (Brenna, 2008). The American swimming star Michael Phelps became the poster child for the positive channelling of ADHD's ecstatic energy (cf. Parker-Pope, 2008), while Norway's silver medallist in the 100 metre breast stroke, Alexander Dale Oen, stated in an interview with the Norwegian Broadcasting Corporation that the secret of his success was not first and foremost his physique or technique but his self-confidence. During the Winter Olympics in Vancouver in 2010 a year and a half later, the tendency to make reference to 'the mental part' was even more pronounced – the support team was made up of four psychologists offering 24-hour acute follow-up of the Norwegian athletes and scarcely a single day passed without 'nerves out of control' or 'emotional fortitude' being offered as an explanation for the difference between victory and defeat. As the president of the Norwegian Psychological Association, Tor Levin Hofgaard (2010), could proudly state in his official blog: 'Psychology strikes gold in the Olympics'.

How are we to understand this development? Is the increased focus on psychology today an expression of the fact that we live in a sicker society or that we have less tolerance for deviance? Or, to the contrary, does it mean that today we have greater openness and better scientific and technological methods, along with more resources than before, which make it possible to both treat unwanted psychological disorders and work with oneself emotionally in ways unknown to previous generations? The question of psychology's status touches in a sense upon the important questions of our time about late modernity and the direction in which society in heading: is everything getting better, or is everything getting worse? Or alternatively: What do we gain and what do we lose? These questions are naturally so general that it is impossible to give a single, conclusive answer. But this nonetheless does not mean that one should refrain from asking this type of question. In fact, the psychology profession is ethically bound to do so, as the ethical guidelines stipulate that a psychologist shall be 'attentive' to and 'responsible' for the society in which he or she is practising (Norwegian Psychological Association, 1998).

Psychology as a science and profession has in a relatively short period of time succeeded in becoming a key social stakeholder and important form of expertise, consulted in areas far afield from its traditional knowledge domains, which have primarily been the therapeutic couch and research laboratory. As psychology acquires more power and influence than ever before, it also acquires greater responsibility. That is as it should be. As the uncle of the super-hero Spider-Man said: 'With great power comes great responsibility.' This Marvel Comics series was produced by the artist Stan Lee during the Cold War and it has therefore been interpreted as a critical admonition about the abuse of science and technology (Genter, 2007). The German sociologist Ulrich Beck (1992) claims in his influential work *Risk Society* that one of the most important changes and challenges of late modernity is society's increasing dependence on scientific and technological knowledge. As scientific and technological advancements entail a greater risk than formerly was the case, with the potential to destroy the earth, it becomes critical to our survival that scientific and technological expertise includes a practice of critical self-reflection, particularly since politicians cannot be expected to have an understanding of all of the dilemmas inherent in new technological developments. Political scientist Erik Oddvar Eriksen (2001) has used the telling image 'democracy's black hole' as a metaphor for the power wielded by the professions today, a power which is, however, seldom the topic of public debate or investigation. Politicians are at the mercy of experts – and it is then to be expected that the experts take their social duty seriously and critically reflect upon the positive and negative consequences of their own enterprise. Although psychology is not in possession of nuclear weapons or atomic power, which is certainly what Stan Lee and Ulrich Beck had in mind, I will show here that psychology's potential to do damage is absolutely not insignificant. Psychology has assumed an important mission: namely, the management of human suffering and – as was the case with its predecessor, Christianity – it can offer relief and comfort, but also in some cases become the very source of the suffering itself. 'Thou who can heal can also make sick', as the old saying goes. The idea that modern, evidence-based psychotherapy or psychology can potentially have such destructive effects is however not to be found in the profession's optimistic 'upgrading programme'. This is cause for concern and the point of departure for this book.

Chapter overview

In the next chapter (2) I address psychology's role in the establishment of the modern consumer society. Here I show how the relation between psychology and economy has been of great importance historically to ensure the functioning of the market economy. 'The economic human being' is of necessity also a 'psychological human being' in that psychological constructs such as 'the empty self', individualisation and self-realisation exert influence on the individual consumer as potent cultural and political imperatives. Psychology and capitalism have therefore a complex interconnection.

Chapter 3 covers the crisis of authority in the West – which would imply the problems that arise in modern society when traditional social roles and norms are abandoned. Here I devote particular attention to Philip Rieff's reading of Sigmund Freud as a philosophical and political theorist. Freud's psychoanalysis and, later, the more general psychology provide *one* possible formula for the nature of the relation between the individual and society in a modern age. Rieff is, however, of the opinion that the social model of Freud and psychology, which we still live with today, is not sustainable in the long run.

In Chapter 4 the investigation of authority continues, but under its traditional name: 'the sacred'. The sacred and religion have, historically speaking, constituted an important social institution which contextualised human beings within a community and motivated them to search beyond the limits of the self. What happens when this institution is dissolved and replaced by a therapeutic expertise that advises the individual to search for the answers within that self? Here I also discuss whether the 'return of religion' and neo-religiosity/neo-spiritualism of recent decades imply that we must re-evaluate whether our perception of the world is in fact secularised and therapeutic.

Chapter 5 explores the role of the therapeutic ethos as this finds expressions in the hands of therapeutic experts in weekly magazines, books and on TV. Here I investigate self-help literature, *The Oprah Winfrey Show* and what I call therapeutic reality TV. In that a number of those researching the propagation of psychology in culture have pointed out that popular psychology, often communicated by TV programmes with a global reach, currently exercises the greatest impact on society today, there is reason to believe that a number of characteristics of the therapeutic culture which until now have been predominantly restricted to the USA are in the process of reaching Norway and other parts of the world.

In Chapter 6 I explore how psychology and the concept of 'the mental part' have entered the sports arena in the past decade. Sports psychology has in a short period of time come to play a highly critical role in Norwegian and international sports – in professional football and in the training period leading up to the Summer and Winter Olympics. The degree to which 'the mental' is or is not of critical importance to performance is here of secondary interest. Instead I employ sports as a mirror of society to demonstrate individual features that emerge when one implements therapeutic explanatory models.

In Chapter 7 I look more closely at neoliberalism, a political ideology that over the course of recent decades has had the same period of expansion and catchment area as psychology. In that both neoliberalism and psychology give the individual a central position, it is natural to presume that they are closely related. As such, neoliberalism represents a litmus test for psychology's ideological resistance and credibility.

Chapter 8 addresses the psychology profession's ethos and position in relation to the ethical dilemmas I have presented in the book. I make the argument that psychologists have a large degree of ethical awareness of client-related factors, but an underdeveloped understanding of socio-ethical problems with respect to how the discipline comes into contact and conflict, respectively, with important social issues. One area where this disparity finds expression is in the Norwegian Psychological Association's political work, which in spite of its good intentions lacks any awareness of the negative aspects of the increased immediacy of psychology in society.

In the final chapter (9) I summarise the book's perspectives on psychology in society and address a number of objections to the book's analyses, before I then highlight some of the more disturbing features of how psychology may develop in the future. For a number of reasons there are (unfortunately) a good many factors indicating that neither politicians nor professionals see any problems with psychology's ideological bias: the use of individual solutions on social problems. The result can be even more psychological ailments in the future, something which both politicians and professionals will, paradoxically, use to justify our need for even more psychology.

Guidance regarding the book's perspective

Some readers may be puzzled at this point by my use of the term 'psychology'. It can therefore be appropriate to give an explanation of how I employ the term throughout the book. *Psychology* is today a science, a clinical profession and a cultural artefact, with a presence as therapeutic expertise in our culture as never before. *Psychologist*, on the other hand, is a professional title protected by law in Norway, as in most other countries. In the therapy market of today, however, a number of different occupational groups exist, all of which offer a form of therapeutic expertise. As the gestalt therapist Elisabeth Arnet (2009) correctly asserts in her book with the fitting title *Therapy: What Is Right For Me?*: psychologists and psychiatrists no longer have a treatment monopoly. With such a multitude of therapeutic experts, there is no point in restricting oneself to psychology as practised by psychologists, even though this is the professional group to which the book devotes the greatest amount of attention. In that this profession has a title protected by law that relies on the trust of society, it is reasonable that psychologists be expected to exercise the greatest ethical awareness. Any disparity here will be more serious and a greater cause for alarm than among other practitioners in the therapeutic market. This is also the professional group with which I have first-hand experience as a psychology student, working psychologist and researcher.

With regard to method, it is challenging to treat psychologists and psychology as a concrete and uniform entity: imprecise generalisations and oversimplifications are a risk. Psychology has since its conception always been characterised by a number of schools and movements which have been from time to time relatively and mutually antagonistic and which have offered extremely different answers to key questions in psychology on the relation between genetics–environment, personality–situation, emotion–cognition, etc. In short, psychology is pervaded by anything but consensus and conformity. Through the profession's rapid development, the differentiation has only increased. Modern psychology includes everything from neuropsychology, which in its microscopic studies of synapses, cells and genes is closely akin to modern medicine, biology and genetics, to disciplines such as environmental psychology or economic psychology, which operate with large macro models of human interaction and as such are closer to the social sciences. Social psychologist Irwin Altman (1987) talks about centripetal and centrifugal trends in psychology, and describes the period from the 1960s and beyond as a period of increased specialisation and differentiation, making it less likely that psychologists could identify with the field as a whole. Given the enormous variation in perceptions of what psychology and psychologists are today, why then insist on trying to understand 'psychology' as if it were one thing?

My answer is because it is an ethical and moral requirement. An anecdote from Aldous Huxley's (1932) future dystopia *Brave New World* can offer an explanation. In Huxley's vision of the future, the ruling, oppressive regime has an express objective of ensuring that all citizens from birth are fully specialised in a single specific work task. In consequence, workers have only one, narrow, niche expertise. The specialisation one is born into serves as an effective buffer against anyone being able to develop a general overview of society and thereby beginning to ask questions and potentially presenting a critique of the regime which could lead to a change of the status quo. If everyone is extremely busy working within the confines of his or her area of expertise, nobody will have the vision and gumption to ask critical questions or become 'evil, general intellectuals', as Huxley humorously has the regime's spokesmen refer to the defunct social critics in *Brave New World*. General knowledge about society and how it is ruled is in other words required for critical thought about social and political conditions. If we can no longer be bothered to try and see 'the big picture', we risk acquiring a non-reflected relation to fundamental assumptions and, in the worst case, becoming blind to these assumptions and their consequences (Taylor, 1999). A lack of self-insight is also particularly embarrassing for a field such as psychology in that the teaching of this is a part of its programme, and it is simultaneously incompatible with the idea of a reflected and ethical awareness of one's own professional activity, something which, moreover, applies to all of the professions. If one looks at psychology today, one sees that it is full to the brim with empirical data but that there is a great deficit in terms of interpretation and meta-reflection about this data. The Norwegian cognitive psychologist Tore Helstrup (2009) and the British psychoanalyst Stephen Frosh (2003) have therefore, in spite of their relatively different professional backgrounds, both maintained that today's psychology is characterised by too much data in the context of too little theory.

In order for psychology to have an awareness of its own fundamental assumptions and its impact on the development of society, it is obliged to assume a position of self-reflection from an external perspective. This implies that psychology must be contextualised in a historical social perspective and analysed in accordance with key issues within modern social theory. In contrast to historical presentations in which psychology's development is tendentiously offered up as a series of successively better theories and methods that bring us closer to the truth with each passing decade, recent historical approaches (cf. Jansz and van Drunen, 2004) thankfully emphasise that the development of the discipline cannot solely be understood through the ideas of leading scientists, but must also be viewed from the perspective of the social circumstances out of which it arose. 'The new history of psychology' challenges the underlying idea of science's straightforward social utility value and asks whether psychology's influence on society is as generally and unilaterally positive as 'the old history of psychology' has had a tendency to depict it as being (Jansz and van Drunen, 2004).

Still, the potentially negative sides of psychology, unlike the positive, are too seldom subject to analysis and debate. This book is therefore not as much about the positive sides. In other disciplines such as medicine, the field with which psychology would aspire to be compared, exclusively critical works are to a far greater extent common and accepted. One of the best known, *Medical Nemesis* by Ivan Illich (1976, p. 3), opens with the following statement: 'The medical establishment has become a major threat to health.' The skewed distribution in the presentation of the negative and positive sides of psychology, however, imposes a requirement on the reader, who is hereby warned against reading this book as if it were telling the full and final story of psychology. Unfortunately, critical perspectives, perhaps in particular those directed at psychiatry, have on occasion been boiled down to simplified, conspiratorial interpretations without any particular understanding of the challenges represented by psychological ailments, neither for the affected parties nor for society in general. A relevant example here is the crusade by the Church of Scientology against the profession. The result is frequently that this critique is dismissed by professional practitioners as rubbish, and, what is even worse, risks leading to an attitude of categorical rejection of all criticism. Let me therefore make it perfectly clear: psychology is an unavoidable part of modern life and the discipline has an obligation that is more important than ever at a time when the individual is more autonomous and vulnerable. The purpose of this book is not to do away with psychology, but to contribute to its development through critical perspectives. This is of particular urgency precisely because psychology has become a central institution in the daily life of modern society. A self-reflecting psychology that is able and willing to promote critical perspectives of itself and the impact it has on society is therefore more important than ever before.

2   The consumer self

The perspective I adopt in my approach to modern psychology seeks to include sociologist C. Wright Mills's (2000, p. 3) well-known insistence that 'Neither the life of an individual nor the history of a society can be understood without understanding both.' A psychology discipline that maintains a unilateral emphasis on a non-contextual understanding of the modern self's vulnerable situation runs the risk, in the worst case, of reinforcing illness and indirectly increasing the incidence of psychological ailments in the population. The process that is called 'individualisation' which I will now present illustrates this paradox perhaps better than any other contemporary phenomenon.

The most important impetus in modern society is the need for individual satisfaction and self-actualisation, according to Beck (1992). The ideal human being in our time is the actively choosing individual who is personally the creator of his/her own life and own identity. The explanation is to be found in a socio-historical process that Beck calls *individualisation*. Individualisation refers to the subjective and biographical aspects of the development of civilisation. The modernisation of society did not only lead to external, structural changes involving a more centralised state system, a concentration of capital, a more pronounced stratification between labour and the market, social mobility and mass consumption, but also the phasing out of the traditional institutionalisation of human life through the extended family, local community, and tradition, where practical knowledge, beliefs and clear guiding norms were passed down from generation to generation. The modern ideal of the individual as free and responsible for the formation of his or her life is therefore a relatively new phenomenon, in that the traditional organisation of society provided no real space for personal expression, bound as most people were by the profession that had been passed down to them from their fathers. Individualisation is as such an inevitable consequence of the large-scale structural changes that occurred in the transition to the modern age. Urbanisation, mass production, the consumer economy, women's liberation, social mobility, etc., resulted in the phasing out of the extended family to make way for a more individual way of life, adapted to a new economy and new working life orientated towards individuals. One consequence of this was that the way of life and living arrangements of a large percentage of the Western population were permanently changed. The number of American households with seven persons or more dropped from 35.9 per cent in 1790 to 20.4 per cent in 1900, and 5.8 per cent in 1950. The number of households with one person increased from 3.7 per cent in 1790 to 9.3 per cent in 1950 to 18.5 per cent in 1973 (Cushman, 1995). In many Western European cities nearly half of the population now lives alone.

The Polish sociologist Zygmunt Bauman (2001) has summarised the consequences of individualisation as follows: individualisation converts human identity from something fixed to a task. A consequence of individualisation is that it gives the population in the West opportunities to choose and realise their own abilities through work, education, place of residence and a variety of forms of cohabitation, opportunities which the majority in previous generations did not have. In spite of the historical opportunities for personal growth and expression which individualisation entails, both Beck and Bauman have a number of critical reservations regarding the changes individualisation implies for society and the individual, reservations that pertain to psychology and psychotherapy.

Although individualisation is an unavoidable consequence of alterations in social conditions and economic development and growth over the course of the last couple of centuries, Beck and Bauman maintain that some aspects of individualisation are also man-made and can be regulated through political governance. They both claim to see an ideological reinforcement of individualisation that has taken place in the course of recent decades, which they connect to late capitalism and neoliberalism, whereby individualisation becomes an obligatory process in which people's capacity for codetermination through their own life choices appears to obscure any opportunity for influence at a structural, collective level.

Individualisation becomes a compulsory, institutionalised individualism in which the individual to an increasing extent is made responsible for their own choices and actions and the results of these, according to Beck. Formerly a clear distinction was made between what happens to people – external events beyond their control – and how they handle these events, in their behaviour and awareness – individual coping abilities (Beck, 1992). Today this is no longer the case. This mentality finds clearest expression in the self-help culture – such as in Rhonda Byrne's *The Secret* (more about this in Chapter 5). The trend is clearly in favour of using the individual as a causal explanation for his or her own advancement or shortcomings. You are personally the cause of your victories, but also of your defeats. Beck's point is not to misappropriate individual responsibility or the ability we all have to make an impact on our own life situation in a negative or positive sense. But by viewing the attribution of life destiny historically, he claims to see clearly that an increasingly larger percentage of society's problems are individualised and placed as a burden on the shoulders of the individual. Unemployment is an example Beck uses, where the explanatory models gradually change from external, structural causes to individual choices and career planning. The family and the individual become the dumping site for society's unresolved conflicts – particularly during periods of economic recession. The Western individualised society encourages us to seek bio-graphical solutions for structural crises – you must be mobile and flexible in order to find a new job or new career (Beck and Beck-Gernsheim, 2002).

This tendency functions to the detriment of class consciousness, which makes it possible to join forces around a common issue. The individual's problems of daily life are no longer helpful in the creation of a common objective and common project, where a sufficient number of these will bring about action and changes. Individualisation leads to the fragmentation of potential collective experiences. This is unfortunate, in that a collective level of action is necessary to gain control of such processes through poli-tical governance, but in order for that to take place, one must have the ability to reverse and see through individualisation. Individualisation has, how-ever, a seductive effect in that it derives from a liberation ideal with positive connotations, which is about liberating the self from former, restrictive ties, so the self is given an opportunity to liberate itself from its allotted place in society. As touched upon in the introduction, the moral side of authority has moved away from external sovereignties to internal convictions. We will later see how the culture is permeated by this seductive message about individual self-actualisation and self-creation.

Beck (1992) makes direct reference to psychology, and specifically clinical psychology and psychotherapy as a social institution that indirectly strengthens such individualisation mechanisms. Political, structural and social phenomena are redefined on a broad scale as psychological disposi-tions such as personal shortcomings, insufficient coping strategies, feelings of guilt, anxiety, inner conflicts and neuroses. Social crises become indi-vidual crises which only sporadically, if at all, are perceived in light of their roots in the social sphere. The last ten years' individualisation explains to a large degree the enormous interest in psychology that arose in Northern Europe throughout the course of the 1980s, Beck claims.

The individualisation hypothesis is then also used to explain psych-ology's penetration in modern society – in particular by the stakeholders of the profession itself – 'in today's society man has become more exposed and vulnerable, and the caring function which the family, relatives or local community previously performed must today be taken over by professionals', etc. But in Beck's analysis, psychology is not only a requisite response, but also a problem and, paradoxically, even further compounds the problems. Psychology has yet to carry out a socio-historical review of its ways of thinking, something which is necessary if it is not to run aground by adhering to the idea of individuality which it profits from by erroneously situating the cause of the individual's problems within the person who has them, is Beck's biting judgement of psychology in *Risk Society*. As the situation is now, psychology and psychotherapy might increase the level of individualisation when society's unresolved conflicts are dumped on the individual and through therapy traced back to the individual's biography and childhood. Beck paints an unflattering picture of psychology and psychotherapy as a social institution that treats individualisation's losers as if they are the very reason and cause of their problems. On the basis of this, individual clinical treatment becomes Western society's preferred response to what Beck holds to be first and foremost a problem that must be solved at a higher, collective level.

Beck is, however, not very thorough in what is, it must be said, a rather grave critique of psychology. Psychology and psychotherapy are mentioned in only a couple of places in the 260 pages that constitute *Risk Society*. There are for this reason a number of objections that can be raised against Beck's critique: is psychology really as individualising as he makes it out to be? A good deal of more recent clinical psychology and psychotherapy seeks to focus on the system surrounding the individual and to understand the client's problems within a larger context. Beck can as such be accused of having created a one-sided, almost caricatured image of psychology. The limited space that he dedicates to psychology in *Risk Society* can serve as an indication that he has a psychoanalytical or a traditional psycho-dynamic model in mind where all answers to the client's problems are to be found in the socialisation of childhood. The objection can also be raised that Beck asserts that it is 'society' that is always the cause of the individual's suffering and that if the problems were to be solved at this level, the problems of the individual would solve themselves. Regardless of the causal connection, imagining that the individual psyche and any problems would be wholly and fully solved by bringing them back to the level of society is a problematic approach. The ailment – even if it is created by society – will always acquire an individual, unique expression and for that reason many will make the argument that it must be met correspondingly with individually adapted treatment.

Although it is possible to raise many such objections to Beck's somewhat cursory critique and thereby defend psychology's necessary position in late modern society, his critique merits consideration and should nonetheless be an ethical problem that psychology takes seriously. If psychology loses sight of the structural level beyond the individual psyche and simply fails to recognise how its own practice is influenced by and influences current societal processes, it is at risk of becoming a social institution with a clear ideological bias that conceals the ailment's cause, prevents social changes and, in the worst case, produces more suffering and indirectly increases the incidence of psychological ailments in the population. As we will see in Chapter 8, on the ethos of the psychology profession, Beck is also on to something essential when he writes that psychology profits from situating the causes in the individual.

To supplement Beck's analysis, we can construct for the occasion an example based on individualisation and psychotherapy. Cleaning assistant Tove is on long-term sick leave due to back and neck ailments, stress reactions and burn-out; little by little in her job she was given responsibility for increasingly larger areas to be covered in the same number of working hours. One day, Tove couldn't take any more. Her body just said 'enough'. And that is how it has been for several months now. Tove's employer has set up a follow-up scheme for sickness absenteeism to address light psychological and complex ailments, due to Tove having been diagnosed with burn-out by her physician. Tove therefore begins to attend therapy with a psychologist, who, after having acquired a good understanding of the situation, helps Tove to work on her attitude to the modified job requirements, and together they look at more concrete coping strategies and techniques that Tove can use to handle stress at work and in daily life in general. Another part of the story is that before her sick leave Tove had gone through a difficult period when her husband fell seriously ill. Some time was also dedicated to this during her treatment, in that in all likelihood it had had an impact on her reaction patterns. Gradually she notes that the symptoms are relieved and after a period of treatment she returns to work. Tove feels that she has benefited greatly from the sessions with the psychologist.

This is how we might envision a treatment process with a successful outcome. The problem is just that the help in this case also reinforces the individualisation: the psychotherapist helps Tove to recover by way of individual explanations and solutions. The structural causes lying behind the problem remain untouched. In this case they are, first, the increasingly more demanding efficiency requirements on the part of the employer – which are in the process of becoming unreasonable – and, second, the fact that the cleaning assistant in question has received no encouragement to contest and protest against the efficiency measures. To the contrary. The treatment has contributed to placing the problem inside of her; she is the owner of the problem. We can also imagine that the treatment professional is an extremely proficient therapist and on the basis of his clinical and ethical remit he has done an excellent job. The example demonstrates psychology's paradox: at an individual level, the right thing to do is offer help. Psychotherapy and the focus on Tove's coping strategies have really helped her, but simultaneously contribute to a reinforced individualisation which in turn makes collective reflexivity, as Beck calls it, and collective resistance to increasingly greater efficiency requirements in working life difficult. The possible structural causes for her disability are not touched, only the individual causes are treated. These have also played a part and contributed to her not being able to carry out her job any longer. The preferred solutions – individual, clinical treatment – restructure the problem into something she can do something about herself. Probably the exact reason why Tove became ill is a combination of structural and individual causes but only the latter are addressed, as that was the 'requisition' and the easiest to handle.

Psychologist Isaac Prilleltensky (1989) has claimed that by starting psychological treatment the client will indirectly be trained to discount the significance of social conditions on his or her life and as a result, the chances of his or her getting involved in activities aiming to challenge the status quo are reduced. The chances of our cleaning assistant Tove doing something about the larger 'problem', such as by getting involved in trade union work, have perhaps been diminished because she has learned how to take responsibility for 'the problem' (accountability) and redefines 'the problem' as a challenge (reframing).

Little research has been done on how psychotherapy can actually reinforce such individualisation processes. Gender studies scholar Kathy Davis (1986) has, however, carried out a unique study of how the individualisation of women's problems can take place in a conversation between therapist and client. Davis analysed how the frustrations of a stay-at-home mother/mother-to-be were interpreted and reformulated by the therapist. Davis succeeds in demonstrating how themes such as gender roles and disparities between men and women are transformed by the therapist into being primarily about the client's personal difficulties in finding expression for her frustration with other people, in this case her husband, in an open and sincere manner. But as was the case in the fictional example of the cleaning assistant Tove, from the perspective of the psychotherapist, there are good reasons for doing this – the framework conditions for psychotherapy are after all based on working on the client's problems. This is probably helpful also for the frustrated woman in Davis's study, but the point of contention is that structural differences between women and men are depoliticised and the conflicts that emerge – predominantly for women – are individualised through therapeutic interventions. Davis (1986) concludes her study by calling for more research on the individualisation problem in psychotherapy, and treatment strategies that have an ambition of resolving women's difficulties in a manner that provides for such a bias.

The Danish psychologist Carsten René Jørgensen (2002) claims that clinical psychology and psychotherapy in today's society are guilty of a self-perpetuating logic which contributes to further individualisation and de-politicisation of the causes behind people's psychological troubles, although without necessarily being aware of this. Examples here are depression and burn-out due to the requirement of an increase in work efficiency/productivity. But the problem is not limited to the therapist's choice of attitudes. Jørgensen connects the problem to the self-reflexive culture in which we live. What before was natural has now become a matter of uncertainty and a problem for many, the solution to which requires expertise. The need for psychology and psychologists who can provide explanations and create a context in our lives therefore becomes considerable, something which in turn will only further reinforce the individualisation and the need for psychological support. The desire for individual explanations for life crises will in all likelihood in many cases come from the client personally. Tove will probably wish to receive a unique answer regarding what lies at the bottom of her disability. There is a strong perception at work in our times that individualisation represents something liberating, whereby people become constantly more autonomous. The seductive effect of individualisation on the individual, as Beck touches upon, is about the intense wish and cultural imperative for self-actualisation. The latter is in fact another category in which the involvement of psychology is ambiguous. Self-actualisation also tells us something about psychology and psychotherapy's role in the consumer culture – where specific psychological categories appear to flourish because the controlling forces in society have a need for this.

Self-actualisation

The historical development through which the individual became more independent simultaneously leads to an increase in the opportunities for self-actualisation. The autonomous, self-sufficient individual becomes more and more of a reality throughout the twentieth century, according to the American historian and psychotherapist Philip Cushman. In keeping with the decline of the extended family, the individual self is now viewed as the ultimate site of salvation (Cushman, 1995). Self-actualisation is an old concept, which can be traced far back in the history of the West, far beyond the proliferation of modern psychotherapy and all the way back to Georg Simmel, Georg W. F. Hegel and even to Aristotle's (384–322 BC) ideal of the development of different abilities in accordance with congenital disposition (Willig, 2005). Nonetheless, the roots of the modern perception of self-actualisation, according to Cushman, are to be found in particular in the humanistic psychology of the USA in the decades following the Second World War. Best known today is probably psychologist Abraham Maslow's (1943) pyramid of needs, where self-actualisation is located at the top as the most evolved form of human need.

The humanistic movement in psychology, also called 'the third force', arose in the USA in the 1960s as a reaction to the dominant tendencies in psychology at the time, such as formalised and elitist psychoanalysis and scientific and detached behaviourism. With a basis in existentialism and the liberation movements of the 1960s, humanistic psychology sought to shift the focus to the unique potential in each individual human being and emphasised choice, self-actualisation and the individual's search for meaning. Humanistic psychology's self was subjective; it broke away from tradition and was first and foremost interested in individual life projects, freedom of choice and self-actualisation.

Cushman (1990, 1995) maintains that a new type of self emerges within the context of the USA's historical and economic era in the post-war years' reconstruction of the nation. The state does not control the population by harnessing the impulses of the latter, as in the Victorian era, but rather by creating and manipulating people's desire to be consoled, told what to do and made whole by temporary satisfaction. 'The empty self' is what Cushman (1995) calls the ideal for this era's self-configuration. An appreciable loss of community, traditions and collective structures of meaning takes place, but this absence is experienced as a personal lack of conviction and values which thereby enshroud the absence, loneliness and deficiencies of life like a chronic, emotional yearning. This undifferentiated emptiness constituted the crucial fertile foundation for the consumer culture which was dependent upon the population's purchasing power and will during the second half of the last century, he claims. For the empty self that arises in the period after the Second World War, consumption is an unconscious means of compensating for what has been lost. Without knowing it, the individual satisfies the consumer-oriented economy with his/her boundless need for material and spiritual replenishment (Cushman, 1995).

The advertising industry and psychotherapy are in Cushman's interpretation comparable professions in a way that many psychologists would prefer not to recognise. The individual in the late-modern era is without any solid community and strives to find meaning in a confusing, new reality. There is little guidance available, the individual stumbles and despairs. New discourses and practices such as the advertising industry and psychology are adapted to respond to and further develop the self's new configuration.

Representatives for both domains are put into a position of healing the empty self without addressing the economic frameworks and historical reasons for the emptiness created by structural and social changes. In the aftermath of the difficulties and illnesses that arise, psychology is the social science best equipped to treat these. But psychology is in itself a product of a larger historical context which both brings along with it and causes these ailments. Psychology cannot reach these symptoms unless it addresses the political and historical causes that create this era, but these are not within psychology's reach. Psychology shall solely offer alleviation of the suffering found within the system and seek to uphold it, not break away from it. Psychology's very remit promotes this view (Cushman, 1990). Psychology is apparently caught on a dead-end street from which it cannot exit. It is reminiscent of the advertisement offering temporary relief. Perhaps advertising campaigns that utilise psychotherapy are an expression of greater structural similarity than we are aware of: 'Calling a psychologist when you're feeling empty doesn't always help' (Pizza Hut) and 'Why pay a therapist to get in touch with your inner child?' (peanut butter) (as cited in Jørgensen, 2002, p. 301).

Most of the discourses surrounding psychotherapy play actively upon the dominant ideology of their era, while the patient's ailments are caused by the same political and economic structures. For example, in order for the economy to thrive, it is necessary that individuals have a strong inclination to desire and consume products. When meeting such individuals, Cushman (1990) holds that many psychotherapeutic theoretical traditions treat the modern self by strengthening the same structures that have created the problem at the outset; its autonomous, boundless nature. The individual is diagnosed as empty and fragmented (as in humanistic psychology) without addressing the socio-historical causes that have brought about this emptiness and fragmentation. Conditions brought about by Western culture, such as loneliness, alienation and extreme competitive instincts, are all viewed as natural and unavoidable. As a result individuals must be constructed to strive for consumption and expansion and live in the faith that this pursuit is an aspect of a universal human nature. Since the symptoms are viewed as being natural and inevitable, they are located outside the sphere of politics and history and they can thereby also not be changed through political action. Ergo the status quo is upheld. In Cushman's account, the self is the very core of the society that perpetuates the status quo, and psychology's and psychotherapy's mission is therefore to assist with this work.

At its best, humanistic psychology offered an alternative, creative, critical voice – which to an equal extent provided support for an extreme individualism and the liberation (in other words, self-actualisation) of an apolitical self. At its worst the movement gave birth to a series of authoritarian organisations selling prefabricated, nihilistic, transformative technologies that harmed the participants. The humanistic movement in psychotherapy, led by authorities such as Abraham Maslow and Carl Rogers, was the faction of psychotherapy that was most successful in leaving its imprint on popular culture and as such played a part in changing our view of the self (Illouz, 2007). Self-actualisation also had a central position in Carl Jung's (1875–1961) analytical psychology. For Jung only an extremely exclusive selection of historical individuals appeared to fulfil his requirements for self-actualisation and attain the final level to become a consummate Self: Buddha, Jesus, Goethe, to a certain extent Nietzsche, and Jung himself (Jung and Jaffe, 1963). Maslow says likewise that only a small percentage of the human population arrives at the point of identity, or self-individuality and full self-actualisation, even in a society such as America where the population is one of the best off on the planet. This is one of the great paradoxes of our times, says Maslow (1993). At the same time, self-actualisation to an increasing extent is viewed and internalised as a universal human right. In this way the perception is created about all those who have not fulfilled this unique inner potential and who therefore could benefit from therapy: people who we call sick are people who are not themselves. They are people who have built up neurotic walls of defence against being human, said Maslow (Illouz, 2007). As a cultural recipe and marketing idea, the idea of self-actualisation is brilliant, in that it both preserves a religious remnant (Vitz, 1991) and instructs the great majority of the Western population who do not feel that they have reached the final level of their full potential to chase after it. From now on, in order to 'be in the world', therapeutic expertise is required – Maslow's (1968, 1993) books are entitled exactly *Toward a Psychology of Being* and *The Farther Reaches of Human Nature*. The journey to the true self is apparently unending. Maslow was indeed sincere and authentic enough in his quest for greater fulfilment of the human potential, but the legacy he left behind entailed the fulfilment of another potential, specifically the self-help industry's need to reach the Western population. As Maslow himself expressed regretfully when he attended a therapy workshop at the Esalen Institute in Big Sur, California, sometime during the 1960s: 'This begins to look like sickness' (as cited in Cushman, 1995, p. 243).

The paradox of individuality in our time is, according to Ehrenberg (2010), that it has become a zone for the highest level of complacency and happiness in our culture, while also serving as the abyss into which the individual risks tumbling, and thereby becoming exhausted and depressed. The individual both judges him/herself and is constantly being judged. In the event of a failure to live up to one's potential the risk is great that the individual will feel impotent, empty, agitated, depleted of energy and paralysed, and finally, depressed (Petersen, 2005). It can appear to be the case that the greater the number of opportunities for self-actualisation, the greater the number of ailments found in the population. A large-scale study of the populations of the USA, Germany, Italy, France, Lebanon, New Zealand and Taiwan from 1915 up to the present day disclosed that for each new generation of young people that grows up, the probability of developing a serious depression has increased (Weissmann, 1992). One explanation can be that there are so many opportunities today that these overwhelm the individual's ability to assess the alternatives and capacity to commit to one of them (Melucci, 1996; Willig, 2005). In the classic study *Suicide* by the French sociologist Émile Durkheim (2010), a theory is developed that anomalistic suicide occurs because society is no longer able to regulate the behaviour of the individual in such a way that their life conduct is satisfactory. In other words, the disintegration of laws, rules, norms, etc., have an impact on the individual and lead him/her to suicide (Willig, 2005). If the individual fails to create a coherent biographical narrative, which can provide a sense of meaning, there is a real danger of existential meaninglessness, which in the most serious cases will lead to depression, and in the worst case suicide (Willig, 2005). Self-actualisation in today's 'you are the only one setting limits on what is possible' culture encourages young people to pursue this project at any cost. For some, that cost is great. As Ehrenberg (2010) puts it: a person becomes depressed because he must abide the illusion that everything is possible for him. The self-help culture reminds us of this requirement all the time: 'Absolutely everything in your life can be improved. And you can do it yourself', reads the characteristic article 'Coach Yourself!' in the Norwegian women's magazine *Women and Clothes* (Koldtoft, 2010, p. 42). A common definition of depression is a lack of correspondence between ambitions and abilities and/or opportunities to realise these ambitions. Not everyone has the parameters required to become 'something big', and the number who can become 'something big' is also limited. Society only needs so many artists and actors, and there are but a limited number of openings in the media-led spotlight on celebrity culture.

What is interesting about Cushman's analysis of the humanistic psychology of the 1960s is not primarily that he shows how a school of psychology that is frequently presented as a positive force in the history books is abused or runs amok, but rather his persuasive analyses of how schools of psychotherapy arise in response to a need in society and, in particular, economic needs in the West's historical eras. There is therefore cause to be sceptical when somebody claims that the new psychotherapy schools rectify psychology's inherent tendency to preserve the status quo (Prilleltensky, 1989) (see Chapter 7 on narrative therapy).

The stock exchange and the cathedral

Capitalism's capacity for survival and potential for growth are found in the spiritual sphere, which in the lifetime of the German sociologist Max Weber (1864–1920) was 'the Protestant ethic'. Weber (2001, p. 31) had a profound understanding of this:

> The question of the motive forces in the expansion of modern capitalism is not in the first instance a question of the origin of the capital sums which were available for capitalistic use, but, above all, of the development of the spirit of capitalism.

Today, the Protestant ethic appears to have been replaced by the therapeutic ethos. Modern capitalism has undergone a development from the production economy of the nineteenth century to the consumer economy of the twentieth century. Its various historical production phases change in accordance with changes in the social economy, in civil life, and in the design and ideal for the self. Protestantism created a human type motivated to live and fulfil the requirements imposed on the individual by capitalist trade and industry (Weber, 2001). Back then, saving was a good thing. In today's times of economic crisis, private savings have become a sin. A natural follow-up question becomes whether psychology/the therapeutic ethos has fostered a human type dedicated to living in accordance with the requirements posed by the capitalist system on the individual today?

Ethos also means that the life of a human being is adapted to the actual phase the world finds itself in, in other words, to the needs of society, according to anthropologist Clifford Geertz (2000). Cushman's (1995) understanding of the self can be viewed in the same way: the self is a product of complex, cultural constraints that bind together elements from society to preserve the status quo and which suit the economic system that fights off stagnation through continual consumption. The classical study of the affinity between market economy and the population's psyche is Weber's (2001) demonstration of a close-knit bond between modern capitalism and Protestant Christianity in his work *The Protestant Ethic and the Spirit of Capitalism*. Weber identified the surprising but convincing concurrence of two seemingly irreconcilable areas of culture: the stock exchange and the cathedral, or Protestantism and capitalism. Weber's study is exceedingly applicable to our times, where capitalism is no longer connected to production but rather to consumption and where Protestantism (although religion does remain a significant factor (see Chapter 4)) exists in a secular version as the therapeutic ethos. Weber's main hypothesis was that the requirements for self-actualisation and economically rational behaviour, respectively, were in reality the same life project. Weber's (2001) study can be viewed as a form of mental archaeology or genealogy – in other words a method that endeavours to excavate forgotten origins from the history of man. What appears self-evident today need not have been so to begin with. In this case it is a matter of looking at how Protestant groups such as the rules for living of the Methodists, Quakers and Baptists created the capitalist mentality in the West. This mentality's requirement for a work ethic and goal-oriented investment arose actually from the objective of increasing God's honour on earth through ascetic strategies. This was done to demonstrate and ensure that the hard-working individual would be one of God's chosen for all eternity.

With time a mentality evolves in which work is accompanied by an inner conviction, as if work were an absolute goal in its own right; it has become an independent calling. At the same time, Weber was interested in getting to the bottom of the capitalistic ideology, which led him to explore Benjamin Franklin's how-to-get-rich-handbooks from the 1700s, where practical advice (such as 'time is money') not only represented a type of wisdom in business or a kind of life technique, but was the expression of a particular ethos. Weber (2001) called the spirit of capitalism an 'ethically coloured maxim for the life conduct'. The ethics through which money becomes an end in its own right go beyond the economic-rational and the individual's material needs and spiritual happiness. In spite of this irrational quintessence, the capitalist economic order represents an enormous cosmos into which the human being is born, and this system is perceived as an inalterable structure within which one must live (Weber, 2001). A potential fusion of the therapeutic ethos with consumer logic can therefore be viewed as such a structure of meaning which has arisen (without the need for any facilitators) in our own time. The development of such fusions which can seem oppressive is not to be understood as being capitalism's or anybody else's conscious creation. Such historical fusions can perhaps be better understood in accordance with a Nietzschean mentality. Weber (2001) indeed plays upon the German philosopher Friedrich Nietzsche's (1844–1900) expression 'the last man' in his predictions about the European bourgeois culture. The merging of the Protestant ethic with the spirit of capitalism can be seen as an alloy that arose in an attempt to give meaning to existence and man's suffering. Such alloys are contingent (not necessary), but all the same influential factors. It therefore becomes the job of the social critic to subvert the status quo by demonstrating that reality need not be this way.

Weber writes of the economic development of Protestants that a particular form of economic rationality arises that is not to be found in Catholicism. A speculative, but tempting possibility, on the basis of these two points of view, is to draw the conclusion that psychology has become an extension of Protestantism's ethic, shaped into the therapeutic ethos. If one looks at religion from the perspective of psychology – as a means of orientating oneself in the world – it is not so far-fetched to view an inward focus, into the self, and an outward focus, towards God in heaven, as two different versions of the same process of searching for meaning – the need for a meaningful framework. It also has meaning to view this as a development whereby the idea of 'God' is pulled down toward the earth. Originally God represented an absolute transcendence above all creation. Gradually, an inner dialogue with God is established which leads up to our own time in which the secularisation of creed is carried out through an ongoing inner dialogue with ourselves (see Chapter 3 for more about the historical shift from religion to therapy). Protestantism's ethic (and the spirit of capitalism) represents an early phase of the development of this ethos leading up to the therapeutic ethos of our time. Are Weber's historical analyses, generally speaking, applicable to today's therapeutic culture where the therapeutic ethos and 'the enterprise self' make up our time's Protestant ethic and spirit of capitalism?

The enterprise self and the therapeutic ethos

Western culture has allegedly undergone a transition from a Protestant to a therapeutic ethos (Lears, 1983). Sociologist Christopher Lasch (1991) claims that the therapeutic ethos has abandoned the Enlightenment project's utilitarian ethic (greatest possible happiness for greatest number of people), and instead serves capitalism in its place. Lasch holds that the professional elite of therapists and other experts on the self have an interest in keeping people dissatisfied, in that dissatisfied human beings turn to professionals for relief and satisfaction. The same principle can also be detected in everything within modern capitalism that seeks to create needs and, thereby, discontentment, which can only be relieved by the consumption of goods and services. The same historical development that has transformed the worker from a producer into a consumer has transformed the citizen into a client.

Sociologist James Nolan Jr (1998) in contradistinction to Lasch proposes a scenario in which the utilitarian ethic and the therapeutic ethos collaborate as two available languages for use in the legitimation of state laws, policies and programmes in the modern state. According to a utilitarian perspective, industry, technology and innovation in communication and transport will thus put us in a position to control the outer world, while the therapeutic empowerment project equips us to master the creation of our inner world.

In both cases these orientations represent a potential for creating and recreating ourselves. According to this mentality, there are no limits to what we can construct and reconstruct in our inner and outer world. The therapeutic and utilitarian mindsets share this orientation towards human limitlessness and represent the main language for legitimation of the state, so it can justify itself today, maintains Nolan Jr.

Religion studies scholar Paul Heelas (1991) has examined the understanding of the political subject as this was nurtured into being during the Thatcher administration in Great Britain during the 1980s. He characterised the ideal self that was cultivated in this period as an 'enterprise self': this means an active citizen who internalises a large individual responsibility and initiative for him/herself, and who manages him/herself like a company. It is, however, uncertain whether this version of the subject is viable, he maintains. The ideal enterprise self needs the backing of an authoritarian agent in order to flourish in the time ahead: 'Yet for this figure to flourish, wealth creation and the Protestant ethic have to be given an authoritative backing' (Heelas, 1991, p. 87). This authoritative agent appears now to be found a few decades down the road – namely, the therapeutic ethos – the message of which is: self-actualisation. The therapeutic ethos represents a secularised version of the Protestant ethic. The enterprise self simultaneously corresponds with the spirit of capitalism, which like its precursor constitutes a force to be reckoned with in society. If the worker begins to have doubts about the hard life on earth and the necessity of the work morality, the Protestant ethic efficiently kicks in to frighten him: 'You must live a life on earth that gives you hope of heavenly salvation in the afterlife.'

Today a therapeutic narrative functions as a factor in society that controls and intercepts the unhappy individuals who no longer manage or want to achieve self-actualisation. The foremost driver is thus not psychologists, but the internalised authority: the perception that one has something inside that it is just a matter of managing in the right fashion. 'Many of us have so many unexploited potentials inside of us,' nutrition consultant Carina Hultin Dahlmann tells *Women and Clothes* (Henriksen, 2010, p. 45). The great taboo today is not having ambitions, but rather having a lack of interest in self-actualisation. The depressed individual represents the involuntary reverse side of this ideal: a human being who is worn out from trying to achieve self-actualisation (Ehrenberg, 2010).

Conclusion

The circle is closed by Nolan Jr who links the therapeutic impulse to Weber: just as the representatives of Protestantism did not understand that their religious orientation would bring forth a capitalistic system, therapy practitioners do not view their ethos as potentially oppressive. In modern democratic society, categories of liberation become a system of empowering values that guide both consumer behaviour and social regulation. Private, sexual liberation takes the place of true social liberation. For the French sociologist Jean Baudrillard (2003) the consumption ideology represents therefore a kind of seductive rhetoric that seeks to convince us that we have reached an entirely new era in which a human revolution is unfolding that separates us from former periods' struggles for the existence that we can now freely enjoy. Psychology constitutes the institutional framework for this consumer society through identity construction as 'the empty self' where consumption and self-actualisation obey the same imperative.

Most social phenomena have as a rule a division between followers, and critics and followers who criticise the critique, etc. The status of the consumer society is no exception. Social anthropologist Runar Døving (2009) claims that the critical presentation of the consumer society of theorists such as Beck and Bauman, cited above, is first and foremost a theoretical construction with a religious dimension of Judgement Day that has no basis in reality: the modern consumer society has increased economic and material prosperity, done away with war (in Europe), increased the average life expectancy, contributed to women's liberation and produced enormous scientific and technological advances, he reminds us. The Hungarian sociologist Elemér Hankiss (2006) has claimed that it is 'the trivialities of consumer society' which in the absence of religion and transcendence now fill up the void and create the meaningful backdrop for our lives. Only if a more authentic and inviting culture should appear will we be willing to abandon the role of consumers. I will not address in further detail the debate about the status of the consumer culture here, but whether one is an opponent or supporter of consumerism is as such not irrelevant to how one views psychology.

The purpose of this chapter has been to demonstrate psychology's role in the establishment of a type of market economy and in so doing destabilise any illusions about psychology representing a critical corrective for capitalism. Capitalism always depends upon a 'friend in spirit', in other words, an ally, or source of legitimacy in the sphere of meaning – whether this be religion or psychology. The critical study of dominant ideologies today should perhaps therefore to a greater extent look at the psychological, historical roots of the self, and studies of the self and its pathologies should perhaps to a larger extent look at the historical organisation of society that has cultivated that self. Here a critical social or societal psychology could have an important part to play. But it must first put its own house in order.

We have seen how marketing and psychology are children of the same era and apparently carry out much of the same function: they offer a form of consolation and intimacy to individuals. Nobody expects the advertising industry to behave morally – in contrast to psychology and psychotherapy. Self-actualisation has salient Gnostic features – every single human being bears a secret and it is up to each individual to find the key to their personal salvation. Sciences about the human being, psychology in particular, can make a contribution to this work with the self – both those with great resources who are not directly exposed to heavy emotional distress – and weak groups of mentally ill individuals who become exhausted and depressed, who cannot cope with exploiting and managing their own resources. Psychology through its presence contributes simultaneously to upholding this culture. Modern psychology as such copies the consumer society's great paradox: the individual's freedom and autonomy are fundamental values, but the freedom to contest the fundamental values of the consumer society is not a real alternative.

3   Crisis of authority
Philip Rieff's critique of Freud's worldview

This chapter is about 'the crisis of authority' in the West, as expressed in Rieff's (2006, p. 13) forewarning: 'No culture has ever preserved itself where it is not a registration of sacred order.' In the late modern Western society at the beginning of the twenty-first century there is no longer any supreme authority to instruct people about what they should do. An immediate reaction would be that this sounds like a situation we have cause to welcome, and many in fact do so, in that they appear to live well with the − historically speaking − radical freedom from all external constraints that we explored in the preceding chapter. But some cultural critics fear that in the long term the authority-less society solely based on the individual's self-determination will dissolve culture's community of meaning and normative basis. There is also a risk that the individual's self-esteem will be undermined because self-actualisation is unilaterally emphasised as an end in its own right, in the worst case resulting in the resurgence of a loss of meaning and psychological disorders.

Religion has traditionally been the guarantee of a superior, transcendent authority which the Greeks called 'nomos', which translated literally means 'the law'. Nomos is the guiding principle in society, an existing ethics (ethos) which induces citizens to do what they *must* do and not simply what they *want* to do. Authority is actually merely a secular term for what traditionally speaking has been associated with 'the sacred' – a cultural narrative that gives the individual a higher meaning and institutes the individual in the cosmos and the social reality. Given the perception of modernity as subject to a process of de-traditionalisation, the authority of today is considerably weakened and finds itself in what is referred to as a crisis of authority (Heelas, 1996a).

The idea of a crisis of authority is actually not new; it has followed modernity ever since its inception. Many have asked what will replace the institutional role religion has traditionally played. One of the largest scale attempts to solve the crisis of authority we find represented in the psychoanalysis of the creator of modern psychotherapy – Sigmund Freud (1856–1939). Freud's 'attempted solution' was to relocate authority within each individual human being and relinquish it to his or her therapist. 'The psychological human being' whom we continue to live with today was thus formed (Rieff, 1987). Psychoanalysis addresses the problem of the modern individual, where repression has become overly dominant and neuroses flourish. In the transition from external control to internal steering, the external threat in the form of physical punishment is also replaced, by a permanent state of inner unhappiness and guilt. In the absence of God it is the new therapeutic culture that is assigned the task of taking care of human beings and their instincts (Casey, 2002).

The horizon is extinguished

As was shown in the last chapter, the individual's freedom to choose his or her own life is a relatively modern phenomenon. Social changes that led up to this over the course of the last two centuries made it easier and more relevant to think and live as if God no longer existed. The traditional, collective religious figures became less credible in that the normative foundation changed and was replaced by the modern individual's self-sufficiency (Casey, 2002). That was apparently how it looked. Some visionary thinkers from the 1800s, however, saw some ominous signs in the development of modernity: specifically, a feeling of alienation over an existence without higher purpose or meaning, and a sense of the emptiness of life in that it was reduced to a purely material existence. Although faith was on the wane in the modern society, guilt, fear or the need for redemption did not necessarily disappear as a result.

Perhaps the most famous contemporary diagnosis of the Western world's crisis of values in the nineteenth century is Nietzsche's (2001, p. 120) statement: 'God is dead! God remains dead! And we have killed him!' Nietzsche maintained that he saw signs around him of a collective crisis of meaning – nihilism – which was spreading through Europe at a rapid pace in the twentieth century, prepared to enjoy the fruits of modernity's progress and elevated to a new existence without material deprivation, spiritual and political unrest, or oppression. Nietzsche's contemporary analysis is based on the idea that the Christian-Platonic worldview and perception of reality had been the dominant truth regime in the West for two thousand years, but in his own lifetime had begun to spring leaks – meaninglessness had therefore begun to creep into human existence. God was truth's guarantor and his fall was an expression of the fact that life and the world were no longer self-evident and given. In meeting with this unfamiliar situation many people reacted with despair, paralysis and resignation rather than actively forming their lives. The explanation Nietzsche gave for this was that the Christian-Platonic worldview had been so successful up to this point in giving humanity an aim for existence that man had become passive and forgotten how to live in an active relationship to existence, recreating its purpose and meaning. This continual renewal of the human cosmos was originally instituted in religion's role in society, where man in an unceasing institutionalised process created a life-space for himself through metaphysical guarantors such as God. Nietzsche's critique of religion was that the Christian-Platonic worldview had been *too* successful in the creation of metaphysical truths; when it finally lost its force after two thousand years, man had forgotten that God was actually created by humans.

It is of interest to note that in addition to the role Nietzsche has been allotted as a Judgement Day prophet, a number of commentators have also called him the father of modern psychology (Casey, 2002). The main reason for this is certainly that Nietzsche represents a shift in the history of philosophy in that he turns the central question in philosophy away from metaphysics and the truth over to questions about values and the impact of the truth for man.

Nietzsche predicted that psychology would one day be recognised as the queen of the sciences, in that it was the path to solving the most fundamental human problems (Rieff, 1979). *The therapeutic turn* that Nietzsche sought was radical in a philosophical sense – human psychology was historically and culturally determined and therefore could change. Freud's understanding of the roots of the crisis in values appears, however, to be characterised by a wholly different psychological perception than that of Nietzsche. Despite being greatly inspired by Nietzsche, Freud sought universal laws from natural science for the human psyche, in contrast to Nietzsche's historical genealogy of Western consciousness. Consciousness was for Nietzsche only a contingent entity defined by valuation and power. Man was for him therefore an extremely malleable being, and psychology a temporary tool that could heal the modern individual's (bad) habit of despairing over the loss of meaning, in that Christianity's evangelism was just one of many possible answers to existence. 'God's death' thus opened existence up, allowing for new interpretations and recreations.

Rieff's culture critique

Today it is said that man has become God. Human beings have been made divine in that they have become fully self-sufficient. Self-knowledge is no longer a path to God but a path to the self. God's features are thereby transferred to the self (Sørhaug, 1996). But do we experience a divine freedom and blissfulness, or is it the case that we ask, 'This heaven gives me a migraine?' in the manner of the British new wave band Gang of Four (King and Gill, 1980). What is the value and the consequence of the therapeutic system of meaning for the modern human being? Has something been lost along the way from salvation to health? Is the modern, psychological human being healthy or ill? These questions to Freud and the entire worldview of psychology are asked by the American religion sociologist Philip Rieff (1922–2006).

The majority of the literature and research on 'the therapeutic ethos' has with few exceptions directly or indirectly stemmed from the works of Rieff (Loss, 2002). Rieff presented in his doctoral dissertation *Freud: The Mind of the Moralist*, from 1959, and later in the popular sequel *The Triumph of the Therapeutic: Uses of Faith after Freud* published in 1966 the theory about 'the psychological human being'. Rieff was one of the very first to produce a systematic and thorough analysis of the significance psychology and psychotherapeutic thought had had for Western culture. In his dissertation about Freud, Rieff claimed that no other philosopher (today) has had greater influence on the formation of the USA's culture and politics.

This comment was made in the 1950s when Freud's popularity was at an historical high. Although the popularity of Freud and psychoanalysis would dwindle in the coming decades, Rieff warned about the ripple effects of Freud in the form of Freudianism and a more general therapeutic movement. The title *The Triumph of the Therapeutic* hints at a contemporary diagnosis wherein Freud has been the source of a series of therapeutic movements which in spite of great internal differences nonetheless defended the same therapeutic worldview. Rieff would prove to be uniquely visionary. Today, at the beginning of the twenty-first century, we have abundant evidence for the triumph of the therapeutic culture, not only in the USA, but in the West likewise (Woolfolk, 2003). The passage of time has in other words demonstrated that Rieff's warnings against Freud and psychology were worth heeding. As I will show through an interpretation of Rieff, although Freud has been declared 'dead' on a number of occasions in recent decades, his ghost continues to haunt us.

Freud's cultural philosophy studies of modern civilisation are found first and foremost in those works written late in his life, *The Future of an Illusion* from 1927 and *Civilization and Its Discontents* from 1929. In these works Freud comes to the conclusion that maintaining culture is inconceivable without powerful psychological inhibitions and repressions. And the more advanced the form of civilisation, the more psychological illnesses we can expect to see. In the modern era, the control of nature with the aim of achieving greater material prosperity is no longer the most important challenge. It is now instead a matter of the psyche and 'the mental life', where the fundamental question to be addressed is whether it is possible to lighten the load borne by the modern individual in that the latter must repress his/ her nature and instincts in the culture (Freud, 1927). Freud, like a number of other philosophers of his day, saw a connection between the extraordinary increase in the incidence of neuroses and the decline of religious faith in the culture of Vienna at the beginning of the twentieth century – which has often been characterised as 'the dress rehearsal for the end of the world' (Eriksen, 2000). Religion, Freud observed, could no longer shape and curb the character, it could now only trouble and bother human beings. Faith had become a form of anxiety. Freud therefore hoped that his own science – psychoanalysis – would contribute to the development of an alternative to the traditional treatment by world religions of the problem of anxiety (man's existential suffering).

Freud knew that he lived in a time of a general collapse in values. Values are, according to him, a modern concept for the edifying belief that the central repressions written into the body are the neuroses of civilisation. The crisis of values was therefore in Freud's hands, transformed into a crisis of neurosis. The moral conflict and political struggle for culture and civilisation were 'repressed' to the benefit of the psychological struggle taking place as an individual life project in the consciousness of each individual. The external conflicts were replaced by the inner struggles of the mind. Psychoanalysis was not solely intended to alleviate the feelings of fear and pathologies that can arise from the meaninglessness of an existence without God, but on the contrary to vanquish this completely, according to the Australian sociologist Michael Casey (2002). But can psychoanalysis and general psychology keep their promise: a final release for the modern human being? Freud attempted to prepare the modern mind for the fact that it would have to live in a world void of sacred powers – where every boundary could be challenged and transgressed, but where sorrow at all times lay just beneath the surface (Rieff, 1979).

The final question in accordance with which Freud's psychoanalysis and general psychology as a modern experiment will be judged is therefore: can man live without God? Or to put this more in terms of secularism and religion psychology: can a human being live in an (anti)-culture that does not put him or her in contact with something beyond the self?

Nature's final bastion

Rieff's ambitious project was to investigate authority's conditions and potential transformations in modernity. Authority was defined by Rieff as a strong law (nomos) which originally informed human beings of their calling and place in life. On the other hand, modernity, permeated as it is by Christianity's decline and the fall of metaphysics, Rieff characterises as *anti-authoritarian*. Modern man's original calling has been turned upside down: now one actively attempts to rid the self of the requirements of the past (see the presentation of individualisation in the last chapter). Rieff claims to the contrary that this repression – the super-ego (the conscience) – which for Freud represented inherited ideal norms and requirements, in short, the moral principle, is something the modern individual never *can* nor, more importantly, ever *should* attempt to do away with.

Freud's project can be understood as particularly ambitious, with the objective of adapting human beings to a wholly new era. Freud revitalised the Enlightenment project's belief in a rationalised future where human beings would once and for all be able to discard superstition and ideologies (Rieff, 1979). The uncovering of man's inner life can be understood as rationality's conquest of nature's final bastion of unknown territory: the psyche. The modern psychological human being becomes the natural endpoint for the Enlightenment's progression all the way from 'the religious human being' and 'the political human being'. Indeed, the number of neuroses and psychological ailments increase, but this, Freud (2002) maintained, was the price we would simply be obliged to pay for the modern culture through which we have subjugated nature and hold the instincts in check. The idea that an increased incidence of psychological ailments is an expression for a gratifying social development is one we can also find today in the ethos of the psychology profession (see Chapter 8).

There are a number of reasons to ask whether this is a sustainable social theory. One objection presented by Rieff is that Freud's vision acquires penetration as a specific outlook on the world, even though Freud himself insisted that he had not created a worldview. Since Freud's day, a displacement from his original purpose has occurred – Freud has been made the inventor of a therapeutic worldview without personally aiming to do so, in Rieff's opinion, particularly due to all of the psychoanalytical and psychotherapeutic schools that subsequently emerged. Rieff points out how Freud is the first theorist in the history of the West who performs a fundamental break in relation to the foundation of morality. For the first time it is not authority (nomos) which is culture's fulcrum, but the self (eros). Rieff's analyses disclose what can be called 'a psychological ethics' which appears today to be universal, and, therefore, to be something we take for granted – wherein values have become synonymous with therapeutic values. 'How does it feel?' has become the fundamental question that the psychological person asks him or herself. But as Rieff shows: Freud's worldview is neither a historical necessity nor universally valid. It just appears that way to us today because we have grown up with it.

Freud as a theorist is first and foremost an interesting figure in the history of ideas in that he expanded upon the therapeutic turn that was prompted by Nietzsche, to develop it further into a distinctive science. The logic, or more specifically the psycho-logic, which Freud represented survives still today. As a clinical theory Freud is dead and his version of psychoanalysis first and foremost an historical anachronism, but if we view him as a social analyst presenting a specific theory about the hierarchical organisation of the relation between the individual psyche and society, it is reasonable to ask whether we are not still living in Freud's worldview. Rieff's (1979, p. 18) treatment of Freud is therefore predominantly indirect: 'It is as a social science that Freudian psychology must be dealt with.' Whether his theories about the life phases of childhood hold water in light of more recent developmental psychology is of secondary importance. An important basis for Rieff's reading of Freud is Freud's alleged ambition of wanting to study man's existential conditions and cultural forms of expression. Freud himself admitted that his entire scientific career was actually just a digression from this objective, Rieff (1979) claims. Through the discovery of psychoanalysis Freud found nonetheless a tool with which to address humanity and civilisation so he could become the philosopher he had always wanted to be. The modern era needed a new science, and Freudian psychology with its intricate interpretation of politics, religion and culture focused on the inner life's psyche was perfectly suited to this endeavour. Freud thus represents a break with psychology as a purely natural science. The latter, according to Rieff, lies outside of Freud's true interest. We must therefore also understand Freudian psychology as a fundamentally social science, is his conclusion.

Between nature and culture

For Freud human desire and instinctual life can be reduced to two types of primal instincts, the sexual instinct – eros – and the destructive instinct, the death drive – thanatos. These two primary instincts are to be understood as congenital. They are the source of needs, but the satisfaction of these needs can simultaneously put the individual in danger. The classical example from Freudian theory is the child who wants to murder his father to gain exclusive access to his mother. But since the child is completely dependent upon his parents for survival, he must repress this desire. In doing so, the child sacrifices elements of his/her opportunities for security, and this sacrifice and trade-off is inevitable for all human beings wishing to have a normal life. Freud's hypothesis of repression also applies in general to culture or civilisation – all human beings have within them a trace of this psychological myth. The consequence of the repression is that the psychological energy does not gain an immediate outlet but, to the contrary, is expressed by indirect means. This generates symptoms of neuroses in a way that is not necessarily pathological, an example being the process he calls sublimation, which is of great importance for the formation and maintenance of civilisation. The repression also creates a distance between impulse and action which makes possible thought and calculation, and as such lays the groundwork for the intellect in the developmental history of man. The repression leads to a shift from external compulsion to internalised control of the self. This then becomes a benchmark for the degree of civilisation in each individual human being and the standard for social and moral order in society (Casey, 2002).

Freud himself emphasised that his psychology was a theory about both the individual and society. What this implies is that although the psychology of the individual and social psychology accordingly are to be considered equivalent, the parts of the analogy are not equal. In Rieff's claim 'the social' can always be reduced to 'the individual', from manifest public actions to latent private emotions. Rieff (1979) therefore makes the argument that Freud never actually developed a truly social psychology. 'Politics' for Freud is first and foremost something taking place in the individual consciousness. Rieff further claims that Freud views the political society not as a superstructure produced to limit man's apparently universal egotistical compulsions, but as an expression of man's irrational wish to return to an authority. Freud's theory about the origins of civilisation was that man committed a primal traumatic patricide in 'the horde', which was later made manifest as an indelible memory in the subconscious of each individual human being (Freud, 1998). Since this postulated primal father was 'murdered', an enormous longing for him emerged.

Freud's view of the political society is therefore that it is equivalent to a universal abomination, and not something that can produce highly divergent and more or less functioning societies, lives and values. Consequently, he always remains sceptical of all forms of politically radical trends, such as the revolutionary movements of his own time in the first half of the twentieth century. Freud reads psychologically the political conflicts of his time over how society should best be organised and views them exclusively as an expression of an eternal psychological struggle between the individual and society (Rieff, 1979). By viewing both social oppression and revolutionary rebellion from a psychological perspective, Freud's sympathies always function in support of the status quo, Rieff argues. Since society is always essentially oppressive, there can never be legitimate revolt. Revolution and the dream of a better world exist only, in other words, as a human illusion.

Freud does not view the individual psyche as a contingent entity as Nietzsche did. Freud therefore explains all collective psychology on the basis of individual action as an unconscious identification with a leader or leader principle that is profoundly rooted in all human beings. The common universal emotional situation that can arise in historical periods is of secondary importance to him. Freud saw no qualitative difference between the hypnotic situation of the therapy session and the emotional organisation of society (Rieff, 1979). It is also (only) the tyrannical democracy of feelings which Freud takes as a model for politics, something which explains in part his deep scepticism of political movements. Freud did not recognise any neutral feelings, either in public or private life. He understands the political leader as a psychological type with few emotional constraints and without any need for the approval of others. He thereby applies the same yardstick to all politics and condemns it to being about authority, Rieff holds. The consequences of Freud's conservatism are that nothing qualitatively new can occur in history. It is possible to take this even further and apply it to the later general psychology in its entirety. Although a number of psychologists and psychology in its own right set out to investigate large-scale social systems or political situations, this is always done from a guiding individual-psychological perspective, to which any conclusions can be attributed. The ideologies or the common human condition is thereby not a part of psychology and the link to how these influence consciousness is lost. The British psychologist Ian Parker (2007) claims for example that the most reductionist and reactionary accounts of collective actions are to be found among social psychologists and political psychologists who in an essential fashion view political questions about power, conflict and change as questions about psychology.

Freud actually reveals his anti-political prejudice and bias – politics can be traced back to a long chain of projections on the part of the individual. With Freud, politics are understood psychologically. This results in analytical psychology contributing to the destruction of the optimistic belief in free citizens who made rational choices by 'discovering' that the average voter was not rational. No distinction is made between different values, only a struggle for identification between different leaders. Public situations become the dramatisation of personal interests. Psychoanalysis has been welcome in the USA ever since the discrediting of political radicalism, because psychoanalysis understands the revolutionary type simply as a neurotic who projects their own aggression on to public life, Rieff claims.

If society is always held together by an irrational cultivation of and dependency on a leader, then society, given that it is stable, is always authoritative. The dream of a society based on equal citizens is therefore an illusion. Acceptance of the necessity of a form of social or cultural coercion (oppression) corresponds with the liberal canon of which Freud is a part, according to Rieff. For that reason Freud also rejects Marxism and other ideas about social development. The necessity of social oppression (in the language of psychoanalysis: repression) does not exactly make Freud a spokesperson for an oppressive system, he emphasises. Freud is first of all a sceptic, unmoved as he is by the possibilities of changing the political order. Politics is not an instrument for rational action, as it is for the Marxists, but is reduced to a collective symptom of catharsis in the subconscious mind of the people. Freud's own sympathies were shaped by a predominant doctrine of individuality, in which society meant sacrifice of the individual, not as in former conceptions of 'society' as an organic community and 'the individual's' fulfilment. Freud adhered to a romantic connection between privation and good governance; he upheld the belief in a permanent antithesis between the individual and society. The relation between the individual and the community and between nature and culture is therefore an inevitable and necessary conflict. The Freudian doctrine is liberalism brought to a preliminary final phase, Rieff claims, where it acts as a medicine for itself. The life of society is only analysed at the moment it fails to respect the individual's right to satisfaction. In consequence it becomes an ethics of social adaptation. Freud remains sceptical of all ideologies about private life, but Freudianism will ironically in fact later come to function as an ideology (Rieff, 1979).

It has been pointed out that Freud's social theory is inspired by the philosopher Thomas Hobbes's (1588–1679) political philosophy about sovereignty, which Freud even refers to in *Civilization and Its Discontents*. Both assert that community and culture arise through the limitation of the individual's anarchistic satisfaction of needs (Eriksen, 2000). The Norwegian philosopher Arne Johan Vetlesen (2009a) has claimed that Hobbes in his time reversed the relation between community and the individual – the individual was from that point onward the unquestionable element in politics that was assumed to inherently exist while the community was considered artificial. Vetlesen (2009a) comments on a feature of Hobbes's political philosophy which Freud's worldview probably has only reinforced: Hobbes too breaks away from the Aristotelian teleological idea that the human being in society has a potential for development into something more. In that the individual simply *is* for Hobbes and Freud, altered forms of society and existence cannot make that individual better, they can only limit him or her.

The famous cultural historian Jacob Burckhardt (1818–1897) lashed out long before Rieff against the Renaissance ideal of 'the private human being' – what man gains as a private individual, he loses simultaneously as a social citizen, he claimed in the well-known work *The Civilization of the Renaissance in Italy* (Burckhardt, 1990). Freud can be accused of the same: individual health rather than social improvement is the psychological message. Freud attributed humans with a nature completely removed from the objectives and meaning of society. Independent of the social values the therapist always prescribed the same medicine: 'man for himself'. Freedom is therefore something that can potentially be realised under any type of regime – because freedom can always be found within the individual if the balance between the psyche's elements is right. Whether we then find ourselves in the modern Western democracy or in the tyranny of ancient Athens is fundamentally a matter of indifference since freedom remains purely a psychological entity. The search for social freedom is superficial; in fact it is an absurdity if one follows the thinking of psychoanalysis, in that freedom and tyranny are merely different states of mind. By turning towards the inner life, psychoanalysis threatens in its consequences the opportunity to discriminate between one regime and another. Freud therefore undermined the ancient interest in political philosophy and replaced it with political psychology, where the opening question and premise for politics becomes in which way and to what extent the individual is bound by social relations (Rieff, 1979). If political protest can be explained by neurotic symptoms and all politics are corrupt, both in a democratic society and in a totalitarian state and if psychoanalysis teaches a private, disillusioned search for well-being, then all resistance to despotism is also futile (Kaye, 2003).

The ethics of self-disclosure

The tendency for a weakening of religious faith in the USA in the beginning of the twentieth century was not created by the entrance of the therapist and psychoanalysis, but as a result of this moral period of upheaval the 'therapist' was summoned to duty in this revolution throughout all of the West, if not the entire world (Rieff, 1979). The analyst then performed a conservative function – his or her task was to pilot the patient safely out of the identity crisis that ensued due to the lack of identification with former authorities. When there is only just enough force remaining in faith to undermine the faithful, the analyst has no other option but to help the patient reach an acceptance of his or her failing beliefs. When the patient has been liberated from the final authority, namely the therapist, the patient has achieved the only real freedom that is still possible – he or she is now wholly alone. Rieff holds that this tearing away is masked as a liberation, in the manner of continual forms of encouragement to live life for its own sake, held up as a freedom ideal.

The psychoanalyst is a new type; he does not struggle against the parish priest, Rieff maintains, in that his therapy is not primarily a therapy about faith. The psychoanalyst instead seeks to instruct 'the psychological human' on how to live without faith. Religion can no longer save the individual from producing his own private neurosis, because he has become his own religion: taking care of himself is now his ritual. Health has become the ultimate creed. Although the goal of therapy is to teach man how to live without faith, the ideological impact of the therapeutic treatment is to replace the moral indecisiveness that the retreat of religion has generated with a new theoretical resolution. Karl Marx also sought to create a substitute for religion as a counter-faith that could provide a basis for new ideological societies. Psychoanalysis does not, however, create much of a fellowship for a counter-faith; Freud creates, Rieff comments, more precisely a faith mixed with theory. Psychoanalysis becomes a mixture of science with faith; a pseudo-religion, but without religion's potency. The therapeutic ethos today seals modernity's gap between science and religion by offering human beings from culturally disparate religious backgrounds a system of collective meaning that resembles religion (Nolan, 1998). The therapeutic ethos therefore becomes a unique alloy which offers the authority from psychology as a science but with a religious weft.

Rieff claims that Freud and the triumph of therapy contributed to the cultivation of a nihilistic universe devoid of values. Freud never provides any grounds for why psychoanalysis' ethics of self-disclosure and sincerity should be any guarantee against wrong choices or evil. Psychoanalysis shares with the rationalists of the Enlightenment the belief in the path of truth. Man should be sincere. If they express their true nature, goodness will come on its own. But in fact, Freud did not believe in instincts any more than in culture; he was first and foremost interested in the balance between the two. The new freedom leads to a calculated type of conformity. It is in this manner that we must understand its nihilistic incentive. Freud believed for a period that only when man is liberated will he or she automatically make rational and well-considered choices, but as Rieff comments, and rightly so – the Freudian ethics help us perhaps to become free, but do not provide any guidance as to which choices we should make (Kaye, 2003). Freud's silence and indifference to moral choices appear therefore to make him vulnerable to accusations of nihilism. This nihilism is albeit wrapped up in a regime of goodness and the language of humanism, but appears to lie beneath psychology's ethos in our times as well. The underlying perception that once a person has been sufficiently liberated from their neuroses, the rest will automatically take care of itself – and everything starts with the individual's self-esteem – continues to dominate the ethos as well as the politics of the psychology profession. This individual empiricism is also highly reminiscent of neoliberalism's view of humanity which emerges later: as long as the individual is healthy, nothing can go wrong. Questions about politics and religion are merely expressions of personal preferences. The psychological system is sufficient to explain all human and social interaction.

Freud's liberating method through psychotherapy offers the patient a unique opportunity to share his or her concerns in a therapy session. This method stands out as the very core activity of all psychotherapy – which is something fundamentally different from a conversation. Here it is a matter of a kind of one-sidedness, where the client initially is not faced with any requirements other than what he or she might want. The model implies an asymmetrical relation between the individual and the surroundings – where one only has rights and no obligations (other than in relation to oneself). Psychotherapy's structuring of the social situation is suspiciously reminiscent of the cultural crisis in the late-modern culture of the West described by social critics. We live in a culture of rights without duties. This is the cultural imprint of psychology's social model and theory about the connection between the individual and surrounding systems that has transported itself into the culture. This is in many ways the psychological human being's fundamental attitude and Freud's dubious offering to the culture.

Rieff positions Freud and Marx in opposition to each other. Self-control is a function of self-awareness for Freud. By making sexual drives conscious we gain control over them in a way that a system of oppression can never approximate. Speech and language therefore become the essential medium for consciousness and therefore also the crucial means of liberation (Rieff, 1979). In a footnote, Rieff cites Marx and Friedrich Engels from *The German Ideology* where they write about the contingent nature of consciousness:

All forms and products of consciousness cannot be dissolved by mental criticism, by resolution into 'self-consciousness' or transformation into 'apparitions,' 'spectres,' 'fancies,' etc., but only by the practical overthrow of the actual social relations which gave rise to this idealistic humbug.

(Marx and Engels as cited in Rieff, 1979, p. 335)

Marx and Engels remind us in other words of the material basis of the nature of consciousness, in contrast to Freud's treatment of the psyche as a universal structure. The contrast is obvious: where Freud's human model is philosophically and politically conservative, Marx and Engels's model is philosophically and politically radical.

Moreover the therapist cannot encourage the patient to seek relief by participating in Catholic, Protestant or social communities. What is needed is liberation from these social institutions. Liberating the 'I' from the 'we' is therefore the best spiritual guidance that Freud can offer. This health perspective results in a personal concern which acquires precedence over social concerns and promotes an ironic attitude towards everything that does not have a direct impact on the self (Rieff, 1979). In a distinctly intimate fashion psychoanalysis defends 'the private individual' from requirements imposed by both culture and instincts. Freud in this manner includes all human beings as his potential subject. From a psychoanalytical perspective, no person has so much self-knowledge that they have nothing more to learn from this type of 'adult education'. The belief that one can always improve 'the mental aspect', increase 'self-esteem' or work with the self has great credence in today's culture, something which we will see finds expression in self-help literature (Chapter 5), sports psychology (Chapter 6) and neoliberalism (Chapter 7).

As mentioned by way of introduction: Freud denied that he personally endeavoured to establish a perception of the world or that psychoanalysis was concerned with questions of values. Freud insisted that psychoanalysis was in the field of science. From the perspective of the patient, what is unusual about the new therapeutic situation is its unique freedom and access to an ultimate authority figure (the therapist and finally oneself). Speech and language constitute the essential medium for communication of consciousness and therefore the ultimate means of liberation. As stated above, Freud offered no hope about changing civilisation. Nonetheless, he did so in his own quaint fashion, as Rieff interprets him. A democratisation of the aristocratic heroic myth occurs and it is replaced by a universal scientific myth. Oedipus Rex becomes the Oedipus complex, something which every human being must live with. The usual is also the unusual, the normal and the pathological are entangled. To say that all human beings are neurotic removes the stigma from the suffering minority. It simultaneously opens up for the therapeutic culture. Even the analysts had to return to analysis every few years to update their self-knowledge.

From a sociological as opposed to an individual perspective, psychoanalysis is an expression of a popular tyranny, Rieff claims. 'The illness democracy' arises, in which everyone can play doctor with themselves and nobody has the right to claim that they have been completely cured. Rieff's descriptions of contemporary society are reminiscent of Goethe's fear about the future: 'Speaking for myself, I do believe humanity will win in the long run; I am only afraid that at the same time the world will have turned into one huge hospital where everyone is everyone else's humane nurse' (as cited in Lears, 1994, p. 56). The hospital replaces the church and parliament as the archetypical institution in the West. What has caused this tyranny of psychology that legitimates self-absorption as the greatest science? In part, the individual's incapacity to find something to cling to other than the self in the modern age. When man lost faith, he also lost faith in himself, which in turn gives legitimacy to a science of absorption with the self. Finally, man understands that he is chronically ill; the psychological human being is found at the end of man's ancient search for a healing doctrine. The experience of the most recent of these, for the time being – Freud's psychoanalysis – can only tell us that each cure will of necessity produce vulnerability to new illnesses (Rieff, 1979). As a result 'the psychological human' becomes incurable and an element of Freud's bleak cultural philosophy from *The Future of an Illusion*, where he has lost faith in the possibility of a better world and that man will ever be happy as a social being (Eriksen, 2000).

The critique and judgement presented by Rieff of Freud's philosophy and mystification of a particular world-view is relatively harsh. What is it that Rieff observes with such great uneasiness in modern Western therapeutic culture? Rieff's conviction is that a society without religion will not survive in the long term. No culture can survive without a transcendent superstructure, is his dire prediction. But modernity is in its essence in the process of breaking away from this idea, Rieff (2006) claims. The late modern Western culture is trying to establish itself without any reference to a transcendent order of existence. Rieff calls cultures without a holy order, such as our own, *anti-cultures* (Zondervan, 2005). Further, he posits a dichotomy between so-called 'positive' and 'negative' societies, where an example of a positive society is archaic cultures in which individuals gain salvation through the community, while modernity is a markedly negative society and historically new, according to Rieff, awaiting an inner salvation. 'Positive societies' will always seek to *transform* human beings, while 'the negative' will solely *inform* human beings (Jensen, 2006). Human beings can never be wholly cured.

Rieff maintains that the idea of man as an autonomous individual first and a social being second is a false dualism. The individual and society can never be understood independent of each other. 'Culture' is just a name for a set of motivations that are intended to direct the self outward, towards a common goal. Only there can man achieve self-actualisation and find contentment (Zondervan, 2005). A cultural crisis arises, according to Rieff, when the culture no longer performs this function and is able to create and uphold symbolic worlds. Modernity is in this sense an experiment since it is the first true attempt at disconnection from any religious basis. This occurs through modernity's efforts to dethrone authority in all of its cultural forms. Modernity and the idea of a collective advancement gradually loses its grip on the Western imagination, which creates a situation of cultural crisis in which several worldviews compete for hegemony.

Eros can be understood as the infinite possibilities of the self. But since authority today only threatens the self with certain limitations, authority is perceived as an enemy. Rieff is critical of the modern emphasis on eros over authority and maintains that we have reached a situation that has turned the situation upside down: existence should be organised around a theory about authority, not a theory about eros or the self (Zondervan, 2005) (see Chapter 4 on how this situation has reversed its original hierarchical organisation).

Conclusion

No therapy preceding the therapeutic movement has produced salvation or healing, unless this was by way of a social system tying the calling to the feeling of a community. We are therefore privileged, Rieff (1987) writes ironically, as participating observers of a historically grandiose experiment based on man's construction of himself out of himself. None of the therapeutic doctrines that Rieff addresses make promises of a connection to collective interests or goals. Instead, the connection is with the therapeutic endeavour in its own right. The therapeutic stakeholder will neither claim nor promise more. The purpose of all forms of therapy, Rieff claims, is to avoid attachment to a specific position, so that no illusion about an objective beyond the feeling of personal well-being can survive. It becomes an effective competitor against other ideologies that promise another and a better world. For Rieff, therapy's triumph represents something new in the history of Western civilisation. The feeling of well-being, self-esteem, has become the goal itself, and not a by-product of the search for a larger collective goal. This represents a fundamental shift in focus for the entire culture. The therapeutic universe becomes an indifferent, nihilistic cosmos that creates an indifferent psyche – a human being who is bored – but more importantly this universe has no evident existential feeling of loss which can function as a sign that things could have been different. The meaningless suffering which traditionally served as a source for rebellion against the establishment, no longer exists when everything can be illuminated and explained scientifically and psychologically (see Illouz's analysis of *Oprah* in Chapter 5 for more about this). The therapy room thereby becomes 'eternity's antechamber' – the connection to both heaven and hell is perhaps only obscured, but for the psychological human being, it appears that the connection has been shut down for good. In this directionless therapeutic universe there is no salvation, only individual formulas for how to endure.

4 Psychology and religion

'The crisis of authority' described in the preceding chapter has run like a red thread throughout the intellectual history of the twentieth century. In recent decades, however, it has become common to speak about a seeming counter-tendency at odds with secularisation in the form of neo-religiosity and neo-spiritualism and the return of religion. The terms neo-religiosity and neo-spiritualism refer to a variety of different religious and semi-religious movements that are either inspired by traditional religions such as Buddhism, Christianity or Islam, or more occult varieties such as New Age, which sprang up in the 1960s as a reaction to the materialism of consumer society and the ideological vacuum of our times. The hypothesis about *the return of religion* on the other hand refers to the observation that religion has today acquired a surprising but renewed political significance since the important historical transitions of 1989–1991 with the fall of the Berlin Wall and the dissolution of the Soviet Union (Habermas, 2006), which were used as signs of the final telling blow of the liberal, secularised democracy (Fukuyama, 1992). The German philosopher Jürgen Habermas (2006) describes the emergence of religious fundamentalism as a reaction to capitalistic modernisation in regions such as the Middle East, large parts of Africa, South East Asia and India, where many inhabitants experience a sense of rootlessness in reaction to these civilisation processes. Simultaneously, religion in a country such as the USA, where modernisation has been the most successful, has also undergone a political revitalisation (Habermas, 2006). The belief that increased modernisation results in increased secularisation, whereby religious faith and practice have increasingly less influence on politics and the life of society would therefore appear to be in need of modification. Habermas and others have therefore defined the era we are living in as post-secular. However, the aspect I will investigate in the wake of this notion is whether the ideas about the return of religion and neo-religiosity weaken the hypothesis that we live in an individualised and therapeutic culture. Is the therapeutic ethos simply in the process of being phased out to make way for a return to a more traditional, collective set of religious values?

Scholars who have studied the burgeoning therapeutic culture and ethos in the USA throughout the development of the twentieth century have neglected the parallel development in the religious culture, claims the historian Christopher Loss (2002). Rieff's influential idea about 'the psychological human being' and the studies of the accompanying therapeutic culture has been established without addressing religious moments to any particular extent, Loss maintains. With a few symbolic exceptions, the connection between religious life in US society and the USA's therapeutic culture remains unexamined. Loss's (2002) appeal is therefore that scholars who are writing about the therapeutic culture must cease to behave as if religion doesn't mean anything (any longer), when clearly today it does.

As I shall demonstrate in this chapter, the return of religion or neo-religiosity need not necessarily be a contradiction to the depiction of the therapeutic culture and the challenges (such as the crisis of authority) it makes manifest. It is not necessary to view neo-religiosity or neo-spirituality as being in opposition with the penetrating impact of the therapeutic ethos; to the contrary, the therapeutic culture encourages precisely all forms of individual search for meaning. New Age and therapy are in this sense to be found along the same continuum (Vitz, 1991). Even more, Western religions today, such as Protestant Christianity, have long since incorporated the therapeutic project, whereby the sacred dialogue more or less assumes the form of a psychotherapeutic consultation or therapy session.

Religion and psychology hand in hand

Modern psychology arose as an extension of Protestant Christianity in particular. Historian Eva Moskowitz (2001) therefore maintains that the USA's nascent therapeutic culture was spread following a minor reorganisation of – and not a decisive schism from – America's Protestant Christian tradition. In this sense we can understand psychology along a continuum. Religiosity today seems to exist within an individualistic-therapeutic worldview, and is not necessarily a departure that implies our returning to a vertically orientated cosmos with a transcendent, symbolic authority. Religion sociologist Robert Bellah (2008), for example, finds in his studies that all of the religions in the USA today revolve around what he calls an individualistic ethos. The French historian Marcel Gauchet (1985) has claimed that Christianity represents the start of the phasing out of religion (in the traditional sense): gradually, 'the sacred' is swallowed up more and more by 'the profane'. Christianity is a religion well-adapted to a post-religious society that is produced by capitalistic modernisation. Martin Luther's (1483–1546) Protestant reformation of Catholic Christianity can be understood as the natural follow-up of an impulse that was initiated by St Augustine (354–430), where faith in God for the first time in the history of man was internalised and reduced to a personal dialogue with God or the self, something which represented a clear departure from the religious tradition which had a particular focus on collective, institutional rituals. Psychology from such a perspective is perhaps only the natural extension of the individualised, Protestant Christianity that gives faith precedence through individual contemplation rather than religious rituals and ceremonies. Norwegian psychologist Steinar Kvale (2003) has remarked that today it is in particular in Protestant countries (the USA and especially the northern regions of Western Europe) that psychology seems to have achieved the greatest proliferation and following.

God as a cosmic therapist

Sociologists of religion Christian Smith and Melinda Lundquist Denton (2005) recently carried out a large national interview survey in the USA about religiosity among American teenagers, in which they discovered that many of them defined themselves as religious, and very few, if any, advocated rebellion against their parents' faith or religious tradition. Accordingly, most American teenagers have an extremely positive attitude towards religion. At the same time, American adolescents, much like American adults, are for the most part deeply individualistic. They therefore instinctively assume that autonomous, individual self-determination is a universal human right and something to be acquired if one should find oneself without it. This perception also has an impact on their relationship to religion as Smith and Denton's findings demonstrate. Most of the teenagers were not subjected to difficult requirements from their surroundings regarding how they were to live their lives and, therefore, nor is their faith associated with any obligations to speak of. The teenagers who were interviewed considered themselves autonomous agents in relation to external factors such as religion; in the final analysis, they are the ones who decide about their own lives. Each individual has their own unique dreams and needs and it is therefore neither possible nor expedient for anyone else to assume the authority to judge another's specific beliefs or life conduct (Smith and Denton, 2005). Along the same lines, when it comes to God there is no right or wrong answer; it is a matter of what you are comfortable with (believing in).

In Smith and Denton's interviews, we find the core values of individualism: each individual is different from all others and in consequence deserves a faith that suits his or her unique self. In other words, it is the individual who has authority over religion and not vice versa. Religion need not (any longer) be practised in a local community. The religious beliefs are even replaceable since it is not the religious creed's traditional integrity that is the defining factor, but the individual's comfort level in believing whatever feels appropriate for them. Through their surveys Smith and Denton (2005) establish emphatically that although the USA must be understood as being religious, it is first and foremost a matter of a religious individualism where the individual has authority over religion and not the reverse, the latter being the position which throughout history has characterised religion's defining function in most societies.

The majority of American teenagers appear to have a purely instrumental relationship to religion: God exists to help the individual so he or she can do as he or she likes. For instance, two of the teenagers give the following description of their faith in God: 'It's always there, helping you mentally, supporting you' [. . .] 'Going to church makes me feel better' (Smith and Denton, 2005, p. 152, 154). Religion is not (any longer) a traditional superstructure or a transcendent authority or divinity imposing requirements that the individual personally does not want. Religion is instead something personal that will cause you to feel good and help you to solve your problems (Smith and Denton, 2005). God can therefore be considered a type of advisor or a *cosmic therapist*; an ever-ready and qualified helper who does not demand any devotion or submission in return. In this sense, one can say that the modern form of religious individualism administrates rights and to a limited extent imposes obligations, wholly in keeping with the therapeutic ethos in which the self is the foremost authority.

What gives religion legitimacy for most adolescents of today is not the life-changing, transcendent truth, but instead that which instrumentally provides mental, psychological, emotional and social benefits. The religion of today in the USA must therefore be said to be qualitatively different from the faith of former eras, which has been about something more than making the right choices and helping people to feel good (Smith and Denton, 2005). The authority has been turned upside down in such a way that religiosity, at least in the USA of today if this study can be said to be representative, exists in full compliance with the theory of the therapeutic rights-based universe and Rieff's anti-culture.

The cultural disorder through which American teenagers navigate shrouds them in the ethos of therapeutic individualism. Therapeutic individualism is not a conscious or deliberate ideology, but a framework for the self, society and the meaning of life that is taken for granted and which has great influence on the morals and boundaries of daily life. Therapeutic individualism exercises considerable influence upon young Americans' religious and spiritual practices and experiences, Smith and Denton maintain. It defines the individual self as the source and goal of an authentic moral knowledge and personal well-being as the main objective of existence. Subjective, personal experiences are the defining characteristic of what is authentic, right and true. And on the flip side, external traditions, duties and society's institutions are inauthentic and impose illegitimate requirements and constraints on morality and behaviour, the liberation from which is the individual's job (and obligation) (Smith and Denton, 2005). Where the self was once put aside and repressed by religion, it is now to be nurtured, actualised and confirmed. An entity such as 'the society' is no longer something the self must adapt itself to, but something the self must liberate itself from. The members of the therapeutic individual culture are encouraged to get in contact with their true feelings and find their true selves, as if they have natural, independent feelings and a self that exists separately from social reality.

The result of seeing God as a cosmic therapist is that everyone is 'religious' and few are critical of this: who am I to criticise the religion of others? But nobody is religious in the traditional sense of the word, and the result is a therapeutic Christianity that to a limited degree provides people with a connection to something that transcends the self. At the same time, faith no longer serves the traditional role of religion in culture – namely, as an authoritative law and order that has a regulatory impact on the needs of the individual and society, and provides the foundation for a well-adjusted balance between rights and obligations.

Neo-religiosity in Norway

A new degree of openness to neo-religiosity and neo-spirituality in many Western countries is evident. An extremely popular item in Norway in this regard that has dominated the bestseller lists is Princess Märtha Louise of Norway and Elisabeth Nordeng's (2009) book *The Spiritual Password*. In the introduction to this book the authors make a distinction between what they call 'the religious' and what they call 'the spiritual':

> Elisabeth was once asked the question 'Are you religious?' What does it mean to be religious, she thought. If it means to meet God through a religion, then I am not religious. If on the other hand it means to meet the divine power that is within and around me, then I am religious.
>
> (Prinsesse Märtha Louise and Nordeng, 2009, p. 8)

Princess Märtha Louise and Nordeng's distinction between 'the religious' as an external force (God) and 'the spiritual' as an inner, divine force can be understood as a distinction between two different approaches to morality – a religious (extraverted) and a therapeutic (introverted). The former is often associated with traditional, institutionalised religion, while the latter is associated with Gnosticism, New Age and therapeutically motivated beliefs (faith based on health and being healthy). My assertion is that a good deal of neo-religiosity can be explained by the development of a therapeutic relation to religion, where people define themselves as religious first and foremost because it has health-enhancing effects.

There are indeed a number of obviously neo-spiritual and spiritual aspects to be found in Princess Märtha Louise and Nordeng's book about guardian angels, chakras, auras, grounding and separation. If, on the other hand, one peels away these supernatural and New Age-inspired stories, what one is left with is a therapeutic core, the message of which is familiar and reminiscent of much of the current self-help literature and popular psychology, something which is revealed through the authors' defining message to the reader:

> Introducing angels into one's existence is about taking greater control over your own life. It is about trusting yourself, so you dare live out what you dream of. You know that in the depths of yourself you have the map to find the road ahead. The angels are loving and insightful life companions. Perhaps the time has come now for you to assume responsibility for your own life?
>
> (Prinsesse Märtha Louise and Nordeng, 2009, p. 171)

The emphasis on the idea that readers should allow angels into their life is essentially about taking responsibility for their own lives. You are the one who must take responsibility for your own life by releasing something embedded in the depths of yourself. The message is easy to recognise. It is about the usual secularised, individualistic conviction that the individual is personally the very key to their own successes and failures, here packaged in a neo-spiritual language with the same characteristics that Smith and Denton found to be the underlying basis of meaning for today's religious American teenagers.

A great deal of contemporary religion can be understood as a worship of the self as God – among other things, a number of New Age movements seek to strengthen the self in the context of modern existence's Babel-like confusion over identity (Revell, 1996). The most central feature of neo-religiosity today is that the self is left as the primary religious arena and foundation for identity. Heelas (1996b) uses New Age as an illustrative example of this authoritative transition to the self. In spite of the fact that at first glance New Age perhaps appears to be particularly heterogeneous – represented by everything from Zen meditation to occultism to astrology – all of these different schools have in common that they first and foremost view the self as the locus of religiosity. It is always a matter of locating something latent in the individual or in one's surrounding environment. The self is described as perfect, wise, energetic, powerful and peaceful. The true self is contrasted with 'the ego' or 'the personality' which has had its vital nature corrupted by socialisation in society. Princess Märtha Louise describes in her book how she struggled with a number of public appearances until she discovered her aura and had it adjusted the requisite number of centimetres. The closer you get to the self, the more authentic the formula, while the outer reality appears increasingly more unfriendly and impersonal. 'More and more people are choosing the inward road – it seems easier to change the self than to change society', observes religion studies scholar Otto Krogseth (2003, p. 122).

Heelas (1996b) draws parallels between New Age and psychotherapy from Freudian psychoanalysis to Rogerian (humanistic) therapy, which he calls a watered-down version of New Age. Both humanistic psychology and versions of psychoanalytic thought, in particular Jungian, have clearly Gnostic elements – one is in possession of a true self just waiting to be released. New Age and psychology have the same period of prevalence in the Modern Age – from the mid-1960s up to today. Even if one classifies New Age as religious and psychology as secular, they are accordingly two sides of the same coin.

'The sacred' has never been about an isolated belief in God, the supernatural or a set of values or norms, according to religious studies scholar Lynn Revell. Regardless of the definition of 'the sacred', its relevance for human beings was its defining feature. The classical worship of 'the sacred' was situated at the core of the conflicts and contradictions in society. New Age in its understanding of the sacred, however, entails a wholly new approach. One characteristic of New Age is its anti-rationalism; in contrast to the Western tradition's requirement for proof of devotion, New Age is first and foremost about whether the faith is acceptable to the individual. It is this inherent relativism in New Age that distinguishes it from the classical perception of 'the sacred' (Revell, 1996). New Age thought instead celebrates as progress the relativisation of authority and truth as opposed to the restriction of old-fashioned dogmas. It is the individual who personally chooses his or her faith and who can abandon the same without any consequences. Since the path of science and reason to the truth has been abandoned, the only guide leading to the truth is the inner self (Revell, 1996).

Historian Suke Wolton (1996) maintains that the current age is characterised by both desacralisation, associated with a decline in traditional religiosity, along with a process of neo-sacralisation, but limited to the sacralisation of the self. This can explain how it is possible that the interest in institutionalised Christianity is waning, while the interest in neo-spiritualism is on the rise in the population. In Norway, belief in God has dropped by 10 per cent, from 78 per cent in 1991 to 68 per cent in 2008, while the percentage of non-believers has increased from 10 per cent to 18 per cent in the same period (Botvar and Schmidt, 2010). Among young people between 18 and 34 years of age, the majority define themselves as neo-spiritual but not religious (30 per cent) (cf. the distinction made in *The Spiritual Password*). What these people have in common is that they 'have their own way of being in contact with God' (Bakke Foss and Sødal, 2009, n.p.). This represents accordingly a clear departure from former experiences of the sacred whereby the individual was integrated into a fellowship. The modern-day psycho- and therapy religiosity, as Krogseth (2003) appropriately calls it, is thus limited to the inner life and the individual.

Bauman (1998) views neo-religiosity as an element of the increasing prevalence of a fundamental uncertainty in the consumer society. Bauman claims that the neo-fundamentalist tendencies must therefore be understood as a modern phenomenon, arising from the joys and sorrows of postmodernism, since its strongly authoritative features are appealing as an excuse to avoid the necessity of having to choose. The development of modernity is characterised by an uncertainty about human existence in its own right, which becomes palpable when people who live in accordance with a traditional ethos (adapted to an external value orientation, such as duty) are more and more in the minority and those who do are perceived as reactionary and often met with requirements to adapt to a more self-driven autonomy:

> People whose already internalised orientations keep being devalued, even ridiculed, by the day, need authoritative guidance; but the guidance they seek and may reasonably expect, a guidance adequate to the kind of agony they experience, is one likely to call on their own resources, aimed at reforming (correcting, improving, developing) their own know-how, attitudes and psychical predispositions.
>
> (Bauman, 1998, pp. 67–68)

This is, in short, the birth of identity – the most significant of all modern creations, according to Bauman. Postmodernity in particular becomes therefore the era of identity experts, he states. Postmodern women and men, either through free choice or coercion, have become choosers. And the art of choosing is predominantly about avoiding one single risk: that of failing to take advantage of the opportunities – either because one did not see them clearly enough, pursue them with enough determination or was too inexperienced to seize them. To avoid this danger, today's men and women need counselling. This postmodern uncertainty does not create a need for religion, but rather for identity experts. Individuals haunted by this uncertainty do not need priests who tell them about their frailty and the shortcomings of human beings. They need support and encouragement to believe that they can do it, and formulas for how to do it (Bauman, 1998). There is a hunger for an expertise or authority in the population, but it is not motivated by religion in the traditional sense.

What then about the neo-fundamentalism witnessed among Christian, Islamic and Jewish movements around the world? Today's lower classes are the consumers who have missed out, who are unable to take advantage of all the opportunities that lie within reach, Bauman claims. The dissatisfied consumers' bitter acknowledgement is that the human individual is not self-sustaining and wholly self-sufficient. The experience of this insufficiency is however unlike the pre-modern morality of religion about man's frailty, but is instead more about the irreparable weakness of the human individual. Bauman (1998) claims that the fundamentalism to be found in the major religions of today is a child of the postmodern and market-controlled society and must be understood as a remedy for risk-filled freedom. Theologian Robin Gill makes an argument along the same lines when he says that the fundamentalism of today within both Christianity and Islam is not primarily about a literal interpretation of a religious tradition or scripture, but must be understood as a modern phenomenon, in which the religious stakeholders' identity is founded first and foremost in opposition to key features of modernity (as cited in Revell, 1996).

Religiosity is defined by Bauman as the human intuition about the boundaries of what we are, what we can achieve and what we can comprehend (Bauman, 1998). Neo-religiosity in our times can therefore be understood as a set of spiritual impulses and resources in the individual, in a culture dominated by the injunction of the individualised and therapeutic ethos to personally manage one's own unique identity in the best possible manner. Krogseth (2001) makes the argument that modernisation and secularisation have resulted in an identity threatened by crisis. Resacralisation and neo-religiosity must therefore be viewed as aspects of an attempt to repair the identity threatened by crisis and heal the loss of a secure foundation. The breakdown of the identity as such opens for neo-religiosity but only under the condition that it helps the individual in his or her self-actualisation and identity building.

Now that we have seen how neo-religiosity does not represent any deviation from the therapeutic ethos but to the contrary can easily be understood as a natural extension of it, it can be appropriate to return to the question of how psychology as a replacement for religion is sustained. According to Kvale (2003) the history of psychology has to a limited extent been concerned with studying the continuity between religion and psychology. The historians of the discipline appear to prefer the rational Descartes over the devout Augustine when they are going to choose an idea historian as the origin of modern psychology (Kvale, 2003). A similar conclusion is drawn by psychologist Paul Vitz (1991) who holds that the religious influence on modern psychology has been systematically and consciously misappropriated in the writing of the history of psychology, something which is of importance with regard to the formation of the discipline's self-perception. Kvale (2003) asserts that there can be a closer connection between Christian thought from Augustine and the diversity of religious sects in North America, with the resultant image of man in recent European and American psychology, than with the history of philosophy. Modern psychology corresponds with religion and with Protestantism in particular, in terms of the individualisation and construction of 'the inner human being' through constructions such as the self and, in its guidelines for personal well-being, in the search for truth and in the consolation found in confession and pastoral care (Kvale, 2003). Protestantism entailed that human beings were set free through their confessions, and the eternal guilt was transferred from the church to the inner consciousness and free will. The very term 'psychology' arose in the sixteenth century and the Protestant individualisation came to dominate the psychology of the Enlightenment project during the centuries that followed (Kvale, 2003). But as we saw above with Rieff, both modern psychology, viewed as a replacement for religion, and the neo-religious movements we have considered here lack the fundamental characteristics and essential qualities that religion has had up to now in society.

Religion's function

Thus far, the investigation of religion and psychology has revolved around whether neo-religiosity demonstrates any signs that we are in the process of abandoning a therapeutic worldview. My answer to this is 'no'. Now I shall, on the other hand, turn the question around and return to the question posed indirectly by Rieff. Can psychology perform the function that religion has traditionally carried out in culture?

The foremost function of religion is to find a meaning for suffering and help people endure it by leading them away from that from which there is no escape in the mundane sense through rituals and faith, towards the supernatural (Geertz, 2000). The problem with suffering has never been how to *avoid* suffering, but how to *address* suffering, in other words, how to learn to endure, in spite of physical pain, the experience of loss and personal defeat. Late modernity, on the other hand, cannot provide for us any longer, the way religion once did, Illouz (2003) claims. The contemporary collective potential for theodicy – interpretations of and explanations for suffering – appears to have been lost. This has, however, been one of the most important functions of culture at all times, specifically, to explain how evil or accidents could strike our lives and how we can come to terms with these in our moral ethos. Where traditional religious theodicy located the meaning of suffering outside of the human being, the therapeutic culture's twist is to locate the meaning and acceptance of suffering within the human being through therapeutic narratives about the self (see, e.g., Illouz's analysis of *Oprah* in Chapter 5). The task of psychology is precisely to alleviate the suffering of modernity's beleaguered self. But can it actually do so? Or does it offer paradoxical solutions which instead put human beings into a locked situation where the pressure of suffering becomes perhaps less acute, but where the problem of meaning has actually not been solved, only temporarily postponed?

Durkheim's view of religion entailed that 'God' was a meaningful entity because the collective worship of God was indicative of the existence of 'society' as a unifying mechanism. 'The sacred' was thus nothing more than the collective power that society had over the individual. Participation in religious rituals actually entailed worship of 'society' (Østerberg, 1974). Durkheim (1971) emphasised the necessity of discovering and creating new ways of giving society meaning. If traditional religion no longer functioned, it was then necessary for human beings to create a new normative order to replace the old. With the demystification and secularisation of the world, this essential work – the regulation of the relation between the individual and society – has come to a halt. 'The sacred' under the New Age and psycho- and therapy religiosity not only emphasises the self, but, even more importantly, it denies potential virtues outside of the self as an illusion (Revell, 1996). 'The sacred' was not just the individual's faith or the physical worship of religion, but a constantly ongoing and vital process in which man created and maintained society, according to Durkheim. Behind Durkheim's (1971) view of religion lay the conviction that without 'the sacred' there could not be any paths to experiences or fellowship outside of it. On his or her own, the human being is only an individual, but connected with other people, he or she can develop the potential to become more than a solitary being. It is in other words 'the sacred' that transforms man into a social being (Revell, 1996). The relation between the self and 'the sacred' is accordingly edifying because 'the sacred' in principle supports the self's extroverted interaction with the rest of society. Today under the relativised New Age religion, this tendency is instead turned around – 'the sacred' generates only an inward search. Neither was there such a thing as an individual relation to God, like the virtually absurd examples we have from the interviews with the 'religious' American teenagers, in that that relationship was already determined by society. Today we live with the perception that the self will become something more than it already is through self-actualisation and physical and spiritual release of your bound-less potential. It is, however, a struggle that is limited to the human being's efforts to disconnect from the requirements imposed by the community/collective. Religion today is therefore a paradoxical phenomenon that glorifies what the self can potentially achieve, without offering any supporting remedies.

The visions forming the basis for 'the traditionally sacred' represented a collective projection of the future. This was a central aspect of society's ability to plan its future as a society. Today the utopias are virtually non-existent. Not only have the individual and the self been elevated above the collective level, but the individual self is also diminished and further at risk, according to Revell. Actualisation of the self becomes both the start and endpoint of our time's search for truth and meaning. The self isolated from the rest of humanity becomes the ultimate guarantor of right and wrong. However, there is no freedom in liberating ourselves from the authority of an omnipotent God if the freedom achieved is only turned inward, she argues. This is not a new liberation, but a self-centred prison without possibilities for shared experiences. The self has perhaps become God, but it is an isolated and lonely self, limited by its fragmented nature and its own constricted experiences and dreams.

In the preceding chapter we saw how Freud understood religion first and foremost as a phenomenon that demonstrates neurotic symptoms en masse (Freud, 1939). Freud located religion inside the individual – for him it was first and foremost a stage in the psychological maturation process that takes place in each individual; religion was not something that was discovered or invented and passed on to subsequent generations. The classical sociologists such as Durkheim and Weber, on the other hand, understood 'the sacred' as a fundamental social phenomenon. Religion was something larger than the sum of individual creeds; it was a force that stimulated and regulated society (Revell, 1996).

The sacred power was never of interest to Freud – the power that Rieff sought to rejuvenate with his sacral sociology. Power is one thing, authority another, Rieff insisted. Psychologists receive their authority from our belief in their roles: as experts in treating our search for the original authority. This new guiding figure in our therapeutic anti-culture makes its presence felt only to depose the religious filaments of our ghost-like forefathers. Rieff calls this an anti-culture because our culture does not meet the criteria for culture's actual purpose – that which steers the self outward towards the collective objectives where the self can become actualised and achieve fulfilment. At the end of the historical journey of the Western self we find only the therapist, prepared to ambush each and every attempt to renew faith and explain away all forms of collective rituals that celebrate recognition of the divine, according to Rieff. The human being is bound to the weight of him/herself and even with enormous therapeutic efforts, one cannot manage anything more than some shifting around of the weight of this burden.

A question of guilt

When we try to do away with religion, we are trying simultaneously to do away with guilt. Rieff criticises the effects of too much psychological knowledge and insight since this serves to undermine our ability to manage the feeling of guilt that is required to uphold the sacred order. This is one of the core characteristics of the modern project. Western culture does not suffer from an overly demanding super-ego, as Freud believed, but rather from one that has become hopelessly weak. Rieff's therapeutic counter strategy was therefore to attempt to reinstate guilt in culture (Kaye, 2003). The guilt that Freud writes about is primarily psychological, not moral. But the therapeutic worldview which remains intact in his wake eventually acquires consequences that weaken morality.

Guilt is not just a dark force to be held in check but our richest and most valuable hidden treasure – the very essence of being human, the Australian sociologist of religion John Carroll (1985) writes in *Guilt: The Grey Eminence Behind Character, History and Culture*. He defines guilt as the human race's sixth sense, the grey eminence that instructs human beings in what they shall do and what they shall not do and what divides the world into good and evil and tears the human being out of the vanity of absorption with the self and its own desires, quite simply that which makes him or her a human being (Carroll, 1985). Guilt is also a messenger from the past, which is of huge significance to the formation of the future. Guilt is at once a psychological, moral and spiritual phenomenon. It rises up in all humans and requires an answer. Without it nothing but a self-situated, emotional ethics is possible. ('How does that make me feel?'). Without guilt we lack channels through which to seek out answers for suffering and meaning anywhere but within ourselves, Carroll (1985, p. 1) writes, and quotes Russian writer Nadezhda Mandelstam's assertion: 'A sense of guilt is a man's greatest asset.'

The Christian culture started with a fundamental transgression when the forefather of the human race was expelled in shame from the Garden of Eden. Since Adam and Eve it has been viewed as abominable not to feel guilt and shame. In the twentieth and twenty-first centuries, guilt has to an increasingly greater extent been viewed as the worst of all illnesses. Has our most important resource been gradually turned into a curse, Carroll therefore asks suggestively, and sets about exploring whether our culture is in the process of failing in its most important task: namely to intercept guilt, give it a framework and give it a meaning.

What is the benefit of modern psychology if the best possible outcome of its application as therapy is to give human beings a consoling delusion, Carroll asks. Freud himself believed in psychoanalysis as therapy. This was Freud as a twentieth-century rationalist, who did his part to contribute to making logical that which would one day be the ever-driving force behind religion; in other words, that the Enlightenment project's belief in progress through science was also possible in the area of the psyche. It is nonetheless somewhat unfair to point at and blame modern psychology for its search for psychological knowledge and scientific advancement at any cost, Carroll warns. Psychology has quite simply followed the Western tradition, the damnation of which began with Adam being tempted to eat from the tree of knowledge, according to Carroll. Adam abandoned faith to follow reason. Freud was a product of humanism and the Enlightenment's idea of a belief that knowledge could heal. He replaced Socrates' axiom that the truth can lead to virtue with the idea that truth will lead to good health. Even as late in his career as 1932 Freud still referred to reason's authority as the hope of the future (Carroll, 1985).

For Carroll it is only the religious language that can put us in contact with guilt, but as long as psychological solutions are all that are provided, guilt's positive resources remain unexploited. People who move too far away from 'the sacred' lose contact with it and become shameless. The Australian aborigines who are an example of such a spiritual people, Carroll writes, would wither away and die if they were to lose contact with these forces. It is no different anywhere else, even if the body survives. The difference between a superficial culture of guilt and a religious culture founded on guilt is that the latter uses most of its energy on upholding a channel to the gods through prohibitions, rituals and celebrations, all of which are steered by a fear of God. Man will feel close to the sacred order, surrounded by it and in constant contact with it. In the opposite case, the sacred order becomes remote and man interested only in himself. The secularisation has entailed an increasingly unclear idea of 'the sacred' and the importance of it. The guilt over making a mistake, for example, is a much greater burden without religion (see the discussion on individualisation in Chapter 2). Psychoanalysis is in this sense morally corrupt, Carroll argues, because it turns psychological health into a goal that exists beyond the scope of good and evil. The scale becomes exclusively therapeutic: 'How do I feel now?' The sick society becomes a self-fulfilling prophecy – everything moral becomes psychological.

For Freud, guilt indicates insufficient self-knowledge, a lack of tolerance for the self on behalf of the natural (in) man (Rieff, 1979). He does not want any part of objectification of the universal dimension of guilt, whereby the question becomes why guilt has apparently always been there, throughout all of civilisation. Freud operates instead with a perception of an initial patricide as the origin of culture: the guilt of human beings stems from the Oedipus complex and was inherited from the murder of the primal father. Modernisation and the culture of individualisation simultaneously lead to the transition from a Christian worldview to a therapeutic and Freudian worldview. The feeling of guilt has been brought down to earth, individualised and has lost its reference to authority but as Jensen (2006) maintains 'the feeling lingers on'. Nowhere is there as much repressed guilt as in the victim culture. Here the guilt cannot be expressed as guilt or as sin but only as anxiety, depression, eating disorders or other illnesses that can only be cured therapeutically. And of critical significance: guilt is in Rieff's words 'the civilising emotion' and wholly decisive for a culture. It is only by retaining guilt as the basis for individual responsibility and obligation in a society that a society is (up)held in which we can become socially well-adapted beings. The victim culture we live in, however, goes in the opposite direction: the citizen has first and foremost rights and few or no duties.

The fatherless society?

In 2006 the Danish historian Henrik Jensen's monumental work *The Fatherless Society* was published, a work that depicts the current culture of rights as a clear departure from former civilisations' authoritative patriarchal cultures of obligation. Jensen, like Rieff and Carroll before him, sees signs of a moral crisis in Denmark and in the West in general. Late modernity is characterised by what he calls 'mother rule' and which indicates that the citizen is apparently liberated from all forms of authority and duties, and the only guidelines imposed on him or her is the welfare state's encouragement of its citizens to pursue self-centred self-actualisation (Jensen, 2006). The social hierarchy in the West up to the present day has been organised around a vertical cosmos, while today we live in a horizontal culture, Jensen maintains, with reference to Rieff among others. 'The fatherly' and 'the motherly' thus become metaphors for the lost, hierarchical culture of obligation and its replacement, the vulgarising culture of rights. Jensen (2006) claims that what he calls one of the basic illusions of liberalism is a prominent feature of the therapeutic culture. Liberalism's basic illusion is the idea that if one only protects the individual, the latter will evolve out of him/herself and the good society will follow (cf. the ethics of sincerity of the previous chapter). Jensen questions this fixation and draws a parallel to the culture of obligation's fixation on order which historically speaking has had a tendency to slide over into a paranoid culture, with the persecution of witches, or Jews, as one of the most horrific examples. On the flip side lies the pitfall of the culture of rights, if it should become an overly unilateral, self-stimulating, mass-individualised victim culture, Jensen argues. In the prototypical culture of guilt, the individual has only duties, and in the victim culture, only rights. The ideal is therefore a carefully weighed balance between rights and duties in the society. Where the individual in the culture of guilt is indebted to God, the parents or society, the opposite is the case in the rights culture: the victim has an eternal claim for recompense. Jensen is thinking first and foremost of the citizen who quickly takes on the role of victim in relation to the state or society and also demands redress. This tendency in our times is not so difficult to glimpse in the media. 'To assume the role of a victim' appears to have become so much a part of the culture that it has become a legitimate media strategy, which politicians and celebrities constantly employ. The culture of rights can also be detected in more or less absurd examples from daily life. For instance, the Norwegian school system where school children have become so aware of their rights that teachers risk committing a crime if they throw somebody out of the classroom and into the corridor for having sabotaged the lesson (Kristoffersen, 2009). For politicians – possibly with the exception of the Conservative Party in Norway which has 'responsibility' as one of its most important virtues – speaking about duties is moreover taboo: politicians and their strategic advisors are remarkably aware that we are living in a culture of rights in which external, authoritative requirements are reactionary. No politicians today have the courage to speak about feelings of duty in a nouveau riche nation made up of individualists concerned about their rights, was the conclusion of *Morgenbladet*'s former editor Alf van der Hagen (2009) in a discussion about community service as an option for weapons-free conscription in 2009.

The second main problem with 'the fatherless society' which Jensen identifies is the liberal individualism's fatigue effect. This is a type of crisis of meaning which finds expression in the form of an increased feeling of emptiness, loss of direction and meaning, particularly among the younger, adolescent generation, in that the individualistic culture does not offer access to anything outside themselves, while it simultaneously encourages us to find the answers within the self. It is not possible to find one's identity without being confronted with authority, Jensen claims, with reference to Adorno's idea that individuation cannot occur without authority, and to Bob Dylan, who is to have stated: 'That lie about everybody having their own truth inside of them has done a lot of damage and made people crazy'.

Self-actualisation is hard work and fewer external reference points make this project confusing and potentially exhausting for many people. The crisis of meaning combined with a cultural perception that 'everything is possible' carries the risk of leading to a situation of extreme despair for many young people. They find themselves exposed to pressures at cross purposes: they feel isolated and lost but all the while with the knowledge that the potential is there somewhere (as a rule, within the self) to turn it all around as self-actualisation. The paradox is that the therapeutic ethos invites people to understand their lives in terms of suffering because pain provides a basis which enables psychologists to give their knowledge legitimacy and construct stories about individuality (Illouz, 2003). The greater the number of causes for suffering that are situated in the self, the more the self is understood on the basis of its predicament – and with more actual ailments produced as a result. Perhaps one formerly located guilt outside of man because one was insightful enough to understand the burdens that situating it within man would entail? Jung's (1972) project was to reconcile religion with psychology and he called attention to precisely the capacity of the myths to liberate the individual from suffering and elevate that suffering to a higher level. Jung often spoke warmly about therapy which elevated the suffering of a general situation, such as the snake bite in Ancient Greece, where it was a matter of demonstrating the archetypical situation through myths. If this failed, the patient was thrown back to him/herself in isolation without any connection to the world (Jung, 1972). This psychological insight appears to a large extent to have been lost today – the preferred explanations are as a rule based on the individual. A reason why Freud's psychoanalysis 'triumphed' over Jung's more collective theories about the unconscious may simply be due to the fact that Freud's individual model was a better fit for the preferred ideology in and outside of therapy. Freud hypnotised the world through his elevation of the 'dream' and 'fantasy' as inner gods. 'The unconscious' with Freud becomes a Western and modern version of 'the beyond', becoming a highly personal and private affair (Sørhaug, 1996). Psychological theory and practice must therefore from now on serve both 'the truth' and 'the sacred'. Perhaps the belief that it was possible to unite science and religion was a modern hubris?

All or nothing

One of the most prominent features of postmodernity is the individual's feeling of omnipotence when something goes well and the feeling of complete incompetence when something goes wrong (Dufour, 2008). The character of the psychopathology has evolved from modernity's neurotic subject who built up a compulsive guilt by disappointing the other (God, parents, etc.) to emerge through the founding of itself, according to the French philosopher Dany-Robert Dufour (2008). Ehrenberg (2010) has demonstrated how feeling ashamed (of oneself) today has come to replace guilt (in relation to others). Where guilt allowed long-term frustration, it must today be vanquished after a long period of introspection and projection into the future – in modernity symbolic purification was possible. Shame directed at the self must on the other hand be removed immediately – and without the relation of meaning one symbolically establishes through guilt. The result is identity confusion. The weakening of religion is accompanied in short by a greater burden in being a self. 'The greater the degree of individualisation, the greater the problem of the self,' Gauchet (1985, p. 205) writes. The post-religious society is a society where the question of madness and everyone's inner uneasiness experiences frenzied growth, he claims. This society is psychologically exhausting for the individual, since it no longer protects or supports them when they are unceasingly confronted with the question: why me? We are condemned to living openly and in a state of anxiety from which the gods have spared us since the beginning of time (Gauchet, 1985). Each and every one of us must work out our own response.

The question I have endeavoured to approach in this chapter is, in some-what simple terms, whether health in fact can be a fully valid replacement for salvation. A conservative critique of the spirit of the times that speaks of 'requirements' and begins to expound upon the idea of the individual human being's self-sufficiency with all rights included, comes across as rather jarring to the ear in the therapeutic rights culture. The critics I have cited here can also be easily understood on the basis of the adult genera-tion's despair over the younger generation's deterioration. It is well-known that all generations believe that the adolescent generation will be the last. The critique of psychology presented in this chapter can therefore be inter-preted as a form of yearning for authority. Carroll and Jensen in particular go to great lengths in making a case for the need for a patriarch in the form of the strong father as possible saviour. This is something which is in con-flict with, for example, the feminist project. The Danish literary scholar Lilian Munk Rösing in her book *The Return of Authority* (2007) takes to task the conservative reactionaries who view with dismay the ideals of the liberation movement, such as self-actualisation and the transcendence of boundaries. Rösing tries instead to find 'a third path' – ironically enough via Freud and psychoanalysis, among others – towards a universal ethics beyond the super-ego and what she calls the ethics of the father's ghost. Rösing's critique of the neoconservatives is that they overlook the fact that duty lives on in pleasure. The solution is therefore not to seek to turn this upside down again, because that will only reinstate old, patriarchal struc-tures, but to effect a radical break from the human image of the super-ego and its obscene dark side: the pleasure principle. Rösing's leap out into 'the unknown' is somewhat reminiscent of Nietzsche who, in contrast to Freud, sought to abandon and break away from man's psychological trappings and its Christian-Platonic consciousness, and move towards a state of eternal becoming, rather than be reconciled with it.

The neoconservative critique of the therapeutic culture can also be accused of exaggerating a current trend – it is not a given that the ethics of self-actualisation must revert to egoism – it can also contain a normative potential involving an imperative to show consideration for the self-actualisation of others, as Danish philosopher Rune Lykkeberg (2007) comments in a fairly critical review of Jensen's *The Fatherless Society*. There is also cause to ask whether duty is in fact as fully absent in the adolescent generation as has been claimed. New studies of the work ethic in Norway and Sweden show, for example, that the work ethic among the generation of young people between the age of 18 and 25 is stronger than in older employees and not in any sense weakened today compared to the 1970s (Bråtebrekken and Emanuelsen, 2010).

In spite of these objections I believe that what can be viewed as falling under the value conservatism critique of society nonetheless has some insights that are worth considering. Rieff maintained that it was possible to find the following social and moral guidelines in Freudian psychology: a liberal defence of the individual against all requirements from social, political and cultural restraints, an attack on a dying, ascetic religious culture and a deep distrust of all forms of collective fellowship because of the latter's potential to produce regressive and destructive movements (Kaye, 2003). Rieff understood early on that Freud was far more sociological in his interests than has been the common conception up until now. Today when the therapeutic culture does not only exist in the USA but in the entire Western world (Illouz, 2008), Rieff's assertions that social considerations were always a hidden underlying agenda in Freud's psychology appear more credible than ever before. In the therapeutic society, institutions no longer exist to discipline or regulate the individual but instead to facilitate his or her deliverance (Jensen, 2006). The therapist therefore becomes the foremost expert but it is naturally the self that is the ultimate authority. The therapeutic culture of rights can at first glance be understood as a care-free culture in enabling us to live out fulfilment in that man's strenuous pursuit to free himself from external constraints is finally over. The only obligation you have left is the one in relation to yourself. This becomes a problem, however, when confronted by situations that challenge the individualist ethos and prompt collective action. The most dramatic example of this in today's global situation is the climate crisis. The problem has been precisely that of convincing people to take action on the basis of a common understanding and a unifying sense of obligation in relation to the world or future generations (cf. Monbiot, 2010). The impact of the therapeutic ethos can thus be to counteract such a collective will.

Vetlesen (2010) recently addressed the problem of collective thought and the possibilities for cooperative action in the age of individualism in connection with the climate issue. One of the main problems that Vetlesen identifies is a misunderstood pluralism of values where the only valid authority is the one the individual discovers for him/herself, which must be respected in the absence of an overriding moral discourse. The parallel to the American teenagers' cultural relativism and insufficient interest in criticism of others' religious life conduct, addressed at the beginning of this chapter, is striking and an expression of the same individual therapeutic logic. Nobody is more valuable than anybody else and all knowledge and information is therefore equally credible. Nobody can make themselves the judge of self-esteem's authority. The result is a collective paralysis. 'Appeals to humanity, cosmo-politics and citizens of the world are in some (intellectual) milieus tractable, that's true, but they have psychology against them: they are too abstract,' writes Vetlesen (2010, p. 25).

Conclusion

We have now looked at how it is possible to perform a religion-psychological critique of Freud and the entire subsequent therapeutic project. Psychology too risks staring blindly at the achievement of emotional well-being and self-actualisation as a goal in and of itself, while throughout history this has been – as Rieff touches upon – a by-product of the establishment of a common culture (cosmos) understood as being indirectly guaranteed for the individual member. Perhaps this is as simple as the old saying about happiness: if we chase it as a goal in its own right, we are condemned to failure. If we on the other hand forget the question of happiness, the chances are better of it taking us by surprise. Likewise, perhaps the conditions for self-actualisation and self-esteem are best when they are not made into an express cultural ideal and a goal in and of themselves, but rather a by-product of a culture that is sufficiently balanced between individual autonomy and a common collective culture, which gives the individual both a feeling of belonging and meaning as well as simple imperatives for how to live. Cultural solutions founded exclusively on the self, on the other hand, would appear to bring about new and serious psychological ailments, particularly in connection with the issue of identity (Dufour, 2008). It is indeed a paradox that the therapeutic project can therefore prove to be in contradiction with what is considered to be a 'healthy' development of society. But as we will see in the second to last chapter, the foremost experts in the field of psychology are in possession of only a limited ability and/or desire to question the basis for it being in such great demand. There is therefore reason to believe that this development will only be further reinforced.

Interlude
Psychology in crisis?

We have seen through the examples of Hall and Freud how modern psychology originated in the Enlightenment project's belief in progress, in which science and rationality were viewed as the road to material prosperity and spiritual happiness. What happens then when cracks begin to appear in this idea – would not psychology then as its legitimate child be thrown out with the same bathwater? The following section is about psychology in our own time, a period often referred to as late modernity or postmodernity.

Kvale (1992) maintained that contemporary psychology was in a state of emergency when considered in light of the postmodern challenge. Modernity put man at centre stage and understood humans as rational beings, followed by a belief in emancipation and development through reason and science. After the atrocities of Auschwitz and Hiroshima, however, it proved difficult to uphold the belief that mankind was evolving away from barbarity towards an increasingly humane society. Postmodernity therefore highlights a condition in which the utopias are dead, a condition of 'what now?', in that the idea of progress has become difficult to substantiate. Psychology's view of human beings as sovereign, autonomous agents with a universal, abstract psyche also appears to be out of sync with the postmodern fragmented identity. The postmodern decentring of the subject can therefore lead to a decentring of modern science about the human subject.

In the early 1990s Kvale (1992) offered the following description of the status of psychology. A journey through the shelves of psychology literature at a university bookstore produces a feeling of boredom. One finds standard works, the collected works of Freud and Jung, a myriad of therapeutic self-help literature and some scientific cognitive works. The new sensational insights about man are no longer to be found in psychology, for this one should instead look to philosophy, literature, the arts and anthropology. Kvale's judgement of psychology in the postmodern era is that it no longer has anything of importance to tell us. The philosopher Alan Bloom (1987) made similar observations in his evaluation of the social sciences' impact on the American universities in the mid-1980s. Psychology appears in a mysterious manner to have disappeared from the social sciences, Bloom notes. And he asks whether psychology's unbelievable success as an applied science has not led to its giving up on any theoretical ambitions. Now that psychotherapy has succeeded in installing itself side by side with the family GP, will one not, from here on in, be interested to a greater extent in more specific problems rather than in comprehensive theories about man? Will this in turn result in psychology education becoming first and foremost a programme of study for a profession, like the study of medicine, rather than a preparation for scientific research (Bloom, 1987)?

The question which shook the pillars of psychology's foundation and cast shadows of doubt upon its entire legitimacy became more frequent throughout the 1990s, in particular the scepticism about psychoanalysis. *Time* magazine in 1993 had, symptomatically, a front cover that asked: 'Is Freud dead?', accompanied by a picture of a fragmented Freud in the process of complete disintegration (Gray, 1993). A sign of the times was that many people were now questioning the status of psychoanalysis as a science – asking whether the idea of the unconscious was solely a product of Freud's imagination and creativity. Nonetheless, psychology is found to be more popular than ever. The *Time* article therefore concludes that in spite of all of the objections to Freud's discoveries and methods that have been raised, he succeeded in creating an intellectual edifice that has greater relevance to people's lives and suffering than any other system of meaning today.

Despite the fact that during the period before and around the turn of the century there were many observable signs in circulation that psychology as a discipline was afflicted by stagnation, either because its potential and meaning had been reached, or because it was judged as passé due to its origins in an optimistic and progress-friendly view of the history of and science about man, this in no sense had an impact on its dissemination and position in society. To the contrary. Although psychology's theoretical innovations and academic influence had suffered a setback, it is in greater demand and more popular than ever on the export market. With an extreme capacity for adaptation and flexibility, psychology seems to navigate like an amoeba towards any type of niche that is receptive to therapy and self-actualisation or the selection and steering of individuals, or so goes Kvale's less than flattering depiction of psychology in the postmodern age. Sociologist Nikolas Rose (2007) has made the argument that an important epistemological shift has taken place in the field of biology, from the nineteenth century's deep biology that sought to reveal underlying organic laws behind living systems, to today's extensive surface mapping of biological genes. Perhaps we can apply this epistemological shift to psychology: we have moved away from the early twentieth century's psychology, which penetrated deep down into the layers of the psyche, to today's popular psychotherapeutic schools, such as cognitive therapy, which focuses more on rearranging the patient's mind map here and now, and which is much briefer in its duration. On the whole, psychology appears like biology to have changed character from deep, esoteric insight to universal application.

This implies that we must 'lower' the gaze from the scientific and professional expertise to focus on 'the surface' and mass culture in order to study today's psychology. We must investigate psychology's presence in examples of popular culture such as the television drama, reality television, the self-help culture and sports in an attempt to discern psychology's place in the culture and in 'the collective unconscious' of the population. A characteristic of the postmodern era is that the cultural and power hierarchies are reshuffled. The traditional distinction between different spheres such as economy and culture is erased and high and low cultures are mixed (Jameson, 1984). The same thing happens to psychology – it acquires penetration in many areas that previously had not been associated with psychology. Research and science become more open to impulses from society and the relation between professional experts and popular psychology is, as we shall see, virtually eliminated.

In order to understand psychology's role in today's society we must therefore investigate today's popular culture and popular psychology. Illouz (2008) holds that it is through these expert tips, magazines, talk shows, and self-help books that psychology has the most influence. The investigation of psychology in the postmodern era entails asking the same question as in previous eras: will the attempts at a postmodern psychology simply reflect consumerism, or does it contain a potential for critical reflection and resistance to the dominant ideology of postmodern society?

5   The self-help culture

Many authorised psychologists and psychology specialists will certainly reserve the right to make a clear distinction between themselves and the self-help industry. This industry is characterised by many unprofessional practitioners; it is a cultural import from the USA and other countries where there is less control over who is permitted to practise and call themselves therapists, etc. This is understandable. But a number of theorists who write about the therapeutic culture have simultaneously pointed out that the distinction between professional and popular psychology expertise is in the process of breaking down. Some would even maintain that the distinction between popular psychology and 'the expert's' psychotherapy has never been as clear as the latter group would have us believe (Becker, 2005). Illouz (2003, 2008) describes the distinction between specialised psychological expert knowledge and popular psychology as porous, since the discourses of both professional and popular psychology address the self by way of more or less the same metaphors and narratives.

Ever since the inception of the psychology profession, psychologists have had an inherent compulsion to transgress the boundary between specialised knowledge and popular culture, Illouz maintains. From an early stage in psychology's history, American professional psychoanalysts and psychologists have employed the market and mass culture in order to reach the entire population with their message. An illustrative example is one of the founders of humanist psychology, Carl Rogers (1961, p. vii), who in his book *On Becoming a Person* makes it clear that he wants to reach ordinary people in their daily lives: 'It is my sincere hope that many people who have no particular interest in the field of counselling or psychotherapy will find that the learnings emerging in this field will strengthen them in their own living'. Illouz provides a number of examples from other branches of psychology as well, among these the cognitive psychology pioneers Albert Ellis (1975) and Aaron Beck (1988) who, like Rogers, in books such as *A New Guide to Rational Living* and *Love Is Never Enough: How Couples can Overcome Misunderstandings, Resolve Conflicts, and Solve Relationship Problems through Cognitive Therapy* have had an express objective of making cognitive psychology accessible to the general public. Psychotherapy's message has accordingly throughout a good portion of psychology's history been directed towards the masses and daily life (Illouz, 2008).

The tendency on the part of clinical experts to popularise both their research findings and elements from their clinical experience in the media and in books categorised as popular psychology and self-help literature is visible in many Western countries. Although the psychological expertise often appears in a context of so-called lighter forms of cultural expression, the impact is not without weight. Illouz (2008) claims that psychology and therapy in all of their manifestations are now being spread around the world at a scale comparable to American pop culture and perhaps even surpassing it. The therapeutic discourse has contributed to erasing former categories such as the private and public, and is now the most important arena for the expression, formation and determination of individuality. The point Illouz (2008) makes here is that this has occurred on all fronts in psychology – scientific, clinical and cultural. On the whole psychology can be said to have achieved a form of cultural legitimacy across social groupings, organisations, institutions and communities. Academic curricula, education programmes, the requirements for psychology professions, treatment programmes, and so on, have been standardised, and in the process the therapeutic discourse has transcended national borders and constituted a transnational language for individuality. Illouz (2008) substantiates this claim through the work of Israeli sociologist Shmuel N. Eisenstadt, who maintains that civilisations have 'cores' that expel and congregate in accordance with different ontological visions. The therapeutic view of the world has, in short, become the centre of the somewhat vague and ambiguous entity better known as Western civilisation. From clinical interventions in people's lives to media claims along the lines of 'Research shows . . . ', through the body of literature comprising psychology research and popular psychology, to fictional TV series such as *The Sopranos* and *In Treatment* or talk shows such as *Oprah* and *Dr. Phil*, psychology today constitutes on the whole a therapeutic matrix – or a formative, basic element in Western culture's self-understanding that regulates the individual and his or her contact with the world (Illouz, 2008). So although authorised psychologists and psychology specialists would prefer not to be compared with all manner of self-help gurus, a preference that can have certain legitimacy, all of these practitioners borrow their authority from and uphold through their cultural proximity what Illouz calls a therapeutic matrix.

Self-help literature

The therapeutic ethos achieves a particular level of penetration through popular psychology and self-help literature which, with time, has become a huge market. The self-help manuals that Kvale began to notice in the psychology sections would come to explode in number in the following decades. The sales of self-help books in the USA increased by 96 per cent over the course of just five years, from 1991 to 1996 (McGee, 2005). From 1972 to 2000 the percentage of self-help books increased from 1.1 per cent to 2.4 per cent of the total number of books printed in the USA (McGee, 2005). According to the NRK television programme *Aktuelt* (NRK, 2010) Norwegian bookstores recently reported an increase in sales of self-help books by 30 per cent, and the interest in self-help courses in Norway increased by 67 per cent from 2008 to 2009 alone.

A popular proponent for the self-help genre is 'Scandinavia's most popular coach' (Women and Clothes, 2010), the Swedish Mia Törnblom (2007, 2010), who has written bestsellers including *Self-esteem Now!* and *More Self-esteem!* of which, combined, she has sold more than a million copies in the Nordic region (Ringheim, 2011). Törnblom is a former drug addict and consciously employs her rough past in her books. *Self-esteem Now!* opens with a scene in which the 29-year-old Törnblom wakes up in the Kronoberg state prison. Her books are typical of the genre in which one frequently follows the author's own transformation from down and out to personal success. Törnblom's message leaves no room for confusion. As the book jacket blurb of *More Self-esteem!* reads: 'This year, 2007, it is about time that you started treating yourself with as much love, respect and consideration as you show others you care for!' Törnblom (2007) introduces the reader to an exercise that she normally uses at her many seminars. All participants are told to write down the names of the three people in their lives who are closest to them. Then Törnblom asks the participants: 'Has anybody written down their own name?' Scant few will have done so. Törnblom's point is that we hold our relationships to others in greater esteem than our relationship to ourselves, when it should be the opposite. If we can manage to have a good relationship to ourselves, our relationships with others will be both simpler and better. Our relationship to ourselves has, in other words, for many become a challenge for which finding a good solution has become a matter of the utmost importance: 'It is the most important relationship of our lives' (Törnblom, 2007, p. 28). In her books the reader receives advice on how to develop 'self-esteem' in friendships, romantic relationships, in the parenting role and in working life. The self-help discourse illustrates clearly how therapeutic ideals can be applied as an explanatory model and guide both in the domain previously understood as private (personal relationships) and in that which was understood as public (working life). If we compare the self-esteem books of the life coach Törnblom with the Norwegian psychology specialist Guro Øiestad's (2009, 2011) books on the same subject matter, the qualitative differences are not particularly great. Øiestad's work is more scholarly, with references to current psychological terms and techniques, and to philosophers and authors, while Törnblom's approach as an author is to draw from her own experience and essentially accompany the reader on the self-help journey. The similarities are, however, much more prevalent than the differences: both are about working with oneself to achieve a better relationship to oneself and to others.

Törnblom is at the beginning of her books careful to emphasise that she is speaking about *self-esteem* as a feeling of self-worth, while she emphasises that *self-confidence* is something else and is more about confidence in one's own abilities. There is something remarkable about the emphasis made by Törnblom and other experts (such as the Danish family therapist Jesper Juul) on the distinction between 'self-esteem' and 'self-confidence'. It is obviously important for Törnblom to make this distinction, but it is nonetheless as if she is personally not fully certain of how different the two concepts actually are. As Øiestad (2009) touches on in her book about self-esteem, in recent years it has been important to distinguish between 'self-confidence' and 'self-esteem', but as she says, this difference would appear to be greatly based on purely linguistic distinctions. An explanation could be that practitioners such as Törnblom want to dissociate themselves from more superficial values that we perhaps with greater facility associate with 'good self-confidence', such as success in life financially, career-wise and in one's personal life. Her books contain a number of stories about people who for all appearances are successful and have 'good self-confidence' but lack 'self-esteem'. Self-esteem is in other words not something related to external, measurable criteria, but is rather something that everyone can achieve. Törnblom can thereby permit herself to be critical of the success ideal of our time and potentially reach everyone with her message. 'Self-esteem' is a deeper psychological metaphor, the achievement of which is less contingent upon external framework conditions.

From a critical perspective is it naturally easy to find objections to Törnblom's positive message which has reached hundreds of thousands of readers in Scandinavia. A sociological or ideological objection would be: Törnblom treats social pathologies as if they were an individual matter, and accordingly individualises and conceals the most important causes of the ailment (cf. Beck's critique of psychology in Chapter 2). The titles of her popular books *Self-esteem Now!* and *More Self-esteem!* accordingly scream out 'identity crisis', or a crisis of meaning, where the sense of self and the overall self-esteem of the population is significantly disabled and to a large extent can be said to be greatly reminiscent of Nietzsche's desperate, meaning-seeking human being of European nihilism at the end of the nineteenth century. The Swedish social psychologist Thomas Johansson (2007) has observed that a remarkable common feature of much of the self-help literature is that it frequently assumes a perspective critical of modernity in terms of contemporary life. One example is the American psychologist Phil McGraw, famous from the therapy talk show *Dr. Phil* (2002–), who often prefaces his books by stating unequivocally that society is going downhill: the number of divorces is on the increase, the crime rate is getting increasingly worse, and so forth. The conclusion drawn by experts such as McGraw is not, moreover, that we must work together to build a better society, Johansson comments. No, instead, the answer is personal development towards improved self-esteem. Reference is made exclusively to working with the self, alone, towards a potentially improved individual future. The rhetorical question put by Vetlesen (2007) in a critical commentary is thus: where are the exercises, techniques and advice on how to imagine a better collective future in self-help literature?

These are timely objections which I personally share to a large degree and have provided for in this book. Nonetheless, I do believe that the critique of the self-help culture must recognise that Törnblom and other self-help experts are on to something essential and, as such, address a need. The relation to the self has become a problem and therefore is 'the most important relationship of our lives'. 'Self-esteem' has in fact become an important psychological technique which coincides with neoliberalism's ideal form of government under which people personally deal with their own problems (this is addressed further in Chapter 7). Another question naturally pertains to the correct solution to any self-esteem problems that might arise. Törnblom offers help towards self-help – people must work on themselves. The question begged by this strategy is whether Törnblom and the self-help literature and popular psychology – through their naked proximity and appeal to readers to work with themselves – indirectly impair the opportunity to motivate and produce attempts at changes that are not about working with the self, but that address instead the external political and structural parameters that dictate our existence. Then self-help comes across as a social anaesthesia, which ensures perpetuation of the status quo.

The books by both Törnblom and Øiestad have been written within the framework of a relatively well-functioning and stable Scandinavian social democracy and they are relatively intelligent and sober-minded, compared with a good deal of the self-help literature to be found, particularly in contrast with more New Age or quantum physics-inspired progeny.

The inner universe

Several of the self-help books embrace postmodernism's ideal of anything goes and happily ally themselves with either hard sciences such as quantum physics, or the soft sciences such as positive psychology or New Age and parapsychology. In spite of the fact that some of these books go quite far in terms of what they encompass and promise, they have nonetheless a common therapeutic core. One curious example is the author Barbara Marciniak (2004) who claims to be a medium for a foreign race from another galaxy – the Pleiadians – who are from the Pleiadian universe where perfect spiritual happiness has been successfully achieved. Through Marciniak's speech and writing the Pleiadians can therefore guide us imperfect beings to physical well-being and spiritual completion. If we take the liberty of peeking behind Marciniak's spaced talk about other existences and dimensions, the creatures from outer space can be understood as being a projection, not solely from Marciniak's personal subconscious, but from the collective subconscious – to borrow a term from Jung – of the desire for perfect well-being and happiness, which is a central theme of a great number of people's lives in late modernity. In the book *Path of Empowerment. Pleiadian Wisdom for a World in Chaos* Marciniak (2004, p. 7) writes:

> Each day, the choices you make are crucial to your well-being, and just as important, your thoughts not only set the course and direction of your life in the physical 3-D world, they also ripple into and affect many other realities. The stakes in this 'game of awareness' are steadily being raised, and you are challenged more than ever to identify your innermost feelings and acknowledge them as a primary source for creating your reality.

If we disregard the reference to multiple dimensions beyond our own, the passage serves as a reasonably fitting description of the situation of the postmodern individual. It reflects the widespread cultural acceptance of the idea that you can personally create your own reality – and that you are thus personally responsible for whether or not you have a good relationship to yourself. We also find here the Gnostic perception, a central concept of New Age philosophy and all forms of psychotherapy, regarding the imperative to liberate something you possess, something that it is important to come into contact with. In that the world around us is in chaos, according to Marciniak, it is now more than ever a matter of urgency to become aware of one's own inner potentials for empowerment and peace of mind.

A better-known example is the film and book phenomenon *The Secret* by Rhonda Byrne (2006, Byrne and Heriot, 2006). Byrne is an Australian TV writer and producer who mixes quantum physics, positive psychology and Dan Brown's *Da Vinci Code* with great success. Both the film and the book have sold by the million on a world basis and topped both the DVD and book bestseller list in the USA in 2007 after two full programmes of *Oprah* were dedicated to it. *The Secret* invites the viewer/reader to gain insight about 'the secret law of the universe' – the law of attraction – and to learn to use positive thinking to achieve wealth, good health, the dream partner and happiness in general. The great secret – which a select few have known about (not surprisingly the most famous philosophers, scientists and artists in history such as Plato, Galileo, Shakespeare, Beethoven and Einstein) – is that our thoughts become things: in other words, your destiny becomes what you are thinking. The psyche's thoughts and feelings are manifested on the material plane. The big problem of the earth's many unhappy souls is that it is common to think about what one fears and hopes to avoid, and this thereby becomes reality. The law that we attract things to us through our thoughts can explain everything in our lives – the individual's psyche is likened to a magnet. As one of the now-living, initiate teachers in the film preaches: 'Do you think it's a coincidence that 1 per cent of the world's population owns 96 per cent of the world's wealth?' *The Secret* takes the perception that 'you become what you think and feel' to absurd and at times infamous lengths – we are told of a homosexual employee who was psychologically and physically harassed both at work and on his way to work, until he learns the secret that he himself and his fear are attracting the unwanted attention.

The Secret represents the self-help idea in its most extreme form – how you personally think and feel is all that means anything. The self can be omnipotent. And anyone can learn this – there are no external barriers or excuses for anyone – with the right attitude to how you think and feel everything can be different. In *The Secret* the stoic Epictetus' (55–135) wisdom about how some things are up to us, other things are not, is broken down. Also our bodies, our possessions, our reputation and position which Epictetus (2004) placed outside of our control are now moved within our grasp. The self can apparently become God. *The Secret* simultaneously plays on the idea that we today live in a godless universe; 'There is no blackboard in the sky where everything is written', as one of the teachers in the film puts it. The meaning of life is then what you personally say it should be. We live therefore in a new age in which the final frontier is no longer outer space, but the psyche, according to another teacher. The Enlightenment project's dream of colonising reality apparently lives on here as well. The idea that we can personally control the universe through our positive thinking and feelings is an extremely narcissistic perception. It is moreover reminiscent of the admonition of one of the early critics of the therapeutic culture – Christopher Lasch (1991) – that the more alienated we feel in society, the more we will value messages that speak directly to us and offer personal gratification. The fact that *The Secret* can become so popular and sell 19 million copies world-wide is testimony to the fact that we live in a cultural climate extremely receptive to messages that thoughts and ideas are all that matter. Barbara Ehrenreich (2009) has written an insightful book about how an epidemic of positive thinking in books such as *The Secret* has undermined the USA, and Ehrenreich shows how cultural formulas that do not take into account potentially negative outcomes can have catastrophic consequences, such as in the world of finance.

Reality and therapy: a happy love story?

The times we are living in are characterised by a hunger for a type of expertise that can help us to choose what is right for us. This need is also apparent in the TV media, where a new genre has undergone an explosive development in the past 10–15 years – reality TV. I have also elected to call a subgenre of this *therapeutic reality TV*. A long series of such programmes now exist, all of which follow a common dramatic structure in which a person or an entire family is incapable of managing a completely fundamental aspect of life: eating, child-raising, personal finances, romantic relationships, the body, pets, the home, and so on, and an expert is required to straighten things out. Through a systematic review of the major Norwegian TV channels NRK, TV2, TV3 and TVNorge in 2010, I found that, combined, these channels currently broadcast about two dozen series that can be classified as therapeutic reality TV. What all of these narratives have in common is a therapeutic dramaturgy – something/one is defined as a problem – and an expert must be called in to raise the consciousness of and give the participants a hand in helping themselves. The body or the self has as a rule been painted into a corner, something is defective or else the participants are not sufficiently making the most of their human potential.

This is a relatively new (TV) reality. It has been said that the function of the media is to contribute to keeping our lives in order and to organise the social space in which we live (Couldry, 2003). How are we, then, to understand the development of this type of programme? On the one hand, this development can be understood as having a democracy-inducing and empowering impact: participants finally receive help with a situation that is often painful and deadlocked. At the same time, the participants on these types of shows are subjected to external pressure in order to persuade them to personally want to become healthy, healed and 'improved versions of themselves', although the values and methods employed by the experts are not subjected to criticism or discussion. The message would appear to be that many people are incapable of taking care of themselves in accordance with the ideals of our culture and therefore are in need of expert assistance. The series even go so far as to communicate an overall message that 'the obese', 'the unhappy', 'the debt-ridden' and 'the hopeless' are personally responsible for their own suffering – of course, not directly, but indirectly, in that the solution to the problems presented is that they must work on themselves.

What is exported through reality television is not specific contents in their own right, but a specific cultural formula (Andrejevic, 2004): man shall (manage to) rule him/herself. The expert role is expanded under neo-liberalism and becomes the central communicative agent between the rulers and the ruled and a representative and guarantor of welfare (Cruikshank, 1996). The ever-increasing popularity of reality television is both a result of the therapeutic culture's enormous interest in the subjective experience, and an expression of the faulty distinction between the public and private spheres (Biressi and Nunn, 2005). Hence, therapeutic TV discloses the reverse side of democracy – the citizen's impotency in the promotion of personal concerns in the public sphere (Biressi and Nunn, 2005).

The increase in the number of series such as *Big Brother* must be understood on the basis of modernity's reflectivity and updating of a life policy that just becomes more and more pronounced when traditional patterns for identity and sociality disintegrate and are opened up to constant re-evaluation (Dovey, 2008). Mark Andrejevic (2004) holds that reality television can be considered a form of staging in which participants are used to rationalise their human capital which is then sold both themselves and all TV viewers as empowerment. Programme concepts such as *The Apprentice* follow a cultural logic which educates viewers in how they can become empowered by fighting – but never fighting against the hard, cynical and shifting forms that working culture has acquired under the auspices of neoliberalism (Couldry and Littler, 2008).

Psychology's experimental and behaviour-modifying techniques have today become television entertainment. A show such as *Big Brother* copies social psychology's famous experiments from the 1960s and turns them into entertainment for the masses (Dovey, 2008). Isolation, surveillance, confession rooms, and commentaries by psychologists who explain the behaviour of the participants give the programme the characteristics of a psychological laboratory. There are also psychologists who are hired by the TV networks to select the right participants for these programmes. As an example, the

American psychology expert Catherine Selden has for a number of years been used on the cosmetic surgery programme *Extreme Makeover* to ensure that the participants do *not* have psychological ailments. Through her professional expertise she guarantees ethics. Therapeutic TV even in its most extreme form does not thus come into any conflict with psychology's professional ethics – as long as it is a matter of mentally sound human beings who are given the opportunity for self-improvement in order to feel better, everything is fine.

Although this reality trend can be understood as a natural consequence of a reflective modernity or neoliberalism's imperative that we are to be the boss of our own life and continuously improve and change, counter tendencies exist. Media scholar Rachel Dubrofsky (2007) studied 13 seasons of the reality TV shows *The Bachelor* and *The Bachelorette*, and she found that the series' underlying moral requirement for the participants was *not* the capacity for change, adaptability and improvement as one might think, given the perception of the flexible, postmodern, neoliberal subject, but the opposite – loyalty to and love for the self. This was consistently more important than winning the dream prince and one's great love, or talking behind the backs of the other contestants. As long as one 'learned' throughout the course of the series to be true to oneself and accept oneself, one was a winner, regardless of how appallingly one may have behaved in relation to others. The findings of Andrejevic (2004) for the British version of *Big Brother* are comparable: the most important thing was to be oneself. This 'true to oneself' theme of these reality shows expands our understanding of the therapeutic culture, according to Dubrofsky. These findings are perhaps not so surprising after all? When our surroundings become more and more artificial, it becomes crucial to 'be oneself'.

Gnostic surgery

In the therapeutic culture, not only the soul but also the body becomes reflective. The body is no longer something that is simply there and that we can take for granted. It has also become a 'project' in its own right. When the programme concept *Extreme Makeover*, in which contestants agree to undergo cosmetic surgery, was introduced to Norwegian TV viewers a few years ago, the reception was one of noisy protest. But this is not the case today; just a few years later the series has become common fare and cosmetic surgery has to a large extent become accepted. Since then a number of similar type programme series have been launched, including local versions, without any real protest of note (Johansson, 2006).

Of the therapeutic reality programmes, the cosmetic surgery programmes are in many ways the most extreme in their methods, but simultaneously are merely the natural consequence of the ongoing enterprise of self-improvement being taken to its extreme in offering people a new physiological restructuring of the self through cosmetic surgery (Franco, 2008). Although here it is the external, physical body that is being treated, there is cause to believe that this is first and foremost about the inner self and self-esteem. From the very beginning of plastic surgery's history, the idea has been that physical defects affected people psychologically. The psychoanalyst Alfred Adler's (1870–1937) theory about the inferiority complex of the 1920s became particularly popular among plastic surgeons (Johansson, 2006; Sæther, 2006). It was believed that by doing away with the physical defects one would also rid oneself of the psychological problems. There is every reason to believe that we have the same mentality today: beneath all the fat is the real me. In the past decade reality series such as *Extreme Makeover* and fictive drama series about plastic surgery such as *Nip/Tuck* (Murphy, 2003–2010) have presumably done more for plastic surgery's penetration than any other phenomenon. The number of US 18-year-olds who had breast implants tripled from 2002 to 2003, something which has led a number of experts to intimate a connection between the programmes and the increase in demand (Albright, 2007; Science Daily, 2009). In the USA the number of surgical procedures has increased by 114 per cent since 1997. The number of non-surgical treatments during the same period increased by all of 754 per cent. Wrinkle treatment by injection of Botox and Restylane, and laser hair removal were the most common.

The consumers of cosmetic surgery are predominantly women. Ninety-one per cent of all of the cosmetic procedures in the USA in 2007 were done on women (American Society for Aesthetic Plastic Surgery, 2010). Men are nonetheless a consumer group experiencing annual growth and far more quickly than the women; the number of cosmetic procedures done on men in the USA increased by 17 per cent from 2006 to 2007 (American Society for Aesthetic Plastic Surgery, 2010). There has also been a dramatic increase in Norway and the import of such TV series has in all likelihood contributed to this. In Norway the annual sales of the nerve poison fluid Botox, used to smooth out facial wrinkles, increased from NOK 2.9 million in 2003 to NOK 8.2 million in 2009 (Sundbye, 2010). In Norway the private cosmetic surgery market has undergone substantial growth in the last 20 years, from a small number of publicly employed plastic surgeons who had private evening practices, to 35 full-time staff employed in cosmetic surgery clinics (Åbyholm, 2003). The development has been so dramatic that there have been problems in acquiring enough plastic surgeons for the public health service (Åbyholm, 2003). In 2004 the Norwegian Board of Health Supervision estimated that there were some 70 practising plastic surgery specialists in Norway.

Cosmetic surgery can be understood as being a type of therapy. The surgical procedures as a method are concrete and remove superfluous or inexpedient layers from individuals and have the objective of giving these individuals closer contact with their bodies and themselves. The idea that within us, behind the fat, lies the real self, ready to be realised, is prominent and is also used by surgeons today in defence of their own activity (Johansson, 2006). Behind the surgical incisions we can detect the psychological self-disclosure ethics, the self-realisation requirement and the idea of your true self. Psychologist Nina Østby Sæther (2006) has even claimed that cosmetic surgery is but a natural extension of humanistic psychology's idea of self-realisation. From the early 2000s until today cosmetic surgery has succeeded in going from controversial to relatively acceptable in Norway. It looks as if an alliance with psychological incentives has been particularly helpful – arguments about correcting physical flaws for purely aesthetic reasons are dismissed as ill-advised in people's attitudes to plastic surgery, but if one claims to have complexes and psychological defects related to physical flaws, it's another story. For who can argue against how a person is feeling?

The boundaries for what is natural are undergoing constant change. Just a few years ago cosmetic surgery was viewed as untenable by the majority of the population (Johansson, 2006). Exercise and diet were viewed as more appropriate cures – that is no longer the case today, it would appear. This can be illustrated by a current feature article from the women's magazine *Women and Clothes* in July of 2010 which follows two women (Førsund, 2010). One of them receives expert help from a personal trainer to lose weight, while the other receives help from a plastic surgeon to get rid of the extra pounds. The article compared the two women's different methods for reaching the goal of a 'new body'. Here one finds no objections or admonitions about how exercise is better or more natural than the other method. It is rather a matter of discerning which method is more suitable for the individual. The plastic surgeon featured in the article, Bjørn Tvedt, explains: 'It won't necessarily make you happy, but can do something to your self-esteem' (Førsund, 2010, p. 18). Tvedt's rhetoric is, as expected, psychological and advanced enough so he avoids being accused of being superficial or cynical in his efforts to help people to find happiness in a new body. The message is instead: 'We can't help you find happiness, but we can help you find self-esteem.' The emphasis on 'self-esteem' itself we recognise from Törnblom's and Øiestad's books. It is, however, worth noting that Törnblom's (2007) statements about plastic surgery are consistently critical in her books, and especially when the motivation is an enhanced self-esteem. What is to be made from this? Perhaps that even though self-help literature and popular psychology can often contain healthy criticisms and a certain level-headedness, as is the case here, the psychological language is nonetheless quickly picked up and adapted to the self-help industry's market logic. Presumably there are no reservations that can halt the dissemination of 'self-esteem'.

From reality television to reality policy

Cosmetic surgery is upheld by a therapeutic idea about the importance of being happy with who one is. This emotional justification was clearly and unequivocally articulated by one of the prophets of this culture in Norway – the celebrity beauty expert Jan Thomas. In the NRK television programme *Grosvold* he defended Botox treatments by saying that for him it was not about the appearance, but at the end of the day, about feeling good about oneself (Grønlund, 2008). Neither seasoned journalists such as Anne Grosvold or guest Marie Simonsen, nor a skilled national politician such as Erna Solberg (now Norway's prime minster), who was also a guest, had any arguments to counter this. And the reason is simple: because there aren't any. Or more precisely – there are arguments, but they have no legitimacy in today's culture. The author Arne Berggren summarises this paradox quite well:

> We embrace a crazy make-up artist with a head and ass full of silicon [. . .] But intellectually I am critical. If I say so, my children claim I am homophobic. They have learned that from the Knowledge Promotion school reform scheme. We have become so tolerant in Norway that there is scarcely any room left for morals.
>
> (Østli, 2008, p. 10)

Jan Thomas in all of his glamorous horror fascinates us because he represents perfection or the extreme of the self-improvement imperative that we personally sense. His enormous success in Norway in a relatively short period of time can appear to be an astounding mystery (Østli, 2008), but perhaps it illustrates simply how what we view as a set of values reserved for the land 'over there' (USA) have now come to Norway on a grand scale. It is women in particular who are made responsible for producing themselves as attractive objects for male desire. This is sold as empowerment, but the concepts of transformation make the participants and its viewers the foremost disciplinary subjects of neoliberalism (Franco, 2008).

Erna Solberg was moreover to fall victim to the same therapeutic logic one year later when the PR expert Kjell Terje Ringdal commented on how her credibility as a politician was undermined in that 'the character is damaged by obesity because it signals a lack of self-control' (Gjerstad, 2009, p. 23). Ringdal took a lot of heat for this claim, among other reasons, for legitimising the imposition of stricter requirements on female politicians who consequently have far less latitude than their male colleagues. The heated protests make it tempting to speculate about how much of the wrath directed at Ringdal was a classic example of shooting the messenger, because he put into words a tendency that many notice but will not acknowledge.

The logic that Ringdal as a PR expert reads out of the spirit of the times found in the voters is testimony to how a politician's credibility as a person trumps the policy she represents, and at the next level how the body has become the primary identity marker for individuals in consumer culture, where the external appearance becomes the authority that is listened to. Our appearance today becomes the carrier of our inner self in the world, as Øiestad writes (2009). Solberg's obesity is understood as a lack of control not just over the pounds, but in the deepest sense, over herself, which in accordance with the therapeutic logic, is the foremost authority, and thereby a politician's credibility. Ringdal's professional advice to Solberg is also striking: to speak out about it; to say that she struggles with her weight. Through a therapeutic self-disclosure technique, she will win over the voters: 'By verbalising what everyone knows and telling the story behind it, she will deflate the balloon' (Gjerstad, 2009, p. 27). In other words, this is not really about being overweight – the voters will forgive as much – it is about Solberg having to demonstrate that she too is a part of, or a victim to, a therapeutic mentality in which the battle with the self is something we all must contend with.

It is of interest to note that the Norwegian Psychological Association (NPF) represented by Chief Advisor Anders Skuterud also got involved in the debate – possibly because Ringdal has established the company Psychology Assistance. Skuterud (2009) came down on Ringdal because as an expert he does not inform the audience about the well-known fundamental attribution error from psychology, which in this case entails that one attributes Erna's obesity to personal character traits, such as greed, rather than to situational factors, such as that she spends all of her time on political service or her free time with her family. NPF's admonition about responsibility on the part of the experts and, indirectly, about rational thought on the part of the voters, testifies to an ambition of assuming a responsible attitude to one's own profession. Nevertheless, the reaction also reflects to a limited extent the historical and social development within politics of recent decades – which collectively has influenced how voters think and choose, and where many have highlighted exactly psychology's negative influence. The most famous example is perhaps sociologist Richard Sennett's (1992, p. 259) work *The Fall of Public Man* which describes the decay of the public sector in the USA in the 1970s:

The reigning myth today is that the evils of society can all be under-stood as evils of impersonality, alienation, and coldness. The sum of these three is an ideology of intimacy: social relationships of all kinds are real, believable, and authentic the closer they approach the inner psychological concerns of each person. This ideology transmutes polit-ical categories into psychological categories.

Ringdal comments on how requirements for politicians' self-representation started in American politics but in the past 15–20 years have become more prevalent in Norway. As such, Sennett's analyses are also relevant for Norway today. This development appears to have been best grasped by PR expert Ringdal and not the NPF.

Universal codes

The Italian social theorist Alberto Melucci (1996) has investigated how new power constellations have become established over past decades in a globalised media world. The establishment of a global media system, which is a relatively new invention dating from the 1980s, functions as the distributor of universal codes on a global scale, he maintains. Large media corporations now determine the language, the information, how the information is organised and how the information is to be distributed throughout the world. The majority of the citizens of the world are pas-sive spectators to this. This production and manipulation of information must be considered a new form of domination, where the power is first and foremost found in the possibility to influence people's everyday thoughts and speech (Melucci, 1996). The programmes become bearers of cultural codes or narratives such as the therapeutic ethos, and acquire a universal character since they are distributed by global TV networks which have the entire world as their potential market. The distance between experts and ordinary viewers becomes increasingly smaller in today's therapeutic TV culture as a result of this development. The programme *Nanny 911* (2004–2009) about a strict governess (early childhood educator) who moves into people's homes and introduces educational theory-based principles about punishment and reward, resulted in a flood of inquiries to the Child Welfare Authorities in the Norwegian province of Hordaland from viewers seeking expert advice after Norwegian television began broadcasting the series. In this way one finds a direct connection between foreign entertainment and the Norwegian public health services. These programmes become bearers of cultural codes that provide a formula for the organisation of the view-ers' lives with the approval of expertise and that acquire penetration across national barriers. A worldwide belief in the rational structures founded on scientific and technological knowledge has to a large extent replaced the Christian Church as the only road to salvation (Meyer, Boli, Thomas, and Ramirez, 1997). The new 'religious elites' are professionals, researchers, scientists and experts who write universal, secularised salvation narratives. This faith is worldwide, and structures the organisation of social life virtually everywhere (Meyer *et al.*, 1997). The same soap operas in the USA, China, Israel or Norway not only promote specific values or behavioural patterns, Melucci (1996) claims, but also structure the mind and the rules for the emotional life. The therapeutic ethos as such becomes a symbolic form which creates patterns in people's mentalities, emotions and feelings. Large portions of what can be called the pre-political or ideology production, which creates the basis for actual policy, concern the production of information and symbolic resources (Couldry, 2003). Reality TV is therefore less about representing reality and more about direct intervention in reality (Franco, 2008). Critical reason is no match for the furious development of the globalised media reality, Melucci claims, and he maintains that we must think in new ways about power and disparity.

The glamour of misery

One of the cardinal features of postmodernism is, according to the influential cultural theorist Fredric Jameson, the USA's hegemonic position – militarily, politically and, most important of all, in this context, culturally. Jameson (2003) highlights the entertainment industry's ever new inroads via the globalised media as an example. Illouz claims that the therapeutic ethos has, if possible, an even greater penetrative impact as a global export article. An inordinately successful example is *Oprah*, which combines pure entertainment with a therapeutic ethos. *The Oprah Winfrey Show* was an American-produced talk show that was broadcast for the first time in 1986 and lasted for 25 seasons before it ended in 2011. By then it had become enormously popular and the highest rated TV show of its day. It is estimated that the show was watched by approximately 15–20 million Americans every single day, the majority of them women, and it has been distributed to 132 different countries (Illouz, 2003). Hostess Oprah Winfrey has not without reason been crowned the most powerful person in the entertainment industry and she figured in *Time*'s list of the 100 most influential people of the twentieth century. It has been claimed that Winfrey exercises a greater influence on our culture than any president, politician or religious leader in the world, with the possible exception of the Pope (Illouz, 2003).

The purpose of the show was, according to Winfrey herself, to empower and enhance the self-esteem of viewers around the world: 'What we are trying to change in this one hour is what I think is at the root of all the problems in the world – the lack of self-esteem' (as cited in Moskowitz, 2001, p. 7). Eva Illouz (2003) has written an entire book about the show and sought to analyse its influence as a cultural therapeutic phenomenon. Illouz claims that Winfrey shows us how to live with the chaos of modernity by offering a rationalised view of the self, heavily inspired by the language of therapy which equips the self with the ability for self-management and change. *Oprah* constitutes a wholly unique narrative about the self, in which the underlying moral structure has collapsed or is threatening to disintegrate. While the West previously struggled with scarcity, chronic hunger and illness which as a matter of course limited individual freedom, late-modern Western society is characterised by material abundance and enormous requirements on the self, without any clear moral resources with which to fulfil such requirements. This provides the basis for a number of types of psychological ailments, Illouz maintains. The victim culture has therefore also become prominent because late-modern society produces real and powerful forms of suffering. Late-modernity can no longer provide us with what religion once did, namely a theodicy to explain suffering. *Oprah* performs the most basic function carried out by religion throughout all of time, as religion theorists Weber and Geertz have claimed, by giving inexplicable suffering meaning (Illouz, 2003). By staging the various ways in which the modern self is suffering, and offering human beings the resources with which to personally produce redemption from it, the show mitigates this lack. Oprah and her guests draw from the therapeutic matrix to give their lives meaning (Illouz, 2003). The show implements a therapeutic biography creating the point of departure for a cohesive performative narrative which becomes an effective psychological technique.

The therapeutic perspective of the world, in both its popular and professional edition, is based on the idea of telling stories about how the emotional self and the change of that self can take place in order to find in the story the (re)solution of suffering (Illouz, 2003). The cultural code that makes this narrative so popular is therapeutic. It is like an emotional secret that can be liberated. Self-esteem has a central position here because Oprah can relate this to any domain whatsoever. Illouz, in her analysis of *Oprah*, illustrates how a therapeutic narrative code can serve to make any problem a starting point for a story in which the self becomes a (specific) problem in its own right and which is then healed by an expert guest who is a specialist in one form of dysfunction or another. Therapeutic themes and narratives can in fact be applied to any and all human action and generate a virtually infinite number of stories because they can be broken down into biographical chains of cause and effect (Illouz, 2003). The self is treated as a highly changeable entity that can be adjusted and transformed in the course of the single hour that the show lasts. Illouz goes a bit far in stating that the show offers not just the guests but also the viewers true healing. However, her foremost critique of Oprah's therapeutic solution is that within it suffering is always understood as the opportunity to learn. All ailments thus represent a potentially valuable, worthwhile experience – in that all suffering becomes a physical and psychological manifestation of a higher meaning.

Strong women

In the secular society it is the experts who have the ability and the authority to heal people. Their abilities are reinforced if they have personally been healed and can thereby demonstrate visible signs of the ability to change (Illouz, 2003). Both Winfrey and Törnblom fit this description in that they are empowered victims. Winfrey has personally told of episode(s) of sexual abuse in her childhood. Törnblom was a substance abuser for ten years of her life. Winfrey and Törnblom become living proof of successful transformations in the therapeutic culture and thereby acquire an aura of authority through their personal life stories. These narratives about long-term struggles to overcome personal problems comprise a specific symbolic structure and psychological battle. Winfrey's well-known weight problems, which she has repeatedly made a theme both on the show itself and in interviews, become first and foremost an exhibition of a psychological, inner conflict, and further, a documentation of the results that can be attained by hiring a private trainer or nutrition expert. This fits perfectly with the postmodern pattern that healing has acquired, according to Illouz – one is never truly healthy; new forms of ailments can arise. Winfrey's yo-yo dieting becomes an ongoing reminder that the battle with the pounds and the self is a never-ending story. It is this battle that Solberg has not demonstrated sufficient willingness to put on display for the voters. Oprah becomes our times' foremost incarnation of the therapeutic ethos – and her show a therapeutic flagship with a global reach and impact.

A new generation of critics

Illouz represents what is for the time being the latest generation of mass culture's cultural critics. She stands on the shoulders of giants, such as the Frankfurt School's earliest representatives Theodor Adorno, Max Horkheimer and Herbert Marcuse. Western mass culture's most famous analysis is perhaps Horkheimer and Adorno's (2002) critique of what they called the culture industry in the work *Dialectic of Enlightenment*, which addressed the emergence of mass culture in the West in the 1930s. This critique has later had great influence on studies of culture's function in Western democracies. In more recent decades, however, the analyses are to a large extent referred to as quintessential examples of scholarly arrogance and contrariness regarding popular culture's ability to offer pleasure as well as create contexts and meaning. Adorno's and Horkheimer's critique, among other things of what they describe as the transition from the subject-friendly telephone to the rendering passive of the radio medium, does indeed seem undeniably out of date and comical today, but the main message remains current. The public sector finds itself at a developmental stage in which free and critical thought has been transformed into a product, and our language a tribute to this product, they claim. It is just a matter of time before the disclosure of this degradation is made impossible by the ongoing linguistic and intellectual requirements of the day. Blocking the theoretical imagination has opened the door for political disillusionment, is their gloomy judgement of the direction that Western culture has taken in modernity.

The Enlightenment project, understood in the broadest sense as the development of the human ability for thought, has always had a mission of liberating man from primal fear and installing him as the sovereign ruler of history. The Enlightenment project's programme was disclosure of or demystification of the world (Horkheimer and Adorno, 2002). The 'happy' connection between human understanding and the essence of things, which Francis Bacon (1561–1626) dreamt of, was by nature patriarchal: by overcoming superstition, man would rule over demystified nature. For the Enlightenment project, everything that did not fit into the standard of calculations for utility was viewed as suspect. For this reason it was totalitarian, claimed Adorno and Horkheimer. The philosophy of the Enlightenment reduced the myriad of mythical figures from former times to one single, isolated common denominator: the human subject (Horkheimer and Adorno, 2002). The idea that truth was to be found by following the path that mapped out consciousness was in itself, however, a peculiar mythology which threatened to restrict reality to the confines of pure psychology. In the therapeutic culture of today, we live apparently with the result that nothing (of value) exists outside of the self.

Illouz claims, as many others have done before her, that cultural critics such as Horkheimer and Adorno are too hasty in their dismissal of popular culture, using what she calls bulldozer concepts such as power and ideology. They did not always understand equally well what they were criticising. Her own approach is therefore far more interpretative in its form. Nonetheless, she ends up with what she personally refers to as an immanent (inherent) critique – what *Oprah* sells is, paradoxically, suffering but a suffering that is always claimed to be meaningful. Oprah's mission is of great importance; the problem is just that the therapeutic ideology she employs is wrong, because she is controlled too much by a religious idea that there is meaning behind every kind of suffering (the trials of Job). Illouz concludes therefore with the same timely note of concern as did Adorno and Horkheimer before her: the subject – this one distinction between human existence and reality – swallows up everything else; nothing is allowed to exist outside of it. Meaningless suffering – which historically speaking has provided fertile conditions for resistance and doing away with former eras' systems of meaning – disappears when the psychologised subject and the therapeutic narrative are apparently able to explain and give meaning to all suffering.

Complain to the stars about your life

Adorno (2002) has written another, less well-known but exceptionally memorable analysis of mass culture and the astrology column of the *Los Angeles Times* at the beginning of the 1950s, after having lived in the city during the war. Adorno is not particularly interested in astrology per se, but wants here to show how this relatively innocent column demonstrates a particular danger inherent in democracy. The astrology system becomes a framework of meaning that people take for granted, and as such they listen for extraterrestrial explanations of their lives from the stars and not from the political system. The astrology column meets unsatisfied psychological needs on the part of readers, while astrology gives all phenomena an individualist packaging that hides contextual factors and causal relations (similar to the reason behind the broad appeal of *The Secret* today). The empirical reality in which readers live is reinterpreted as destiny. The expert advice of the astrology column functions as a conservative ideology protecting the status quo. The column gives the impression that all problems stemming from objective circumstances, such as financial difficulties, can be solved through personal initiatives or by finding the correct psychological insight within oneself. The astrology column's function appears to an increasingly greater extent to be upheld by popular psychology, as Adorno noted, even back in the 1950s. When psychology's analyses are done well, they can provide insight to the self or a better understanding of others, he argues, but they can also serve as a social anaesthesia. This is particularly the case for objective circumstances which, although they undoubtedly have something subjective about them, are presented as if they are wholly and fully up to the individual (Adorno, 2002). The flattering formula of astrological advice that 'everything depends on the individual' is not just an exaggeration and false truth, but functions as a confining veil that descends over our heads. Narcissistic gratification drives out any critical ideas. Adorno commented that a feature of the dawning consumer culture is the classical liberal idea of unlimited individual development, while at the same time a strict organisational requirement on the part of society is at work. Culture's psychological conflicts and oppositions must be solved, and in Adorno's analyses this was the mission of the astrology column. In the 1950s, the world was on the brink of a new era, in which consumption and psychology would come to be important elements. Adorno's analyses of the irrationality of the astrology column's expert advice from Los Angeles – California's metropolis – was perhaps an omen of what was to come.

Life imitates good television

Another American export, the television drama, has been said to be experiencing a unique golden age with respect to level of ambition, complexity and available resources, as evidenced by series such as *Six Feet Under*, *The West Wing*, *The Sopranos*, *The Wire* and *Mad Men*. Several of these series reflect the important role of therapy in late-modern life. The most obvious use of psychology is found in series such as *Tell Me You Love Me* (Rozema, 2007) featuring couples therapy, and *In Treatment* (Garcia, 2008–2010) in which the entire plot is set in a therapy room where we follow the therapist Paul and his clients five days a week. The series, beyond being an exceptional drama using little more than dialogue between two human beings, reflects what many have commented: psychology and psychotherapy have in a short period of time been demystified and made accessible (Johansson, 2007). Another much-lauded series, *Mad Men* (Weiner, 2007–), takes the more recent cultural history of the USA seriously and shows how psychotherapy had an empowering impact on the liberation of women in the 1960s and played an important part in the marketing industry, although Freud literally ends up in the dustbin in the first episode. However, the first TV series to convert therapy into entertainment and material for common consumption was the mafia series *The Sopranos* (Chase, 1999–2007) in which therapy is frequently featured throughout the six seasons of the series. The series' main character, the mafia boss Tony Soprano, agrees to enrol in psychotherapy with the psychiatrist Dr Melfi after experiencing a number of uncomfortable episodes of panic and anxiety attacks. Through therapy Dr Melfi teaches Tony how to gain control over his panic attacks, which turn out to stem from a traumatic episode in his childhood when Tony inadvertently witnessed his father perpetuating extremely brutal violence on a butcher who had not paid his debt. The panic attacks arose every time he came into contact with raw meat.

The panic attacks moreover lead Tony deeper into therapy and the labyrinth of his soul – where the central conflict is his relationship to his mother, a woman with a personality disorder. Eventually, as the series evolves, Dr Melfi comes to realise that Tony in reality cannot be healed. In the end she chooses to terminate the therapeutic relation after being convinced by research findings that demonstrate how psychotherapy with sociopaths or psychopaths simply makes them a bit more controlled and better adapted. Through therapy with Dr Melfi, Tony learns to handle his difficult feelings and anger outbursts in a more adaptive manner and he becomes as a result a better mafia boss and professional criminal, enabling him to go even further in his lies and manipulation of family members and colleagues. *The Sopranos* functions therefore as a good illustration of psychology's paradox in a pathological culture. Therapy can offer individual adaptation strategies, but provides no tools to change society. Tony learns how to become an improved psychopath in an unchanged psychopathic culture.

The Sopranos is, in addition to being an exceedingly well-written contemporary drama and a subtle postmodern flirtation with Italian-American culture, an exploration of the identity crisis of the modern self. Tony personifies many of the contradictions and conflicts of the late-modern Western society. A recurring theme is the conflict between new, feminine values and the old culture of honour. Tony's livelihood is torn between 'the old world' − the patriarchy − and the new world: a liberal USA that is democratised and feminised, in which education, equal rights, social mobility and globalisation undermine the mafia world's former core activity: blackmail and protection of the local community. When the dangers become global − Al-Qaida or the SARS virus − the protection they have to offer no longer has the same value.

Tony is, in spite of a certain dependency on Dr Melfi, simultaneously a sharp critic of the therapeutic culture − 'Talk, talk, talk. It's all talk!' he bursts out in frustration during a therapy session. It is of course possible to interpret this clinically − people with Tony's psychological profile − sociopaths or psychopaths − will never reach any true insights about themselves and achieve change. If on the other hand we view the series with a more general gaze, Tony's outbursts can just as well be understood as the modern self's frustration over what the therapeutic system of meaning actually has to offer. In other words, what it *cannot* offer − a form of redemption, or salvation from modern life's frustrations and disappointments.

Popular culture's take on the mafia culture has almost always focused on the transition from the feudal to the modern era and the painful and problematic adaptation of the pre-modern, Italian code of honour to the modern USA, where something equivalent perhaps no longer exists. *The Godfather* trilogy (Coppola, 1974, 1990; Ruddy and Coppola, 1972), referred to frequently in *The Sopranos*, illustrates this conflict. The caporegime Frank Pentangeli agrees to collaborate with the police and testify against Michael Corleone. The Corleone family's counter-move is to fly his elder brother Vincenzo in from Sicily, who through his mere presence and penetrating gaze in the courtroom reminds his culturally confused brother of what he must do: keep his mouth shut and commit suicide in the bathtub, as his Roman forefathers would have done. Vincenzo communicates the culture of honour's sense of duty that his reckless brother was in the process of forgetting after having lived for too long in the USA's norm-eroding consumer culture. This archaic value system is flown into the USA on a few occasions in *The Sopranos* as well – as a rule when somebody is to be liquidated. For the series' cast of characters *omerta* – the code of honour – has, however, been weakened far too much to function correctly. The therapeutic culture is obviously stronger than the universe depicted by *The Godfather* trilogy, where men are still men – and the law (nomos) rules. Tony must constantly struggle with disloyal employees who put their own desires and needs first. The irony of *The Sopranos* is that its cast of characters use popular culture's renditions of 'the old world' such as *The Godfather* to try and preserve tradition, often with tragicomic results.

The reception of *The Sopranos* by psychologists in and of itself is illustrative of the profession's use of self-deluding, therapeutic, cognitive techniques designed to give everything the best possible interpretation. In spite of the latent social criticism of the therapeutic culture which the series clearly conveys, it has been lauded by professionals because it has reportedly contributed to men also rushing to therapy in droves to seek help (cf. Gabbard, 2002).

6   Psychology and sports

Sports are a mirror of society, or so it is claimed. I will therefore outline psychology's entrance into the sports arena and attempt a contemporary analysis on the basis of the 'psychological revolution' that has taken place in sports such as football and skiing, and which can perhaps tell us something about the position psychology has otherwise acquired in society.

Psychology's entrance into the world of sports can be demonstrated by a striking increase in the tendency on the part of athletes, coaches and commentators to explain athletic performances, whether good or bad, with 'the mental aspect'. Recently former world record holder Ingrid Kristiansen (2013, p. 33) wrote an article about the upcoming Oslo marathon where she stressed that: 'There are other things than the mental aspect that are important on the day of the race'. It looks as if people in 2013 need to be told that there is more to completing a marathon than the mental aspect. 'The mental aspect' is generally not further specified, but appears to have become virtually self-explanatory. If one follows the discourse of sports, no doubt remains about the fact that 'the mental aspect', whatever it is that this might refer to, has become extremely important. A search done for the phrase in Norwegian newspapers for a period of just one week in 2010 clearly demonstrates this. 'The most important thing of all is to adjust the mental aspect', maintains Stabæk football club coach Jan Jönsson (Dale, 2010, p. 16). 'Everything must tally. The mental aspect becomes important, especially at the starting line', reasons André Fosså Aguiluz about BMX supercross (Sel, 2010, p. 17). 'In addition to everything related to technique she also works a lot with mental aspects', a journalist writes about showjumper Malin Betten Hansen (Bergsli, 2010, p. 30). 'It is good to be on top of the mental aspect in a sport that to such a great extent is about handling mental pressure', ski jumping national coach Mika Kojonkoski tells NTB (2010, p. 6). 'I believe that predominantly it is about the mental aspect, that it's more important than the physiological', swimmer Alexander Dale Oen philosophises (Andersen, 2010, p. 5).

These statements, from a random selection of newspapers during a week chosen arbitrarily from the summer of 2010, illustrate the position that 'the mental life' and psychology have acquired virtually across the board in the sports world. The statements indicate that there is now a consensus in a number of sports that 'the mental aspect' is the most important success factor. On the basis of the quotes, it is also worth noting that 'the mental part' has come to inhabit a given place alongside the technical and physical domains of sports while, at the same time, psychology has acquired this place to the detriment of these other areas. As an example, the swimmer Dale Oen affirms that 'the mental aspect' has become more important than 'the physiological' (Andersen, 2010). Now certainly this does not mean that Dale Oen would maintain that great mental fortitude will replace broad backs and a long arm-span in future swimmers or that he personally puts his faith in the replacement of pool laps with mental training on the therapeutic couch. Nonetheless, it does say a great deal about how 'the mental aspect' has perhaps become the most central explanatory model or metaphor used by athletes today in the understanding of their performance. It can in turn tell us something about the central position psychology has gained in society and in our understanding of ourselves. 'Naturally, the mental life is important,' one might perhaps think, there is nothing sensational about that, is there? But it has nonetheless not always been the case. A systematic search in a Norwegian newspaper database reflects a clear increase in the use of the phrase 'the mental aspect' from just two hits in 1981 to an accelerating increase towards the end of the 1990s, and a particularly high frequency rate around 2007 and up to today of more than 450 hits per year.

The magic 'mental part'

'That's another thing that's coming big into football, the psychology' Manchester United's centre back Rio Ferdinand (2009, n.p.) explained in a conversation about football and politics with the then Prime Minister and football lover Gordon Brown in *The Observer*.

Psychology and 'the mental aspect' have made their entrance in football around the globe despite the sport's conservatism regarding new training methods compared to other sports. 'The mental aspect' has succeeded in becoming a beloved and frequently employed explanatory model in the world's largest sport – both in the moment of defeat and the euphoria of victory, at the national as well as international level, and it is apparently widespread in both women's and men's football. For instance, women's football coach Trine Lise Andersen said after Frøya had lost yet another match: 'It is because of "the mental aspect" that we lose football matches' (Sætre, 2010, p. 23). And Netherlands' Arjen Robben affirmed with satisfaction: 'The mental aspect is perhaps the most important thing at this level' after his team had eliminated Brazil in the football World Cup in South Africa in 2010 (Johannessen, 2010, p. 2).

In the modern football coach's job descriptions the ability to exert a psychological influence on one's surroundings – as regards players, opponents, the media and supporters – is therefore a requirement. The modern coach must cover a therapeutic role, both in terms of his dealings with players and in his relations with coach colleagues. 'The military commander' or 'the strategist' has been replaced by 'the therapist' as the leader ideal in modern football. Psychological qualities have become as important as tactical skills. In what is presumably the world's best league – the English Barclays Premier League – ongoing psychological warfare is now often at work between coaches who seek to employ the media to their own advantage. 'If we beat them it doesn't involve psychology,' Sir Alex Ferguson was virtually obliged to inform the press before the big showdown between Manchester United and Liverpool on 14 March 2009, providing a reality orientation that would take the sting out of Liverpool coach Rafael Benitez's claims that Ferguson had, among other things, been manipulating the referees at Old Trafford (Taylor and Hunter, 2009, n.p.). According to Ferguson, Benitez's verbal attack required a solid knowledge of Freud to understand.

There is also a widespread perception that changing a coach can have an immediate psychological effect on the players just days and hours later. Tottenham, the London club that seems to perform often below par, is an example of this. The then Tottenham striker Dimitar Berbatov likened his new coach, Spaniard Juande Ramos, to a professor thanks to his extraordinary capacity for analysis and clinical calm and ability to prepare his players. 'The mental aspect is paramount', added *The Guardian* (2008, n.p.) in praise of Ramos. Despite his special abilities Ramos was discharged from the position in October 2008 due to a lack of results, in spite of a promising first season. One of the explanations was that the Spanish-speaking Ramos had never learned much English and could not communicate directly with his players. The new coach, the quintessentially British and apple-cheeked Harry Redknapp, on the other hand, had immediate success, in fact just 24 hours after taking over the team. Explanation: '"Harry can talk to people one-to-one, have a proper conversation" according to forward Darren Bent' (Hytner, 2008, n.p.). In other words, Redknapp's traditional talking therapy appears to be preferable to Ramos's more non-verbal shamanism.

The Norwegian men's football team has had limited success in recent years. Norway hasn't taken part in a final championship since the European Football Championship in 2000. But 'the mental aspect' and psychology have been successfully established as important factors. In the winter of 2008 the tabloid *Dagbladet* announced on the front page of its sports section: 'The national team needs a psychologist' (Kvam, 2008, pp. 22–23). The article was about the national manager of that time, Åge Hareide, and his perplexity about the lack of results in the WC qualifications for South Africa. Hareide speculated about whether it could be due to mental blocks on the part of the players: 'It's possible to carry out some mental improvements' (Kvam, 2008, p. 22). Perhaps it was actually the brutal fact that the player material that Hareide and Norway had to work with was simply not good enough to qualify for the football World Cup in 2010, but the belief in psychology's apparently infinite potential nonetheless instilled hope. One can never become sufficiently proficient when it comes to the mental part.

It is remarkable that a coach and character like Hareide in particular *should* deploy a psychological vocabulary such as this. As a player he was known as a hard-playing, no-nonsense centre back, qualities which among other things have given him a successful pro career in England at Manchester City (1981–82) and Norwich City (1982–84). As a coach he has continued this line and as the manager of a national team, he spoke about 'big balls' and criticised the players for 'skipping around on their high heels like women do'. When an old-fashioned macho man such as Hareide demonstrates such an interest in 'the mental aspect', this gives us cause to believe that football during recent decades has in fact undergone a formidable process of psychologisation. The news article 'TIL receives mental assistance' described how the struggling elite series team Tromsø would receive expert assistance from sports psychologist Anne Marit Pensgaard in a bid to let in fewer goals (Holte, 2009). The Finnish defender Miika Koppinen formulated his expectations in this way: 'Pensgaard can offer all kinds of ideas and advice that we can apply, but when it comes to the players' self-confidence and sense of security out on the pitch, they are personally responsible' (Holte, 2009, n.p.). For sturdy football players it is the same as for everyone else today: a matter of finding 'self-confidence and a sense of security out on the pitch'. And in football as in self-help literature, it is a matter of help towards self-help. Koppinen emphasises that the sports psychologist can only serve to inspire – that at the end of the day, the players are personally responsible for whether or not they have self-confidence and a sense of security when out on the playing field.

In the interview with Hareide he speaks of a closer follow-up of individual players, and he introduces the concept of 'the whole player' (Kvam, 2008). His argument is that Norway has so few players that they must ensure individual follow-up and a close dialogue with the clubs about strain and treatment of injury, thereby ensuring the availability of the greatest possible number of players. Hareide's language here seems suspiciously like a form of therapeutic new-speak – where the players become clients who, like users of long-term and coordinated social and health care services, have the right to an individualised scheme. And neither is it just the players who have a need for a mental overhaul. 'Also those of us in the support system need a coach,' Hareide tells the reporter (Kvam, 2008, p. 22). The modern sports coach also needs an expert who is in direct contact with 'the mental aspect' in order to do his job. The problem was of course not as serious or acute as it was for the players, who needed the foremost in expertise: a psychologist.

However, Hareide never had the opportunity to utilise 'the mental part' – at least not in a way that showed any results; the national team for the first time did not win a single game in the course of an entire calendar year and in December 2008 Hareide stepped down, to be replaced by an old, familiar and beloved figure: Egil 'Drillo' Olsen. Where Hareide had sought to find solutions by embracing a therapeutic model, albeit in a tough edition – the 'football professor' Drillo was known for his precise, scientific and statistics-based approach to football. In other words, the rehiring of Drillo does not fit in with the image seeking to depict football as increasingly more therapeutically oriented, and more and more about psychology. But even though Drillo does not fit as well into the formula, press reception of him has changed since the last time he was national team manager in the 1990s (1990–1998).

There were great expectations surrounding the comeback of Drillo in the match against Germany on 9 February 2009. As a pre-match warm-up, the newspaper *VG* ran the story 'The Hunt for the Drillo Magic' (Øgar, 2009). The angle of the article was that something else must lie behind the strategic and calculating mindset that Drillo is so famous for – a pedagogical core or a psychological force that had been neglected in the presentation of his impressive achievements as a national team manager. Former national team player Jan Åge Fjørtoft made the following comment: 'Egil has not been good enough at speaking about himself as a leader. Far too often he has become involved in debates about playing style' and 'Does Egil understand that he is a good motivator?' (Øgar, 2009, pp. 9–10). The underlying theme of the article, to find a therapeutic explanation for the mysterious Drillo magic, can be an indication of a change in atmosphere in Norway from the 1990s up to the end of the twentieth century. Physical educationalist Rolf Ingvaldsen (2009) provides an interesting analysis of Drillo's successful comeback as national team coach when Norway won 1–0 against the football super power Germany in a practice match. Ingvaldsen comments that when Drillo receives the natural question about the secret of his success and answers with technical analyses based on a match's profile, it does not (any longer) appear to be a satisfactory answer for journalists and other self-proclaimed experts. There must be something more underneath it all. And the explanatory models reverted to are terms such as 'self-esteem', 'team spirit', 'leadership qualities', 'charisma' and a coined expression: 'the Drillo effect', which plays upon exactly the alleged psychological change that can occur in the heads of the players overnight when a new coach steps in. Ingvaldsen (who has a PhD in sports psychology) warns against what he calls the psychologising of sports performances, particularly if it entails the gradual replacement of both match analyses and the development of strategic playing models by a unilateral focus on psychological factors – or the cultivation of coaches who are personally and charismatically attractive, rather than in possession of actual coaching knowledge (Ingvaldsen, 2009). However, after a troublesome qualification for the World Cup in Brazil 2014 that looked set to go about without Norwegian participation, the fans and the Norwegian Football Association seem to have run out of patience with the 'structuralist' Olsen. Drillo was asked to resign. One of the main differences between Drillo and his successor Per-Matthias Høgmo, which commentators hope will revitalise the national side, is the belief in how mental training and cooperation with psychologists can turn things around for a football team (Overvik, 2013).

With respect to the tendency toward the psychologising of football and other sports performances, one can ask what it is that is introduced by sports psychology that is new. What we can call 'everyday psychology' has of course been there all along – the players have naturally always had a psyche that could be influenced – for example, the home pitch advantage has a great deal to do with psychological factors. The particular emphasis, cultivation and making scientific of 'the mental aspect', however, appears to be something new. To investigate this in further detail, I will take as a point of departure the example of Sven-Göran Eriksson's period as a coach for the English national football team (2001–2006). After the regrettable loss to Germany in the autumn of 2000, which was a farewell to the old Wembley Stadium and led up to England's qualification for the World Cup in South Korea and Japan in 2002, Kevin Keegan, the team coach at the time, resigned. The English Football Association did something they had never done before, and that was to hire a foreign coach. The choice fell on the highly qualified cosmopolitan Swede Sven-Göran Eriksson. Eriksson managed to turn around England's poor start and win the Qualifying Group, with a 5–1 victory over Germany in Munich serving as a particularly memorable highlight. Eriksson's apparently miraculous transformation of the English national team was explained by an alleged psychological revolution connected to Eriksson's many years of collaboration with the professor of performance psychology Willi Railo at the Norwegian School of Sport Sciences. This work has been documented in the book *Inside Football – the Mental Game* (Railo, Eriksson, and Matson, 2001) and by the BBC documentary *The England Patient* (Gibbon, 2002). The TV documentary explains Eriksson's success based on the application of Railo's scientific methods. We are shown an in-depth study of Gareth Southgate's famous missed penalty kick in the EURO 96 semi-final, again against Germany. We are told that Southgate's movement just seconds before the fatal kick were mechanical and choppy. This is explained as being due to a fear of failure that is greater than the desire for victory. This penalty kick becomes the very personification of 'the English psyche'. The players were suffering from performance anxiety. Now that the diagnosis has been made, the 'England patient' is treated using Railo's scientific methods, which quickly produce results. The opposite winning psyche is illustrated via David Beckham's deciding, last-minute free kick, right before full time against Greece, which secured England's World Cup participation in South Korea and Japan in 2002. The secret to Beckham's success is his psyche; the desire to win is greater than the fear of failure. The solution therefore is to be found, according to Railo, in what occurs in Beckham's mind during this free kick. We are shown a graphic image of a brain that shows us that activation of the dorsal stream produces natural movements and success, while activation of the ventral stream creates anxiety and failure. Based on these findings Railo explains his model: every single team's success is dependent upon a 'common mental model' for how a team is to play. The coach uses this model, but he needs an extending arm on the pitch to communicate it – a 'cultural architect'. This is a player who personally has vision and the best understanding of the coach's mental model.

England's cultural architect is not surprisingly David Beckham. If a team plays using a common mental model, the idea is that the players will enter the 'flow zone'. In the flow zone the players stop thinking and do everything automatically. Railo's principles are then superimposed on the images from England's 5–1 victory over Germany. It starts out badly. At first England is 0–1 down, but then the psychology of Railo and Eriksson begins to take effect. The cultural architect takes control. The team begins playing using a common mental model and Michael Owen finds the flow zone. The BBC documentary ends full of expectations on behalf of the English national team for the World Cup in South Korea and Japan (Gibbon, 2002). The hope is that since they are playing on the same team as science and psychology, this will help England to finally once again win a huge championship. England has only won the World Cup on one occasion – and has ever since had an unfortunate tendency to be eliminated in the knock-out stages, particularly on penalty kicks.

But things did not exactly turn out as hoped. England was eliminated in the quarter-finals against Brazil who later won the entire championship. How could this then happen? Was Railo's method just a bluff? England was still without any title since the World Cup at home in 1966 and Eriksson too turned out to be only human. Even though Eriksson's status had been shaken, the man behind him, Willi Railo, representing psychology, remained secure in his position as a victor. Railo and sports psychology had effectively introduced a set of concepts that were complementary, in other words, concepts that could be used both when the alleged psychological effect emerged, and when it failed to materialise. The fact was that England failed again in a big championship. The explanation was that the fear of failure was greater than the desire to succeed. There was no common mental model. The cultural architects did not assume enough responsibility.

Those of us with an interest in football will have registered from time to time the following explanations of losses: 'The results do not come about on their own'; 'The interaction was poor'; 'The players are not willing to give their all'. A new set of explanations is now lined up to replace these clichés. All of Railo's concepts can be easily translated into ordinary speech:

- Cultural architect = key player
- Fear of failure greater than the will to win = player with shoulders too high
- Will to win greater than fear of losing = player with great self-confidence
- Common mental model = interaction, teamwork

One can easily code these psychological concepts back into a common vernacular and it is unclear how Railo's concepts actually introduce any new knowledge, qualitatively speaking, to football. Previously one missed a penalty if one's 'shoulders were too high'. If the development continues as sports psychology intends, in the future players will miss penalty kicks because they are 'activated in the ventral region'. The new explanation, however, does not introduce anything new; it is solely a new description with the same prescribed solution. The solution in both cases is still 'to keep a cool head'. The paradox, however, is that there does not appear in this case to be a requirement for sports psychology to introduce any genuinely new knowledge; it is sufficient to adapt everyday language to a more pronounced scientific jargon, which thereby acquires greater credibility and weight. Perhaps it is, to the contrary, the case that psychology is welcomed exactly because it can be reconciled with football's existing explanatory models with such facility and does not actually change anything?

Eriksson continued as national team manager after the World Cup in Germany 2006, with a relatively good record as a manager for England, but without success in any large championship. England was eliminated on penalty kicks in both the UEFA European Championship in 2004 and the World Cup 2006, on both occasions against Portugal. The English football association promoted Eriksson's assistant Steve McClaren to manager for a short period of time without any success worth mentioning and in 2008 placed its faith once again in a successful foreigner – the authoritarian Italian Fabio Capello. Capello's explanation for England's lack of success in recent years was simply fear. He observed that the players had the abilities but that they also had 'a big problem of the mind' (*The Guardian*, 2009, n.p.). The history from Eriksson's period repeated itself – England made an impressive showing in the qualification but in the World Cup in South Africa in 2010 the team struggled with its game and was knocked out in the last 16, once again against its arch-enemy Germany. Capello's explanation for the poor performance: 'It reminds me of when I first started as England manager, I saw the same fear when we played at Wembley' (Beasley, 2010, n.p.). In other words, it's back to square one and group therapy sessions for 'the English patient'. And once again it was time to return to familiar ground, as Roy Hodgson was appointed manager of England's football team on 1 May 2012.

Psychologist on call round the clock

The Winter Olympic Games in Vancouver in 2010 were in many ways the ultimate breakthrough for sports psychology in Norway. Before the Olympics, sports psychology came into the spotlight of the media and was made the object of a light and humorous rivalry between the neighbours Norway and Sweden. It all started with a news segment from national broadcaster NRK claiming that the Norwegian troupe of athletes in Vancouver could come to require 24-hour help from a psychologist. Among the 68 persons constituting the support system for the Norwegian athletes, there were four psychologists. Elite sports manager Jarle Aambø justified the 24-hour service in this way: 'This field has now been integrated into the implementation of the Olympics in order to give the athletes the same security factor as they have otherwise' (NRK teletext, 2010, n.p.). The Swedish media quickly picked up on the item and the reactions from the other side of the border were not long in materialising: 'Only losers use sports psychologists. Good Lord, when athletes start crying for a psychologist, one knows that they have already lost,' was the biting opinion of the Swedish newspaper *Aftonbladet's* commentator Lasse Anrell (2010, n.p.). The Swedish cross-country skier Marcus Hellner was no less outspoken and claimed that a psychologist was somebody to be consulted when one had problems (Flinck and Thorén, 2010).

It is clear that not everyone had followed along in the development that had taken place in 'the mental part' of sports to the same degree. Psychologist and football referee Tom Henning Øvrebø was quick to jump in and maintain that the statements testified to ignorance: 'Anrell could just as well have said that only losers bring along ski waxers' (Askeland, 2010, n.p.). Sports psychology and 'the mental aspect' had in other words become just as important as ski wax and gliding surface in the cross-country sport in 2010, at the very least in Norway. The national competition between Norway and Sweden culminated in a clear Norwegian victory when the medals were tallied in the end. Norway took a total of 23 medals, nine of these gold, while Sweden took only 11 medals, five of these gold. The biggest winner was nonetheless sports psychology. For it would dominate the media coverage of the Olympic Games as never before.

One of the Norwegian athletes for whom there were great expectations leading up to the Olympics was the Alpine skier Aksel Lund Svindal. He came through as well, with a gold medal in the men's super-giant slalom as the highlight. Immediately following the winning race, the NRK sports journalist Line Andersen exclaimed live from the finish line: 'That's the whole point, how strong he is mentally.' Expert commentator and former elite alpine skier Kjetil André Aamodt nodded in assent. What was impressive about Lund Svindal's performance lay in the management of his mental resources – the ability to handle the pressure, to shut everything out and concentrate exclusively on the task at hand. TV viewers did indeed, in addition, receive expert commentary which throughout the race offered insights on the purely technical aspects of his skiing performance, but once the gold medal was a fact, and this was to be communicated to the people, what was viewed as being important to emphasise was mastery of 'the mental aspect'. Many are those who can ski fast, but only the true champions are able to master 'the mental aspect' when it really matters.

The first week of the Olympics started off rather miserably from a Norwegian perspective and was characterised by Norwegian athletes who were unable to meet the expectations imposed on them. The ski jumper Anders Jacobsen failed to 'solve the mental blocks' while the winner, Swiss Simon Ammann, was both more experienced and 'psychologically stronger' than Jacobsen, according to Jacobsen (Borud, 2010). The cross-country skier Marit Bjørgen had in the previous season struggled mightily to live up to her impressive achievements from her early cross-country skiing career. She had, however, received help to 'correctly adjust her nerves', as one commentary had expressed it. For the women's 10-kilometre this resulted in a bronze medal, but despite a respectable third place, her nerves here had also played a role beforehand and had had an impact at the start of the race, as Bjørgen herself had disclosed. Luckily she found her stride, and the remainder of the Olympics was for her a huge success. For the next distance, the individual sprint for women, Bjørgen took the gold. She won two more gold medals and one silver medal. The transformation was a fact. As early as in the autumn of 2009 rumours had circulated stating that she was back. Bjørgen then told she had acquired some 'mental scars' due to her lack of results in past years (Skjerdingstad, 2009). The most important help had therefore come from psychologist Britt Tajet-Foxell who had helped her to erase the negative thoughts. It all fell into place for the ski jumper Jacobsen, too: when teammate Johan Remen Evensen was asked what they had done to cheer him up, he answered that they had sent Jacobsen to have therapy with his wife. The reward was a bronze medal for the Norwegian ski jumping team after Jacobsen came through as the final jumper and where he, as a result of there being too much wind on the slope, had been forced to endure some nerve-wracking minutes of waiting on the barrier before being allowed to jump. 'It is my greatest mental achievement,' Jacobsen told the press afterwards (Eriksen, 2010, n.p.).

After Tora Berger took her first Olympic gold in the biathlon, sports commentator Esten O. Sæther (2010) wrote that we cannot simply conclude that Norwegian success is due to the excellence of sports psychology, in spite of the fact that the first thing Berger mentioned after the victory was the psychologist who had helped her to find her way back to 'thinking like a winner'. The president of the Norwegian Psychological Association, Hofgaard, was less reticent. In the blog entry 'Psychologists strike gold in the Olympics' he took advantage of the occasion to comment on how the Olympics had been an impressive demonstration of the significance of 'the mental aspect', and a powerful wake-up call for those who 'continue to believe that this is merely a matter of knowing how to ski' (Hofgaard, 2010, n.p.). According to Hofgaard, the Olympic medal statistics, in which Norway had twice as many medals as Sweden, were clearly evidence of the fact that it was time for the Swedes to wake up. Hofgaard had apparently not heard that it had been disclosed that Anrell and Hellner were not representative of the attitude towards sports psychology in Sweden. It was revealed that as many as between 20 and 25 per cent of the Swedish Olympic athletes had received psychological assistance before the games and that the proliferation of sports psychology is just as great in Sweden as in Norway (Christiansen, 2010). However, the Swedes had a culture in which this was addressed before rather than during large-scale competitions.

Mirror of society?

Whether sports psychology truly makes an impact and improves performance and, as such, was a contributing factor to the Norwegian triumph in the Vancouver Olympics in 2010 is certainly important for the athletes, coaches and, not least, the reputation of the sports psychologists, but it is actually not what is of most interest in this context. Impact or no impact, that is not the question. All signs would seem to indicate that sports psychology has come to stay and that psychology's defenders, such as Øvrebø and Hofgaard, are absolutely right about psychology today being an essential part of sports. What is of interest is therefore to try and find some features of the metaphor 'the mental aspect' that can contribute to explaining elements of psychology's pervasive impact in social spheres such as the sports world.

(1) What is most striking is how 'the mental aspect' seems to be an inexhaustible source, not just in terms of explanations of sports performances but also in the express hope of improving them at some time in the future. The picture that emerges in self-help literature and sports psychology is one that depicts the psychology found in these spheres as containing the Enlightenment project's optimism for the future, and its belief in happiness or success through science and rationality. The magic 'mental part' hovers there, at all times, containing unexploited potential: 'Sports tries at all times to develop in terms of equipment, nutrition and technique. In the mental field, a great deal remains to be done and I am certain that we will only see more such coaches in the future,' said Ole Einar Bjørndalen about his own personal motivation expert Øyvind Hammer in connection with the feud with the Swedes (Askeland, 2010, n.p.).

(2) Psychology became established in an astoundingly short period of time as something extremely important. From being something ridiculed by those who weren't paying attention to the development – such as backward Swedish skiers and commentators – 'the mental dimension' and the psyche are now being utilised in full measure to explain the difference between victory and defeat, and success and failure. Even macho types like Hareide and Capello now make active use of it. Sports psychology is nonetheless a relatively new sub-discipline of psychology. It acquired its first international organisation in 1965 – the International Society of Sports Psychology – and it was not until 1986 and 1993 that sports psychology was accepted as a separate branch of psychology by the psychology associations in the USA and in Great Britain (Jarvis, 1999). In Norway, sports psychology arrived even later. In the official evaluation report by Olympiatoppen (the Norwegian elite sport organisation) on the Winter Olympics in Turin 2006, which was a sports fiasco for Norway, mental training and sports psychology were introduced, at the request of athletes and coaches, as a measure also to be employed during competitions. This was feasibly the reason why the decision was made to employ it at the Vancouver Olympics during the competition (NRK teletext, 2010).

There is every reason to believe that 'the physiological' has for a long time been far more important than 'the mental'. However, the founder of the modern Olympic Games and the first president of the International Olympic

Committee, the Frenchman Pierre de Coubertin (1863–1937), was also a visionary with respect to psychology in sports. Coubertin was possibly the first to use the term 'sports psychology' (Kornspan, 2007). But he was relatively alone in his interest in 'the mental aspect', something to which his lament from 1900 attests: 'These days the physiological effects of sports are studied in great detail. Curious experiments are being conducted that will fully elucidate that matter. But the psychological side has remained in the shadows' (Courbertin as cited in Kornspan, 2007, n.p.).

(3) 'The mental aspect' functions as an explanatory model regardless of whether the results it has contributed to cultivating are good or bad. The examples of Bjørgen, Jacobsen and Capello illustrate how psychology and 'the mental aspect' are flexible and expedient as explanatory models whether it is one's success or failure that is to be explained. Through relatively simplistic metaphors such as 'negative thoughts', 'mental scars' and 'dealing with mental blocks' one can offer an expert explanation of just about everything through the use of psychological language. Sports psychology as such functions more like a reference work that has come to stay, rather than a simple causal explanation. Sir Karl Popper's (1963) well-known critique of Freud and psychoanalysis as an illustration of a totalising theory that cannot be falsified would prove uniquely visionary. Psychology functions, regardless of the outcome, like a suitable explanatory model that never runs dry. This is not unlike the special logic Joseph Heller (1994) describes in the novel *Catch-22*: one has to be mad to fly bombing raids. If one declares that one does not want to fly bombing raids, one proves that one is not mad, but rational, and in consequence one must fly bombing raids. In the therapeutic culture perhaps the opposite applies. Because if one rejects psychology as a significant factor, one ends up in madness, which then confirms the importance of psychology. Freud's therapeutic formula was, as is known, based on the idea that the therapist is always on track, regardless of whether the patient has confirmed or denied a symptom. In the 'feud' with Sweden leading up to the Olympics, Hammer summarised concisely the entire debate and − indirectly − the all-encompassing logic of sports psychology during the Olympics in Vancouver: 'I would say that it is insane not to bring along any mental coaches to the Olympics' (Askeland, 2010, n.p.).

(4) 'The mental aspect' has in sports succeeded in becoming established as a domain with the same rightful place as 'technique' or 'the physical'. Empirical evidence for it includes Øverbø's statement that psychology has become as important today as the ski waxer in cross-country skiing, or Dale Oen's comment that the mental aspect has perhaps become more important than the physiological in swimming. It is also possible to envision that these domains operate on a principle of energy constancy, whereby when 'the

mental' is given prominence, this occurs to the detriment of something else, which becomes less important and retreats into the background. Within sports this implies perhaps what Ingvaldsen warns us against – a unilateral focus on psychological variables on the part of the coach – to the detriment of systematic training knowledge. This is perhaps not so significant? Amongst all unimportant subjects, football is by far the most important, as Pope John Paul II supposedly once said. Sports exist first and foremost as modern day bread and games for the appeasement of an audience. If the presence of psychology should lead us astray, this is after all relatively benign. It is greater cause for concern when psychological explanations prevail at the expense of other explanations outside of sports, such as in social policy. In the next chapter we will see how Tony Blair and the British authorities have claimed that the biggest problem about poverty in Great Britain is that many of the impoverished have a 'poor self-image' (Furedi, 2004). More traditional demographic explanations such as 'lack of a place to live' or 'unemployment' are suppressed with the very best intentions.

(5) 'The mental part' can always serve as an explanatory model when the material or economic elements are not in place and accordingly can also be abused. The camouflaging power of psychology is perhaps particularly convenient in a sport such as football, characterised by finance, large capital and shady agent and trading activities on the one hand, and loyalty, a sense of belonging and strong emotions on the other. Psychology can indirectly help out in misrepresenting how football's winners and losers on the whole reflect large economic differences. Certainly exceptions are to be found, here and there, of clubs with limited funds that perform better than clubs with greater resources. But in the long run it is the richest clubs in the world that are the most successful because they can afford to pay the best players. There are of course always opportunities to work with 'the mental aspect' but probably less than football itself and its supporters would like to believe. Kuper and Szymanski (2009) implemented regression analyses and came to the conclusion that around 90 per cent of the variance in the league placement of English Premier League and Championship clubs between 1978 and 2007 could be attributed to the size of the salaries clubs could afford to pay their players. The underlying assumption of the analysis is that the market at all times will have a regulatory effect, so that the best players are for the most part the best-paid players. This uncomfortable truth is something most of those who follow football throughout the world are aware of deep down but it is preferable to believe the illusion that this is not the case. And here psychology comes in handy.

The Norwegian national team is perhaps an example of this. A reasonable assumption for why the Norwegian team did not take part in the World

Cup in South Africa in 2010, and failed to qualify for Brazil in 2014, could be that it is simply not good enough. That implies that the standard of the Norwegian players compared to that of other nations is worse now than it was a few years ago, a point which is reflected by the reduced number of Norwegian professional players in the Barclays Premier League and other big leagues, and in the performances of the Norwegian club teams in Europe. The same can also in fact be the case for the English national team. Kuper and Szymanski (2009) make the argument that the popular perception that England always underperforms when it comes to big championships is a myth. Based on a calculation that takes into account the size of the population, the gross national product (GNP) and a team's international experience, they demonstrate that England has in fact performed a little above the average expected in recent years. In both of these examples psychology gives athletes and supporters the belief that success is possible if one releases one's (inner) potential. 'It's about the mental dimension, as well as a belief in the impossible,' orienteering runner Audun Hultgreen Weltzien recently said in an interview (Halvorsen, 2010, p. 11). Here we perhaps approach a key to understanding 'the mental'. The mental dimension in this statement figures in tandem with 'the impossible' – the mental becomes an infinite resource which can make impossible dreams possible. As such, we can say that 'the mental aspect' can represent a positive metaphor that highlights the sports ethos that everyone can participate, or that everyone can become good, if they just have the right attitude and the will. Footballer Koppinen says the following when he comments on all of the goals his club have let in: 'We have suffered an unbelievably hard punishment for all of the errors we have made this year, but behind it all lies a lot of psychology' (Holte, 2009, n.p.). The message that psychology sends is like Adorno's (2002) studies of astrology, the idea that if one just has the right mental attitude, everything will work out fine. In the world of football, psychology becomes the perfect mythology whereby an authoritative, scientific explanation sets aside the arbitrary facts of reality, economic inequalities and/or limited abilities. The hope lives on, in other words, thanks to psychology, because in terms of 'the mental dimension' everyone has an infinite potential. In the next chapter we will see how psychology finds its given place in the political ideology of neoliberalism.

7   Psychology and neoliberalism

'The Stanford marshmallow experiment' led by Walter Mischel is one of social psychology's famous experiments from the 1960s and 1970s. In the experiment, four-year-olds were each given one marshmallow and were promised one more if they managed not to eat the first one right away (Mischel, Ebbesen and Raskoff Zeiss, 1972). The leader of the experiment then left the room, leaving the child alone with the marshmallow. Some children gobbled up their marshmallow as soon as the leader left the room. Other children managed to wait for a few minutes, but then succumbed to temptation. Some of the four-year-olds managed to wait until the adult returned after 20 minutes with another marshmallow. These children employed different strategies and techniques during the waiting period, such as putting their hands over their eyes, putting their heads down and resting, singing or playing games by themselves. More than ten years later, all of the four-year-olds from the experiment were assessed by their parents and teachers in terms of how well adapted they were, and they were asked to take a general academic skills test (Shoda, Mischel and Peake, 1990). The results showed that those who had managed to wait for 20 minutes as children were consistently better adapted, more popular, had more determination, were more self-confident and more reliable than those who had not passed the test as four-year-olds. Since then the Stanford marshmallow experiment has been used as an widespread argument for the theory that the ability to delay gratification and control one's impulses is a more reliable variable for success than more traditional ability rating scales, such as an IQ score (cf. Gibbs, 2001; Goleman, 1996). Self-control appears, in other words, to be a skill that it is wholly critical to master in today's society. A potential explanatory model can be found in the strategy of political governance that goes by the name of neoliberalism, where the ideal is that 'You shall govern yourself' (Neumann and Sending, 2003). I will now show how neoliberalism entails a displacement of conflicts of values from traditional politics over into professions such as psychology. The expanded mandate which the expertise of governmental science acquires under neoliberalism imposes greater accountability requirements on the professions.

What is neoliberalism?

Neoliberalism refers to a market-friendly politics that first appeared in the post-war years and which became particularly manifest in the form of government found in countries such as the USA, Great Britain and China towards the end of the 1970s. Social geographer David Harvey's (2005, p. 2) influential definition of neoliberalism reads: 'a theory of political economic practices that proposes that human well-being can best be advanced by liberating individual entrepreneurial freedoms and skills within an institutional framework characterized by strong private property rights, free markets, and free trade'. In Norway the Labour Party in particular, including the terms in office of both Gro Harlem Brundtland (1981, 1986–1989 and 1990–1996) and Jens Stoltenberg (2000–2001 and 2005–2013), has been referred to as Norwegian neoliberalism (Marsdal and Wold, 2005; Nilsen and Østerberg, 1998). Neoliberalism in Norway has also been examined from a political science perspective on public reforms, where the conclusion on the basis of the empirical analyses is that 'neoliberalism is only in part an apt diagnosis of society' (Mydske, Claes, and Lie, 2007, p. 369). A discourse analysis of the incidence of verbal expressions and values associated with neoliberalism in Norwegian newspapers during the time period 1984–2007, however, supports the hypothesis of neoliberalism's penetration in Norway (Nafstad, Blakar, Carlquist, Phelps and Rand-Hendriksen, 2009). Typical neoliberal terms such as 'founder', 'entrepreneurship' and 'freedom of choice' experienced a clear upswing during this period. Parallel to this, terms such as 'solidarity', 'unity' and 'cohesion' underwent a corresponding decline. The analysis indicates that the use of several of the terms associated with neoliberalism stagnated or experienced a slight decline towards the end of the period (2005–2007) under assessment, something which can indicate that neoliberal individualism had reached a preliminary peak in Norway, and then experienced a small ideological decline. What are presumed to be verbal expressions for individualism such as 'I/me' have increased by 45 per cent, while 'we/us' have only increased by 10 per cent during the same time period (Nafstad *et al.*, 2009). The media language seems on the whole to be moving in a more personal direction in this period, and the analysis also provides evidence for the emergence of the culture of rights: the use of the word 'right' increased by 22 per cent in the period while the use of 'responsibility' dropped by 21 per cent (Nafstad *et al.*, 2009).

There are different and at times conflicting perspectives on neoliberalism and the changes which are frequently attributed to or associated with it, such as individualism. The British sociologist Anthony Giddens (1990, 1998), for example, views the neoliberal policy promoted by New Labour in the 1990s in Great Britain as a necessary modernisation project and emphasises the dynamic of activating and empowering the citizen. The formation of a new type of citizenship that is more autonomous is both necessary and desirable through this form of rule. Approaches to neoliberalism inspired by French philosopher Michel Foucault's (1926–1984) analyses of power understand empowerment as a rhetoric that conceals systematic forms of power and protection in Western capitalistic states, institutionalised through welfare and the public sector, and embodied by social citizenship (Clarke, 2005). This execution of power is, however, necessary in order for the constitution of subjects as free, autonomous citizens or users. These approaches often put the normative question regarding whether the development is 'good' or 'bad' in brackets. The Foucault perspective will first and foremost stress that power changes under neoliberalism. There are also more explicit critics of neoliberalism who claim that it is a well-concealed ideology that introduces a specific market logic and an ideal for governance which abuses the concept of freedom and instead leads to new forms of coercion and oppression (cf. Bourdieu, 1998a; Dufour, 2008).

Neoliberalism's social psychology

Regardless of how one views neoliberalism there is a consensus about the fact that the relation between the state and the citizen is undergoing change. In neoliberal thought, the individual – *homo oeconomicus* – becomes the central point of reference (Lemke, 2001). In contrast to classical liberalism, it is not the state's interference in the market that must be regulated – rather the opposite – the state is needed to establish the market mechanisms and the impact of competition can only occur if it is produced by the government's practice (Lemke, 2001). Neoliberalism removes the delimiting, external principle and puts a regulating, inner principle in its place: it becomes the market that serves as the organising principle for the state and for society (Lemke, 2001). The same occurs with the human being under neoliberalism. He/she becomes *homo oeconomicus*, who differs from the political subject of the eighteenth century's liberal philosophers, where the individual's freedom is a precondition for a rational government which the government cannot tamper with without the risk of putting its own foundation in danger. Now, to the contrary, neoliberalism works by connecting the rationality of governance to the rational actions of individuals, but the point of reference is no longer a human nature that is given, but an artificial, constructed type of subjectivity. Neoliberalism, Thomas Lemke (2001) writes, no longer situates the rational principle for regulating and restraining the actions of governance in a natural freedom that we all must recognise, but brings in an artificially arranged freedom: in the entrepreneurial and competition-oriented behaviour of the economically rational individual.

With neoliberalism the autonomous individual therefore becomes the all-encompassing political reference point per se, regardless of whether it is postulated by the traditional liberal parties or by modernised social democrats with the English New Labour as a model (Jørgensen, 2002). This is thus not solely a political rhetoric, but a reality that all of the political parties on the right or left are obliged to relate to. This development, even though it has to a large extent become a reality, is also understood as an effect of neoliberalism as an ideological process, even if neoliberalism's followers would like to depict it as a natural development. For example, the French sociologist Pierre Bourdieu (1998b, n.p.) connects neoliberalism to individualisation processes which it supports under a semblance of economic and individual freedom: '. . . the economic view which individualizes everything'. In the labour market this finds expression in the form of individualisation of wages, positions and expertise and an atomisation of labour in general (Bourdieu, 1998a), which in turn makes the formation of reflexivity and collective protest against neoliberal, political reforms difficult. Neoliberalism is a programme for getting rid of troublesome collective structures, Bourdieu claimed. We have already seen one form that such individualisation can take in the imagined case of the cleaning assistant Tove (see Chapter 2).

Great changes also occur in the social psychology of daily life. The cultural idea about self-actualisation is reinforced under neoliberalism (Willig, 2005). The use of the term 'self-actualisation' increased by more than 240 per cent in Norwegian newspapers from 1984 to 2007 (Nafstad *et al.*, 2009). Neoliberalism is founded on the conviction that social justice can be achieved through the market. A well-functioning market-based society will give the individual sufficient opportunities for self-actualisation and in competition with other individuals their self-worth will increase in step with the reputation derived through their accomplishments. Everyone is a winner, in other words. The Danish sociologist Rasmus Willig (2005) stresses how neoliberalism is underpinned by an assumption that it can emancipate the individual from limited opportunities and future prospects to a more open horizon of choices by way of political measures such as deregulation and privatisation. With a full-scale de-institutionalisation from ties to the state, the prevailing political idea is thereby at all times upheld by the individual's faith in increased chances of realising his or her talents and abilities. However, Willig (2005) warns against the individual willingly allowing him/herself to be enraptured by this promising dream, because the individual risks being entrapped within a false autonomy inflicted with self-actualisation projects where each and every one of us is forced to motivate, optimise and examine ourselves in order to improve our human capital. A common feature of neoliberalism on the one hand and self-developmental psychology and New Age movements on the other is that it is the individual's or individual human being's consciousness that creates the surroundings and not the opposite (Vetlesen, 2007). Fittingly enough, the opening passage of Øiestad's (2009, p. 13) *Self-esteem* expresses quite precisely this prevailing mentality:

> Without self-esteem the world stops. The man-made society would come to a complete halt if human beings did not have self-esteem. The reason for this is that what takes place in our inner worlds determines what we do in the outer world.

It is worth noting that this view of the relation between the individual and society is diametrically opposed to Marx and Engels's (1998) well-known fundamental premise that it is life's economical, political and social conditions which create man's consciousness and not consciousness that creates the material conditions. Psychology, defined here as the science of the universal psyche, is at particular risk of acquiring an ideological bias if it always posits the individual as 'the first mover'. Psychology and neoliberalism have apparently a number of common features and structural similarities, which I will now address in greater detail. Is there a close connection to be found between what has been referred to as our age's dominant ideology (Johnston and Saad-Filho, 2005), and what has been referred to as our age's cultural hegemony, the therapeutic ethos (Lears, 1985)? If so, what type resistance then does psychology possess to enable it to withstand the existing contemporary cultural logic? It would be cause for great concern if psychology were to legitimise and support a political ideological project. At least unconsciously. Neoliberalism – the most prominent and possibly only ideology of our time – becomes in other words the ultimate test for whether psychology is aware of its social responsibility, or if it simply moves about in accordance with market demand as Kvale's amoeba metaphor would imply, without any thought about where it is headed, but with a formidable ability to adapt to new and foreign environments.

The art of governing

In the eighteenth century a shift occurred from political science to the art of governance: from a regime dominated by so-called sovereignty structures to a regime characterised by governing techniques. This change marked simultaneously the birth of the modern political economy, according to Foucault (2007). This is no coincidence. With the emergence of advanced liberal democracies in the Western world throughout the nineteenth century, a transformation takes place in the state's manner of governing. From predominantly having ruled over territories, a transition occurs to that of governing (over) populations, gradually in increasingly smaller entities, until finally down to every single individual (Foucault, 2007). Advanced liberal governments therefore involve a profound change in the traditional manner of thinking about and practising politics. While welfare strategies traditionally speaking seek to rule through society, advanced liberal governing strategies ask whether it is possible to rule outside of society, and instead govern through the measurable and easily regulated choices of autonomous agents, such as citizens, consumers, parents, employees, etc. This specific formula for governance encompasses a unique relation between political subjects and expertise where the experts' advice and orders (ideally) coincide with the citizens' own projects for self-governing and improvement of their lives (Rose, 1996). What is being sought here is a form of politics that is independent of the state, a life politics or ethics that emphasises instead the important political values by way of the mobilisation and establishment of individual capacities and governance. This is an autonomised and plural formula for government, which is dependent upon regulating elements at a micropolitical level in the form of experts. Here all 'psy' disciplines – such as psychiatry, psychology and psychotherapy – acquire their historical currency.

Inspired by Foucault's historical study of the art of governing in the West, Nikolas Rose has investigated psychology's historical development in Great Britain and in the West in general. Rose's (1996, 1999) studies can be characterised as a genealogy of subjectivation, which means the exploration of how our relationship to the self has changed. The objective of such a genealogical method is not the history of man but, more specifically, the relation which man has established to the self, how he or she has come to relate to him/herself as a specific self. The art of government entails in this case the development of strategies based on defined technologies, so-called self-governing mechanisms, in accordance with how the individual experiences, understands, judges and controls him/herself.

The psy-disciplines, such as psychology and psychotherapy, have, partly due to their heterogeneous nature and lack of a definite paradigm, achieved a unique capacity with respect to practices that pertain to the governing of governance. Not only do they offer a selection of models of the self, but also practical recipes for action, provided by professionals in different settings. Their currency has been further reinforced through the ability to support these practical recipes with a legitimacy based on access to the truth about human beings. It has become impossible to experience one's own or another's personality, or to govern the self or others without psy. This government rationality's efficiency can be illustrated by an example. The humanist requirement that one shall live and act authentically and true to oneself essentially runs at cross purposes with political or institutional requirements for collective responsibility, such as economic freedom of trade. Here one has accordingly an apparent contradiction for which the art of government has a prescribed solution. The answer is 'autonomy', which is the final word in governing techniques: the individual is directed to govern the self in accordance with the goal of governmental politics. Individual self-actualisation by way of consumption is a perfect match for the political economy that is dependent upon a consistently high level of consumption in order to enable general growth. Not being an active consumer becomes extremely difficult, if not impossible.

Rose views psychology as a technique whose production of psychological truth effects is inextricably bound to an ongoing psychologisation of countless domains, problems, practices and activities in accordance with the new ideal government. These fields become psychological because they are problematised – they are perceived as cause for concern and incomprehensible, and psychology is injected. It is a constructive relation between what is considered to be an adequate psychological theory and the process by which psychology becomes visible and legitimate within these domains, such as in raising a child, changing a problem child's behaviour, curing a hysteric, administering a military troop, running a factory. The ruling of people becomes comprehensible and visible when it can be brought into a psychological framework. In this way reality is ordered in accordance with a psychological logic, and abilities, personalities, attitudes and the like become key components in authorities' decisions and calculations. This implies for psychology's part a large demand, but also an undermining of the power of definition over the contents of psychology. Psychological epistemology is therefore to be understood as institutional epistemology. The rules for what can be knowledge are structured by the very institutional relations within which they have been formed.

Rose views psychology not just as a way of thinking, but as a specific way of life, a type of practice or action in the world. He uses Aristotle's term *techne*, which signifies a type of practical knowledge about the workings of psychology in society, in the form of techniques: psychology receives its truth through its techniques. Throughout the twentieth century, psychological norms, values, images and techniques have shaped the way different social authorities think about individuals, their vices and virtues, their condition of illness and health, their normality and their pathologies. Objective psychological terms such a normality, adaptation and accomplishment have been incorporated into the programmes, dreams and outlines for regulation of the governance of human beings. Psychology has been implemented in the techniques and agencies created for governmental rule and is practised not only by psychologists themselves, but also by other experts such as doctors, priests, philanthropists, architects and teachers, or as we have seen, the coach, the cosmetic surgeon or football coach. The strategies, programmes, techniques, devices and reflections of the administration of government which Foucault calls 'governmentality' have been psychologised. The execution of modern forms of political power has been inextricably connected to knowledge about human subjectivity. Psychology's authority therefore stems from the fact that it has in its own right produced a series of new authorities whose office is the governing of the governance, control of subjectivity.

Psychology is associated with new fields and problems over which expertise must be exercised; even normality is related to a type of expertise. Psychology is also connected to already existing systems of authority: we could have added the officer in the military, the school teacher, the company executives and now the football coach to Rose's list. These forms of authority accumulate a type of ethical basis through their use of psychology's terminology and techniques. Authority becomes ethical to the extent it is performed in light of knowledge about those who are its subjects. This no longer entails simply giving orders, controlling, demanding obedience and loyalty, but also improving the individual's capacity to execute authority over the self. Ergo 'help towards self-help', the example of what the sports psychologist Pensgaard was going to give the Tromsø football club. Execution of authority becomes thereby a therapeutic activity; the most powerful way to control the actions of others is to change the way in which they govern themselves. Over the past 50 years, the language, techniques and personnel of psychology have influenced and transformed the ways people have been required and led to become ethical beings. We define and regulate ourselves in accordance with a moral code that rules our lives and set moral goals for ourselves. Human beings have been opened up in different ways for interventions performed in the name of subjectivity. As Rose sees it, the psy sciences have thereby created the modern subject and function in daily life as a guarantor of and repairman for human beings' autonomy and freedom.

This development towards the neoliberal system of government and view of man is made manifest today in the form of the requirement that each individual citizen shall govern themselves. Political scientists Iver Neumann and Ole Jacob Sending (2003) highlight how in Norway today there is a welfare state government rationality which contains an inherent expectation that each of us should govern ourselves. We do so by way of the ideal and scheme of a welfare model which makes citizens into 'users', 'clients' and 'consumers' who personally choose services, whether the product is a cable TV provider or public service such as a hospital or treatment programme.

The new social glue

We can better understand Rose's perspective of psychology as a governmental science through a psychological category that we have already addressed several times: 'self-esteem'. The most common means by which the therapeutic culture assesses health is through 'self-image' or 'self-esteem'. A high degree of positive self-esteem characterises a desired state of emotional and psychological health, while a negative self-image is a symptom of a self that is ill and on the verge of a crisis. Self-esteem, as such, can encompass both the positive and the negative in life (Øiestad, 2009). It is accordingly not a matter of a superficial search for happiness, but an emotional platform which safeguards life's ups and downs, run by the simultaneous requirement to be the 'agent of one's own life': in other words, empowerment.

As mentioned earlier, beneath the therapeutic culture is the underlying belief in the idea that by enhancing the self-image or self-esteem of a population, society will thrive. Striving for this becomes a form of civic responsibility. Sociologist Frank Furedi (2004) refers to the research on self-esteem, such as the work of Neil Smelser which shows that the variable 'self-esteem' has become a key factor in terms of understanding and explaining social problems. It is a specific therapeutic sensibility in relation to the self's emotions which has led to complex social problems being reduced to simple psychological factors such as self-esteem. Self-esteem has a free-flowing character that can be attributed to any topic. It has become a popular mythology which is given continuity in our cultural awareness (Furedi, 2004). In *Therapy Culture* Furedi claims to see the therapeutic ethos as a defining feature in the New Labour party's modernisation of the welfare state in Great Britain. The British government can be said to operate in accordance with an escalating therapeutic imperative which finds expression as modernisation of the welfare state. The rhetoric of New Labour is characterised by a therapeutic discourse. According to Tony Blair the main problem with social inequalities was not material poverty but the destructive consequences of this for self-image (Furedi, 2004). Official governmental statements in Great Britain imply that a low self-image is a significant cause of child prostitution, homelessness, teenage pregnancy, substance abuse and anti-social behaviour. Social problems thereby to an increasing degree are interpreted in such a way that their causes are found in psychopathology requiring therapeutic treatment. The therapeutic culture not only gives society a narrative about the self, it also passes on ideas about how people can give meaning to their life conditions and how to address these. According to Furedi, under neoliberalism, a new social contract is formed between the state and citizen that is characterised by an inherently paternalistic perception of the vulnerable subject in need of guidance and support from the public sector. This implies a devaluation of the citizen as an autonomous and rational agent. Therapy is to be understood as merely a means of survival, Furedi argues – where people are not cured, but instead receive confirmation, only to be then sent back out into society. This sounds like an echo of Rieff's critique of the triumph of therapy.

Furedi's critique is classical liberalism – in that he attacks the therapeutic state for its soft paternalism and a well-concealed assault on freedom. Although Furedi provides a convincing documentation of how typical neoliberal systems of government such as the British New Labour party find themselves depending upon therapeutic strategies, his understanding of psychology's constituting role in the creation of identity and meaning is nonetheless somewhat limited. Furedi's explanation of the growing therapeutic state is supported predominantly by the hypothesis about the need for state control and an anti-liberal and/or overly zealous wish to carry out treatment on the part of psychologists and psychiatrists. He offers no deeper explanation for why these problems are arising at this particular time or that there can be new, real phenomena and problem areas that are appearing, and for which control is sought, to be acquired through therapeutic solutions.

A more interpretive approach to a therapeutic concept, and techniques such as self-esteem or self-confidence can be found in the so-called governmentality literature (cf. Dean, 2009; Rose, 1996, 1999), inspired by Foucault's analyses of the history of the art of government. The governmentality literature has engendered a number of studies that address the new discourse fields or dispositifs that open up under neoliberalism. The analyses are not critical of power from above and down, but are more micro-political in their approach, in accordance with the fragmentation and division of power and the altered expression of modern forms of government.

The self-esteem movement

Political scientist Barbara Cruikshank (1996, 1999) shows how the self-respect movement in the USA promises to solve social problems by heralding a revolution – not against capitalism, racism or patriarchy, but against the incorrect way in which we govern ourselves. The very perspective of potential political and social interventions is hereby altered from a perceptual horizon where it is social and structural factors that determine whether problems such as unemployment, crime, child abuse, and so on, can be solved, to make room for categories of understanding and solutions based on subjective, individual grounds (Lemke, 2001). The self will therefore always be measured, evaluated and disciplined to adjust personal empowerment to collective standards. An extremely important harmony must then arise between the political objectives of the state and the personal self-esteem status of each individual (Lemke, 2001). Cruikshank (1996) shows how the question of governance becomes a question of self-governance through the discourse of self-esteem.

The most well-known example of this is the social movement 'California Task Force to Promote Self-Esteem and Personal and Social Responsibility', which was formed in California in 1983 to offer a programme that claimed to be able to solve social problems such as crime, poverty and gender discrimination by leading a social revolution against the self and its form of self-rule (Cruikshank, 1996). The members of the movement are a number of experts, social workers and grassroots activists working in accordance with the basic principle that social problems threaten democratic stability. But these problems cannot be solved by the state or experts, but solely through each individual citizen's personal empowerment:

> Self-esteem is the likeliest candidate for a *social vaccine*, something that empowers us to live responsibly and that inoculates us against the lures of crime, violence, substance abuse, teen pregnancy, child abuse, chronic welfare dependency, and educational failure. The lack of self-esteem is central to most personal and social ills plaguing our state and nation as we approach the end of the twentieth century.
>
> (California Task Force, cited in Cruikshank, 1996, p. 232)

Adorno's social anaesthesia mentioned earlier has here become a social vaccine. Self-esteem becomes a type of liberation therapy that presupposes a complete restructuring of the approach to the solution for social problems which will ideally mobilise all residents of California. Self-esteem becomes a means of subjectivising citizens, which makes them receptive to incorporating self-esteem in their vision of a good life and society. Those who go through an inner revolution are citizens who do the right thing, they join programmes, volunteer, but most important of all they work to improve their own self-image (Cruikshank, 1996). Self-esteem is a technology for citizenship and self-government which equips us to evaluate and act in relation to ourselves, so that the police officer, doctor or psychologist is not needed. Our relationship to ourselves is understood as being directly connected to citizenship according to the California Task Force: 'Being a responsible citizen depends on developing personal and social responsibility' (Cruikshank, 1996, p. 234).

Cruikshank (1996) holds that up to now we have gravely underestimated the degree of self-government already to be found in society. Government is not something that is done to us by those in power, Cruikshank claims, but something we do to ourselves – it is a complicit empowerment that involves no external threats. The norm of self-esteem connects subjectivity to power in a particularly effective manner, in that it seems to appear from within each individual's independent goal, it appears to be a part of our freedom. But the self-esteem movement is not just about our relationship to ourselves; it is a strategy for the democratic development of the individual and society. It opens up a wholly new set of social factors and strategies that can evolve under the empowering liberation therapy of experts.

The self-esteem discourse seeks to constitute a just and democratic society, but in a new way. The formation of self-esteem has little to do with the old, living public authority, Cruikshank claims. Self-esteem is founded to the contrary on the basis of the self's inner dialogue with itself. It has been a necessity ever since the formation of mass democracy and the republican public authority's decline, which Alexis de Tocqueville famously described from his America journeys in the 1830s. De Tocqueville overlooked the significance of the social sciences, Cruikshank maintains – democratic participation gradually came to rely upon a new type of scientific politics which governs and guides the citizens from inside. The American democracy could not reach the isolated citizens through a public sphere. It was therefore necessary to establish a form of government that created an ethos in which citizens were made personally responsible for governing themselves.

From liberation to empowerment

We have now looked at Cruikshank's descriptions of therapeutic hygiene movements, such as the California Task Force, which has a programme of creating increased empowerment among citizens: 'In the twenty-first century every government level in the state and each of its programs are designed to empower people to become self-realizing and self-reliant' (California Task Force, cited in Cruikshank, 1996, p. 239). 'Empowerment' appears to have become an extremely popular term in recent decades as a replacement for 'liberation'. Empowerment entails in the simplest sense that people or groups in a situation of powerlessness can personally develop the strength and power they need to overcome this.

Welfare scholar Ole Petter Askheim (2007) warns against an uncritical implementation of empowerment in the Nordic countries. He suggests that empowerment has already succeeded in becoming a popular term in health disciplines, where lifestyle influences, among other things, are meant to strengthen the patient, in accordance with goals others have set for them, perhaps at the expense of what they personally feel to be important. An example which illustrates how citizens are intended to govern themselves was the green prescription scheme introduced in 2003 by then Norwegian Minister of Health Dagfinn Høybråten. The idea behind the green prescription is to give physicians another tool to change the health behaviour of patients with high blood pressure or type 2 diabetes, but only for patients who are not already on medication. The principle is that the physicians write out a detailed 'prescription' containing instructions for 25 minutes of walking every day. The most important form of government is, as stated, to govern along with the individual rather than across them. An interview with an exercising 'patient' on a green prescription illustrates this idea: 'I have not felt any obligation or pressure, because that would have just gone all wrong' (Skogstrøm, 2004, p. 5). Here the exercise imperative functions in accordance with exactly this principle: the state and the citizens want the same thing. The effectiveness of such governing measures such as green prescriptions is precisely that the citizens feel as if they themselves own them. The exercising patient claims that he wants this and has felt no coercion. Critical objections to this governing rationality become in principle more difficult to present. The encroachments are well hidden, if it even has any meaning to call them that.

Criticism of empowerment has been raised which, particularly in the USA, is often depicted as comparable to an individual self-actualisation which seeks to bring out the individual's authentic self, while the social relations and structures are neglected (Askheim, 2007). What keeps people down is viewed as being emotional phenomena without any social basis or connection. Psychologist Dana Becker (2005) describes how therapy uncritically focuses on frustrated housewives in the USA, where individual self-actualisation has come to replace the struggle for women's rights to level out social inequalities. While the external framework conditions such as equal rights for men and women, rights in working life, day-care, equal pay and family politics remain untouched, an entire industry now caters to these women with a message of how they should organise and make better use of their time. The group of women whom Becker describes also constitute the core of *Oprah's* viewers and they are the most active consumers of both self-help and psychotherapy. Eighty-four per cent of the clients of private psychotherapists in the USA are women (Illouz, 2003). Becker (2005) therefore requests that therapists exercise caution in their eagerness to view women's ailments as personal rather than political, also in the way they employ empowerment strategies. When poor and disadvantaged women are encouraged to 'take responsibility for their health', then poverty as well as social and gender-related inequalities are given a medical, psychological explanation and are obscured by the discourse of empowerment. Becker therefore states that the tendency to understand women's problems as personal rather than political – through the stress discourse, for example – entails that we must be particularly suspicious about promises of empowerment. The stress discourse emphasises not only that men and women experience stress differently, but women personally are held responsible for the fact that they are more stressed than men, biologically and psychologically: 'Stress hurts: a wake-up call for women' was the title of an ABC News story (Becker, 2005, p. 176). In this case, Beck's charge that psychology and psychotherapy 'short-circuit the causal circuit' would appear to be woefully on the mark. In her recent book *One Nation under Stress* Becker (2013) now maintains that the stress discourse, especially in the USA, takes on ideological proportions ('stressism') as it increasingly emerges in explanations of the troubles experienced by vulnerable groups in society.

Transfer of power?

In more areas of life than before people are expected to behave like consumers, and citizens also want to be treated as such. The distinction between consumers who purchase goods and users of services is with increasing frequency being erased (Keat *et al.*, 1994). Consumer power, user power – influence and empowerment are terms that appear both among commercial consumers and among users of health services such as psychological health care. One way of understanding this is to view it as a democratisation of traditional power hierarchies, where politics do not disappear but seep out into the market as it is undergoing a process of politicisation (Jensen, 2010). Power is dethroned as something external and authoritative to become something individual and microscopic and is portioned out to each individual. Traditional voter power is thereby replaced by consumer power whereby the former ideology-based party politics is dissolved in the transition to questions that are more about life politics. The expert and not the politician becomes therefore the authority to be heeded.

Others are more doubtful about the advantages of this form of depoliticisation and empowerment and point out that an elimination of traditional authorities is taking place which undermines the value basis and experiences that arise outside of the market (Keat *et al.*, 1994). Neoliberalism gets rid of bothersome structures that can inhibit the free flow of the market, was Bourdieu's warning. Under this ideology, liberation has become the central value, or method, for increasing the individual's opportunities to become master of his/her own life and to rule over his/her surroundings. But this responsibility and the freedom citizens as consumers and users wield can turn out to be a charade. The authoritarian control and the role that the public authorities at times still assume is viewed with great scepticism and as politically incorrect – because the self-proclaimed ethos dictates that one personally knows what is best for oneself. This anti-authoritarian attitude, however, conceals a strengthened social control which is made even more efficient because it is not presented as a traditional external control, but in a subtle fashion has become an internally situated control, according to Vetlesen (2007).

Neoliberalism develops indirect techniques to lead and control individuals without being responsible for them, predominantly through the social technology that is called accountability. This entails that subjects are made accountable by inducing them to view social risks such as illness, unemployment, poverty, and so on, not as being primarily the responsibility of the state, but as being within the domain of the individual who personally wants to be accountable, in accordance with the cultural ideal of empowerment, and who thus becomes complicit in transforming the problem into a problem about governing the self. The danger of these political solutions is that the pressure and responsibility placed upon the individual increases in the choices regarding the therapeutic solutions. And our understanding of responsibility and power is shifted from external authorities to internal self-government. Perhaps it is here 'the missing class debate' should have its renaissance? Class division of the future must perhaps be derived from how well/poorly one manages the requirement to govern oneself and the incidence of psychological ailments? I will now look at a diagnosis that makes precisely the claim that the new class distinction must perhaps be drawn between those who manage to govern themselves and those who do not (Ekeland, 2006).

The ADHD epidemic

In my introductory presentation of the Stanford marshmallow experiment we saw how the ability to postpone impulses and gratification would appear to be one of the most important qualities for managing well in the Western culture of today. Four-year-olds who managed to resist temptation managed across the board better as teenagers, but what about those who did not master this as well?

One of neoliberalism's defining features is its requirement for citizens that they must govern themselves. The individual's capacity for self-government becomes critical in terms of achieving success in education, working life, career and good health. In the Norwegian school system there has been a clear tendency since the 1980s to speak about 'responsibility for one's own learning', while entrepreneurship today has become a new field of knowledge. The abilities that are installed as guarantors of our freedom along the same lines as political goals are an enterprising spirit and independence (Rose, 1992). An enterprising spirit implies energy, initiative, ambition, planning and personal responsibility. The enterprise self wants to make its life a project and as in an enterprise, seek to maximise its own human capital. Independence is to assume control over our obligations, define our goals, and plan to meet our needs through power. The autonomy of the self is one of the objectives and instruments of the modern emphasis on personal control (Rose, 1992).

One of the most widespread psychological illnesses of recent decades is ADHD. ADHD stands for 'Attention-Deficit/Hyperactive Disorder', and the diagnosis entails over-active, poorly adapted behaviour with clear concentration difficulties and the tendency to change activities or not finish things, and that these behavioural features endure over time. In Norway ADHD is one of the most frequently used diagnoses. The most common treatment of ADHD involves counselling, special adaptations in the classroom, support for the child's family and surrounding community, and medication. Figures from the Norwegian Prescription Database show a tripling in the number of ADHD medication users in the age group 0–19 years in the time period 2004 to 2011. While in 2004 there were 8,543 users, the number had doubled to 16,788 users in 2009 and then more than tripled to 30,525 users in 2011. In 2004 the sales volume of ADHD medication was at approximately NOK 75 million. In 2012 this figure had increased to NOK 170 million (Sakshaug *et al.*, 2013). The majority with the ADHD diagnosis are to be found in the age group 10–19 years old. Among these more than 70 per cent are boys (Dåstøl, 2010). The Norwegian Directorate of Health and Social Affairs estimates that between 3 and 5 per cent of all Norwegian children have ADHD. Norway has thus a relatively high rate both with respect to diagnosis and the treatment of ADHD with medication, where as a rule psychostimulants are prescribed, a medication which has a calming and regulating effect, such as Ritalin and Concerta. An explanation for why Norway has such a high level compared to other nations can be found in a specific type of treatment culture – for example, that we have better developed support services. I am also interested in discerning whether there are possible social explanations for this explosive growth rate. Are the many cases of ADHD found in Norway in recent decades merely the flip side of the neoliberal ideal of the self-governed human being?

If we look at the criteria for the ADHD disorder in the diagnosis manual DSM-5 (American Psychiatric Association, 2013), we find two sets of main categories: (1) *inattention*, difficulties with concentration and attention span, and (2) *hyperactivity and impulsivity*, where the specific criteria indicate the inclusion of behaviour such as problems with organising activities, with being a self-starter, with delayed gratification and with controlling one's desire for something to happen here and now. As we saw by way of introduction with the four-year-olds in Mischel's marshmallow experiment, it was the children with a large degree of self-control who managed best as adults, while the impulsive children did not fare as well and they make up, based on the criteria, in all likelihood the group in which one would have found the greatest frequency of the ADHD disorder. Self-control has in other words become an essential value in today's society: something which is seen in working life, education and schooling. Individuals with ADHD have a lot of energy but they have difficulties structuring and channelling this energy constructively towards a future project. The criteria for meeting the ADHD diagnosis appear to be the utter negation of neoliberalism's political require-ment that citizens govern themselves. The ADHD disorder can therefore be viewed as the cultural expression of the flip side of the neoliberal governing strategy which emphasises a large degree of internal control.

Over time, a lot of research has been carried out on the causes, prolifera-tion and treatment methods for ADHD. A great deal of the research today connects the reasons to neurological and genetic vulnerability, for example, connected to dopamine uptake or a serotonin hormone deficiency in these children's brains. It is thus held as being an established fact that ADHD is a neurological disorder – the Norwegian Institute of Public Health (2013) defines the disorder as such. Although today there is broad consensus that ADHD is biologically determined, great uncertainty remains regarding what it is exactly that causes the disorder. Norway's leading chain of chem-ists, Apotek 1 (2009), states on its website that genetics are a central factor and estimate that 60–80 per cent of the cases are genetic, while they also write that the cause of ADHD is unknown. Despite a lot of research in the field one question that is *not* asked is why the incidence of ADHD in Norway right now is so high.

The Norwegian psychologist Tor-Johan Ekeland (2006) holds that explaining ADHD as a type of genetically determined disorder represents a huge paradox. Genes operate always *in* environments – it is therefore also important to ask what is unique about today's requirements for children and the conditions for children's upbringing in Norway and other Western countries which leads to a genetic variation (genotype) developing into a phenomenon that is socially problematic (phenotype) in our time. Given that the biological variation has 'always' been there – in that the human genotype changes very slowly and only over the course of hundreds of thousands of years – why do the most impulsive 3–5 per cent of the chil-dren become a problem at precisely this point in time? Biological variation becomes in other words a problem to be solved at the moment it meets with the functional requirements of a given culture, Ekeland argues. Even if we accept that a considerable component of ADHD is genetically deter-mined, we must search elsewhere to understand the entire phenomenon and the problem of ADHD. In the case of both ADHD and a number of other ailments that are explained biologically, it is the case that in biology there are no problems, deviations, disorders and diagnoses. There is only variation (Ekeland, 2006). It is in our interpretation of a biological phenomenon that something becomes a problem. Ekeland (2006) illustrates this with the diagnostic inclusion criteria for ADHD such as 'concentration', 'hyperactivity' and 'impulsiveness'. One must always be concentrated *on something*, active *in relation to something*, or impulsive *in relation to something*. Behaviour can in other words not be understood in isolation but only in a specific environmental and cultural context. For this reason ADHD will always be a social phenomenon. Vetlesen (2009c) has also highlighted this difference: it is one thing to state that a child has, for example, a low serotonin level, as an explanation; it is another thing to ask the question why this has become an ailment that many children have today. To focus on the structural causes is something else entirely, he points out.

Ekeland (2007) identifies a number of features of our times that can explain why the ADHD disorder appears on such a scale. Parental authority has been dismantled – the corrective community of the adult world has been weakened. As Ekeland writes: adults intervene less frequently to correct their own children and even less in relation to the children of others. Another aspect of the school and daily life is the gradual transition from external disciplining to internal forms of discipline – the self-control requirement has increased, both in working life and in the school. On the whole the school has become more theoretical and less physically challenging, while the pedagogical structures have been loosened up and presuppose greater inner discipline (Ekeland, 2007). When the external walls disappear, many will have problems establishing 'inner walls', he argues. He also asks whether secondary socialisation arenas such as nursery school/kindergarten and the school have been feminised, in the sense that a constant focus on problematic masculine values has also undermined positive masculine values in the socialisation process. Of the children diagnosed with ADHD, three out of four are boys.

The self-control requirement today is an intentional policy that accommodates individual development but which imposes large requirements on the individual's ability to take responsibility for him/herself and, in many cases, those requirements are too large. The increase in the incidence of the ADHD disorder can be viewed as an example of this. But the increase is understood as everything but a political phenomenon, and more as a natural science phenomenon. In this manner psychological expertise can contribute to the evasion of society's unresolved conflicts by disguising them as science. ADHD is politicised and should therefore also provide a basis for a debate about values. Tens of thousands of Norwegian boys on medication, with problems adapting to the school system and perhaps with a permanently affected self-image is possibly the price being paid for carrying out pedagogical reforms in the school and education system which emphasise a large degree of internal motivation and responsibility for own learning.

The newspaper *Aftenposten* had in July 2010 a number of articles about all of the referrals that child and adolescent psychiatry receives stemming from a suspicion of ADHD. The number of children taking ADHD medication has increased by 80 per cent over the last six years, the article claims. Psychology professor Willy-Tore Mørch is critical: 'Then there is something wrong with the child. So the parents relax about their own parenting methods' (Sandvig, 2010, p. 5). Of course it is possible to call for greater accountability on the part of the parents, as Mørch does here, but at the same time, Mørch is a member of a profession that takes part in giving ADHD legitimacy and accommodating the possibility for schools and families to utilise this knowledge and the diagnosis. Perhaps one should therefore direct a critical eye towards one's own profession as well? For psychology, the ADHD 'epidemic' implies an increase in demand in the form of public requirements for more research, investigation and treatment. Large discrepancies in the incidence of ADHD in the different counties of Norway have been established which can be interpreted as an indication that the diagnosis is not made solely on the basis of scientific criteria, but is also culturally contingent (Hinshaw *et al.*, 2011).

It is difficult and has virtually become taboo to even question the ADHD diagnosis and the dominant causal explanations (Ekeland, 2006). 'Everyone' – users, parents, peer organisations and many teachers – are *for* the diagnosis. Very many families will, understandably, certainly experience a huge sense of relief, the recognition of their frustration by the public authorities and a longed-for explanation in the form of scientific knowledge when their son or daughter is finally diagnosed, often after a long period of suspicion. For this reason, a critical analysis of a disorder such as ADHD can easily provoke and upset. Part of the reason for this is perhaps that we have a tendency to think in either-or categories: either ADHD is a true ailment, or it's a fallacy.

Philosopher Ian Hacking (1995, 1998) has studied the history and nature of medical and psychiatric diagnoses – and his findings indicate that diagnoses sometimes become a channel and expression for people's suffering. In the case of ADHD this can mean that children who are struggling at school or entire families who are struggling in daily life, through a diagnosis such as ADHD gain an outlet and support in the form of an accepted medical explanation. In contrast to what one might perhaps believe, that does not mean that the sudden incidences of disorders – such as ADHD – are therefore a fallacy. It just means that it is a more complex phenomenon than a purely biological explanation would imply, with considerable inter-personal and social components. Psychiatric diagnoses can in many contexts be the culturally acceptable way of expressing suffering – so it intercepts discomfort, unhappiness or rage. These negative feelings will arise if many children today feel alienated and unable to adapt in the modern school due to pedagogical reforms derived from ideological and political governing ideals.

One hypothesis can then be that the neoliberal governing mechanism's strong emphasis on inner governing and self-control creates an environ-mental basis that causes the manifestation of a problem and a disorder that previously did not exist to the same extent. An expanding psychological disorder such as ADHD becomes an expression for those who do not fully master this ideal. Psychology acquires a function as the helpful servant that frames the problem in a medical and scientific context and which changes the phenomenon from being about political values and the negative conse-quences of specific government ideals. We could in contrast to this envision a kind of psychology that understood the powerful increase in a disorder such as ADHD in correlation with development traits in society, such as the school system and thereby employ its professional expertise to warn of the negative aspects of putting too great an emphasis on responsibility and inner management in young children. A possible 'opening up' of ADHD in this way as something more than a purely biological deviation can also be viewed as something positive for people who are affected by it, in that the disorder will also be connected to relevant cultural, social, pedagogical and political factors and in this way made more comprehensible and manage-able and less arbitrary and deterministic.

We have now seen how a specific ideology's governance ideal – huge requirements for inner control – *can* help to explain increased incidences of a given diagnosis. We have seen how psychology to a limited extent investigates the socio-historical foundation of the disorder, as it understands it in individualised, biomedical terms, from which it then in turn profits. The phenomenon ADHD could be used as an argument against the neo-liberal government formula, but it is not. An explanation can be that the neoliberal government policy's increased used of an expertise as a connect-ing link between the state and the population entails psychology losing its autonomy. Psychology's role in society dictates that it is not the task of psy-chology and psychotherapy to ask questions that challenge the economic and political frameworks.

The postmodern subject

Kvale (1992) is interested in this paradox and has remarked that with postmodernism as the ideology of the consumer society, it remains to be seen whether the attempts to establish new postmodern versions of psychology will reflect consumerism or whether it is the case that psychology has learned from history and can nonetheless contain the potential for a critical opposition to the dominant ideologies. Is there a critical psychology and psychotherapy that could carry out an alarm function as outlined in the example of ADHD above? Jørgensen (2002) outlines a schematic division between modern therapy forms, such as traditional psychodynamic treatment, where the cultural and political factors are viewed as irrelevant for psychotherapy, and postmodern therapy forms, such as narrative and interpersonal psychotherapy, where the prevailing cultural and political discourses are taken seriously. Narrative therapy (cf. White and Epston, 1990), which is perhaps the most popular postmodern therapy form, claims that it takes into account psychology's uncritical tendency to reflect contemporary society ideologically. Explained in brief, narrative therapy is about creating change by understanding a human being's life as a story, where our ability to create a somewhat systematic, coherent and not least meaningful biography of our lives is of great significance to our mental health. People suffering from psychological ailments are often locked in dysfunctional stories about themselves (depression, compulsive disorders, neuroses), or they have fragile and unstable narratives that threaten to break down (anxiety, dissociative disorder, psychosis). Narrative therapy became particularly popular in psychology in the 1980s and 1990s and its strength lies without doubt in its distinctly pragmatic and solution-oriented perspective on creating change which many find useful in clinical work. But does narrative therapy fulfil the requirement Jørgensen imposes on postmodern therapy, which in addition to carrying out treatment is also attentive to the society-related ethical challenges outside of the therapy room?

The trials done on critical psychology have, as in the case of narrative therapy, a tendency to criticise mainstream psychology and psychotherapy for not taking into account contemporary philosophical trends. The remedy lies often in importing philosophical impulses in order to guarantee that to a large extent one is epistemological and ethical at a level corresponding with the political questions and challenges of the day. Humanistic psychology sought in its time to import philosophical impulses from German and French existentialist philosophy from the mid-twentieth century, and this was intended to counteract the dominant schools such as psychoanalysis and behaviourism at that time. The humanistic tradition in psychology was as stated subjected to harsh criticism from Cushman, who accused it of fitting hand in glove with the requirements for citizens' economic behaviour at the time.

Does not narrative therapy in the same manner attempt to incorporate postmodernism in psychology by drawing from the linguistic turn and anti-realist impulses of the contemporary philosophy of a few decades back? A narrative idea about the self appears also to be a natural extension of humanistic psychology's empty self. Everything is possible, but the physical reality shall now no longer stand in the way; everything has become a network of identity constructions and stories which one is free to turn on or off. The self-actualisation project has not disappeared from narrative thinking but rather been updated for a new age. The stable boundaries for the subject which characterised humanism/existentialism were perhaps too strongly connected to a single specific life project for the consumer society. The narrative philosophy can be described as 'postmodernism with a happy face'. Krogseth (2001) emphasises how the narrative identity perspective is particularly adapted to postmodern thought and concepts of time. All possibilities are apparently within the individual's reach, everything can be dissolved, everything floats around; it is just a matter of following the flow of the circulation of goods. Advertising and marketing of course brazenly exploit this postmodern rhetoric – the opening of the 'experience centre' Xhibition in the city of Bergen, a shopping mall for a new millennium, was launched with the message 'Are you ready for a whole new self?'. The narrative thought found in psychotherapy appears to be simply a mentality that is appropriate for its time. If therapy has been successful, the repaired souls are sent out into the culture again with instructions and better conditions for success in sewing together their own biography and the story of themselves in a new way. It is difficult to see how this form of postmodern psychotherapy challenges the established system's encouragement of each individual to create his or her own life. Or how it can be used to disclose and criticise new ailments that can arise in response to neoliberalism's image of man and government ideal.

Perhaps it is such that psychology, like marketing, must follow the cultural impulses of the times to remain current? One need not envision scenarios where sycophantic capitalists and salesmen knock on the door of psychology and request that she develop her forms of therapy so as to create new needs. Historian of ideas Dorthé Jørgensen has claimed that psychology can never be a critical science because its programme is pragmatic by definition and it inherently absorbs the dominant trends of the culture (Jørgensen, 2002). This is in turn dictated by psychology's obligations in relation to the client: if one is going to work with a number of different people, one must of necessity assume a pragmatic and relatively open attitude in order to understand and help as many clients as possible. One's personal values and opinions should not be too extreme in that this can get in the way of achieving trust and forming a good relation to the client, which has been proved necessary for all successful forms of psychotherapeutic treatment. Pragmatism will therefore always come before any critique. The model which is expedient in working with clients' problems is, however, of necessity a poor model for solving psychology's socio-ethical challenges (more about this in Chapter 8).

Birds of a feather flock together

The sociologist Eliot Freidson (1988) found in his study of the medical profession that the profession's autonomous development implied that physicians developed limited and self-satisfied perspectives of their social role, establishing a strong belief that they knew best what society needed. When we then find ourselves in a political situation in which the society requires ever more psychological services – which is a natural consequence of the neoliberal project's need for government expertise within both the implementation and management of self-government, there is little cause to believe that any type of reservations will occur on the basis of self-critique. If there is a great demand for individual solutions under neoliberalism, psychology will benefit from this. This relation between government and expertise will also only have a self-perpetuating effect. Individualisation can as such be understood as an effective governing technique for a neo-liberal government ideal (Rose, 1996). Through individualisation, the individual subject becomes a manageable entity which, ideally, will govern itself. A transformation of politics occurs. Individuality formerly remained situated below the level of description, as Foucault (1991) explains government in *Discipline and Punishment*, but this is now reversed: the modern psychological human being is installed as a subject and object for expert knowledge, so that it can in the simplest possible fashion be transferred and transported between different institutions.

Studies of psychology's resistance and critical potential in relation to the cultural logic of its time are rare. One of the problems is naturally that the interaction between a science and profession and a large social system or political ideologies is extremely complex, and difficult to submit to any type of purely scientific study. Little literature exists that investigates neo-liberalism in Norway and even less that is specifically about the psychology profession. Psychologist Karen-Merete Bruland (2008) investigated in her master's thesis the content of the *Journal of the Norwegian Psychological Association* in the period from 1974 to 2007 and used discourse analysis to disclose possible ideological constraints in the field of psychology. She concluded that psychology throughout the course of the past three decades had allowed itself to be shaped by neoliberalism, something which found expression in the journal's format and scientific content. It would nonethe-less not be all that surprising if the psychology profession had been coloured by the times – the question here is essentially the opposite: has psychology also played a part in influencing the development of society and paved the way for neoliberalism?

The theoretical force of the term 'governmentality' is found in the fact that it constructs neoliberalism not solely as an ideological rhetoric or a political-economic reality, but as a political project that does everything it can to create a social reality which it claims already existed before its own existence (Lemke, 2001). Neoliberalism is a political rationality that seeks to present the social domain as economic and connect a reduction in state welfare services and safety nets to the benefits of the ever louder call for personal responsibility and self-help (Lemke, 2001). Just listen to how Margaret Thatcher and her ideologist Michael Heseltine express themselves about the political objective for how the citizens of the state should behave in relation to themselves: 'Wherever possible we want individuals to control, influence and determine their own destiny . . . the psychology of independence is to the fore', and 'People should exercise their abilities (serving as authors of their own decisions, seizing opportunities, and so on) in order to help themselves' (as cited in Heelas, 1991, p. 77). Critics of neoliberalism point out how this creates a mass individualism that does not add up. The need for self-actualisation and recognition is simply greater than the resources that can be offered to the population. Very many people's needs for self-actualisation therefore end up in an illusory spiral of gratification – where the neoliberal individual will of necessity feel violated in that his or her expectations and compulsion for recognition are not satisfied, despite the massive portfolio of options they are equipped with (Willig, 2005). The result can perhaps be seen in the prevalence of depression in the Western population. For example, according to the World Health Organization, 'unipolar depressive disorders were ranked as the third leading cause of the global burden of disease in 2004 and will move into the first place by 2030' (as cited in World Federation for Mental Health, 2012, p. 2).

Cruikshank (1996) warns against understanding the self-esteem movement as purely an ideology; it is not a trick, a universal medium or a cynical plot – it is simply a form of governance. We are on our way towards neither an omnipotent therapeutic state, she claims, nor a condition of complete subjectivation of all citizens. The critics of the self-esteem movement have trains of thought that are too reactionary, employing dichotomised oppositions such as individual and collective, public and private, political and personal, Cruikshank argues. Nonetheless, she admits that social protest and open resistance have become less common fare today, something which is cause for concern. In spite of the fact that we still have large inequalities on the basis of race, gender and class, society is relatively speaking politically stable, thanks to the regulating role of the social sciences.

Rose (1987) advocates in her writings that we discard the old concept of critique. In our dealings with analyses of power we must liberate ourselves from the belief in a pure oppression of the self. Inspired by Foucault we must understand power and freedom as mutual conditions for each other. The subject is first made possible through a specific politics of truth. As a replacement for such critical perspectives, which are frequently global and general in nature, he instead wants to explore specific problems and the conditions that make them possible and the advantages and disadvantages they produce. Such micropolitical studies, however, require that the professions understand themselves and their own times. The interpretive approach of Cruikshank and Rose does not necessarily rule out normative questions – even if they suspend traditional critical approaches in brackets. The clear answers in which liberation and oppression are clearly distinguished become perhaps less obvious. The political rationality that appears transcends the concept of ideology (Barry *et al.*, 1996). They constitute parts of our manner of thinking and acting. Liberalism becomes more a form of ethos rather than a traditional form of politics. Oppression and freedom are intertwined. The psychologists are, in the midst of this paradox, agents for the state. An important ethical reflection involves asking oneself: if the neoliberal form of government is only one of infinitely many political constitutions of the subject – what could we have acquired through other forms of social organisation that we currently do not have? As a philosophical speculation, Rose (1999) maintains that the subject would potentially have been different without psychology's cultivation of it.

Neoliberalism encourages individuals to shape their lives in a specific entrepreneurial form. The participation however has a price tag – the individual must personally assume responsibility for the activities and for any unsuccessful outcomes (Lemke, 2001). Accordingly, it is a matter of a structural shift here, where the individual potentially has perhaps more to gain, but also more to lose. But this individualisation and radicalisation of destiny is camouflaged – and those who draw the shortest straw are not given any possibility to turn down this destiny, even though one can always speak about the individual's freedom to choose to take responsibility for his or her own life. The commandment 'You shall govern yourself!' exists as a commandment for all citizens and it is not possible to free oneself from it today. The possibilities for individuals to achieve an awareness of the significance of factors larger than themselves that play a part in their life destinies, which in turn are a condition enabling them to work to change structures outside of themselves, appear to have been depleted under the individualisation of psychology and neoliberalism.

Conclusion

Psychology has gained increased legitimacy in that to a far greater extent the individual is being made accountable for him/herself and as such the need for expertise at both ends of subjectivation (the constitution and support of the modern subject) would appear necessary in many cases. Whether or not one applies a critical perspective to psychology's expertise in the neoliberal form of rule depends upon whether one works on the basis of a critical attitude to the entire development of society. It is fully possible to object to the revisionists in the governmentality tradition, such as Rose and Cruikshank, claiming that they have no clearly normative concept of quality or measure of the potential human consequences of social development. Many psychological disorders apparently continue to proliferate. Can this be due to something more than the redefinition as psychological stress and strain of what formerly were social crises? Are we closing our eyes to an unhealthy development in society assisted by psychology where the political solutions produce too great a burden and strain on the individual? What happens to the possibilities for another kind of politics when in spite of continued inequality on the basis race, gender and class in society there remains a silent acceptance of this, as Cruikshank quite rightly notes? Have the possibilities for revolt also been lost in the transition from external to internal revolution? Is the empowerment of the self the only possible liberation struggle that remains? The debate about the paradoxes of neoliberalism and late modernity will continue into the future as well, but the psychologists are largely absent there. As we will see in the next chapter, on the psychology profession, there is much to indicate that the profession remains baffled by these questions because they are not a part of its vocabulary nor, consequently, of its ethical horizon.

8　The ethos of the psychology profession

Contemporary society depends to a large degree on the professions and their members for the safeguarding and administrating of the interests of individuals and the community. This development has been called *The Third Revolution* (Perkin, 1996). In the same way that pre-industrial society was run by landowners and industrial society by capitalists, post-industrial society is run by professional experts. The professions have become extremely important providers of the prerequisites for the design, implementation and regulation of public policy. Professionals, as such, are to be viewed as the agents of the welfare state and therefore exercise considerable influence on the development of society (Eriksen, 2001). The professionalisation of society is thus dependent upon serious stakeholders who carry out their profession in accordance with established professional requirements and ethical standards. There is a lot at stake. The professions' management of their mandate and professional ethics is of critical significance – both for society and for the individual user's trust. When it comes to questions about ethics and psychology, we can distinguish between ethical questions pertaining to responsibility for the individual, as a rule the client or testees, and questions pertaining to the society, so-called social ethics. I will now show how the former set of obligations is safeguarded well in the teaching and practise of the professions while the latter set is by and large neglected.

If we ask the psychology profession itself, in particular the Norwegian Psychological Association (NPF), the association will certainly claim that it attends to its social responsibility through its measures and political objectives of improving the treatment scheme for the population and its work in general on increasing the influence of psychology in society. This work of getting psychology and psychologists out into society is also clearly evident if one looks at NPF's (2007, n.p.) explicit objectives from recent years – 2004 to 2010 – which are:

- Better representation of psychological perspectives in debates in society and social planning;
- Increased access to psychology in public services;
- More psychologists in management positions;
- Psychology outreach programmes for the population.

An overriding objective for all of these strategies appears to be to increase psychology's dissemination in society, both in a purely concrete and an overall sense. Psychology needs to be strengthened at the local level in order to better help people and it should to a greater degree seek to acquire the influence to build a more humane society, either in the concrete sense through management roles or more generally by wielding greater influence in debates in society and social planning. Viewed as a whole, these objectives from the last two national assembly periods attest to a proactive and self-confident profession. The more psychology, the better for society, would appear to be the underlying conviction. A quicker, earlier and closer mentality is reflected in the areas of investment cited.

The intention of all objectives in this period has accordingly been to secure a greater catchment area and influence for psychology than it has at the current time. Of particular interest is perhaps the objective that 'psychological perspectives must be better represented in debates in society and social planning'. If one understands this objective of the NPF as an expression of a general consensus among psychologists, it means that the profession maintains that psychology up to now has not had sufficient impact on society and that it would be advantageous if its influence was increased. The overall mentality that is reflected in these objectives can appear peculiar in the context of the current social analyses of psychology presented in this book thus far, which are also reflected in contemporary diagnoses such as 'the age of psychology' (Havemann, 1957) or 'the psychological society' (Gross, 1978). Theories about psychology's increased influence on society have from time to time been relatively critical, but if one were to interpret the prevailing expansive professional policy, the profession itself is either indifferent to or ignorant of this critique. Here we are, regardless, faced with a challenge: the psychology profession itself appears to recognise only the story about all of the good that psychology has contributed and consequently the solution and professional policy becomes 'more psychology/more psychologists'. On top of this, the solution is presented as wholly without problems and it is established without any further debate about any potentially negative side effects.

This selective self-awareness is due in my opinion to the absence of critical perspectives on basic ideology. Philosopher Harald Grimen (2008) recently made the argument that professional ethics on the part of the professions must to a larger degree reflect that they have been given political legitimacy for a social assignment, which provides the basis for the professional ethics. The psychology profession appears, however, to focus on this to a very limited extent. A study done about the psychology studies programme at the University of Oslo provides an indication that questions about professional ethics are limited to matters regulated by law regarding the relation between the therapist and the patient (Solbrekke and Karseth, 2006). Ethical questions related to clinical settings are what is emphasised. This is naturally extremely important but seems to overshadow the focus on social responsibility in the curriculum. Psychologist Hilde Nafstad (2008) has further argued that the ethics curriculum for Norwegian psychologists-to-be is to far too great an extent about prescriptive rules for how one should *not* behave as a psychologist, something which is important but far from being sufficient. This is wholly in accordance with my own experiences as a student at the programme of psychology studies at the University of Bergen. The lectures in ethics largely addressed how, as a psychologist, one should conduct oneself in order to avoid having patients file complaints. It was striking how ethics was about good morals, and very little about the ethics constituting the norm and value foundation of that morality. Nafstad (2008) therefore makes an appeal for greater moral and ethical sensitivity, and this can only be developed if one addresses the discipline's underlying values and implications, which can in turn provide greater awareness about how psychology in different ways is related to and influences both the client and society.

Ethical thought in psychology has been, like society otherwise, individualised. A displacement appears to have occurred in the ethical reflection within the psychology profession because the automatic assumption is that good patient care means good social development as well. This is also in harmony with the social model which we have seen was advocated from Freud to the self-help culture, to neoliberalism. Healthy, well-adapted individuals are considered a guarantee for the good society. This position, which has become extremely prevalent, can be understood as a school of thought about the society and the community in the form of systematic individualism. It is thereby also difficult to make an appeal for criteria regarding the nature of psychology's social responsibility, because the appropriate system and categories for thinking about the question of 'good social development' do not exist and 'social responsibility' has come to be synonymous with 'good treatment'. This is not necessarily an expedient development at a time when ever new areas in society are being viewed through clinical spectacles, so that therapeutic forms of understanding mask problems which are in principle of a social, political or structural nature.

Psychology in modern Western democracies has, as we have seen throughout the twentieth century, had its social mandate constantly expanded. This coincides with the neoliberal governance rationality that seeks to govern as efficiently as possible by governing as little as possible. The citizens' self-governance is the aim. And as shown, psychology in particular is an extremely effective theoretical and practical science which opens up a space making this possible. Higher educational researchers Tone Dyrdal Solbrekke and Berit Karseth (2006) have, as an extension of this idea, claimed that disciplines such as psychology should to a greater extent make room for a critical evaluation of the profession's value basis and practice. The politically legitimated social mandate of which the profession is the conveyor must be articulated and made the subject of more morally deliberate evaluations in own professional practice.

The psychology profession on the other hand is quick to maintain that it conducts itself on the basis of a political legitimacy and intention to give those who are psychologically ill the help they need. Simultaneously, the ethical debate within the profession about the background for its expanded social mandate lacks the desire to offer help other than in the form of purely clinical assistance. At a meeting under the auspices of NPF Hordaland in Bergen on 11 September 2009, which president Tor Levin Hofgaard and vice president Aina Holmen attended, this social mandate was referred to as 'the crystal clear social mandate' and 'society's increased need for psychological expertise'. A recurring theme was that society has now begun in a serious fashion to open its eyes to what psychology has to offer. Social responsibility was understood as meaning exclusively giving the governing powers what they wanted, namely more psychologists, as opposed to discussing what can be the basis for this increasingly greater demand and whether in fact it is auspicious. In terms of *realpolitik*, psychology is in other words acutely conscious of its social role and is aware of the important part it has come to play in modern Western cultures. Pre-politically or ideologically speaking, psychology is on the other hand relatively unreflective about its social role and is not aware of how the role it is being asked to fill can have ambiguous and in the worst case even destructive dimensions.

The great discussion about the future of psychology?

The big questions in psychology are to a large extent being replaced by 'small questions' about professional policy. In 2010 NPF initiated what was presented as being 'the great discussion about the future of psychology'. The questions raised here are about the challenges of meeting the need for psychological expertise. One of the most important questions is then whether the programme for professional psychology studies in Norway should be strengthened in order to educate more psychology graduates (cand. psychol.) annually, or whether everyone who had a master's degree in psychology should be allowed to pursue a clinical post-graduate programme and receive authorisation to also practice as psychologists. The discussion about psychology's future is based on a larger narrative in which psychology is a success story that has won and driven out psychiatry from specialist health services. At the same time, this takes place in an historical context where there is a great political willingness and demand for psychologists to provide outreach services and primary care in the outlying districts of Norway; health sector executives, politicians and society at large are demanding with greater and greater frequency the expertise of psychologists. This is of course flattering for the members of the profession but even more it militates against rigorous and critical thinking. To ask the question of whether psychologists also should discuss the politics behind this social mandate, for example: 'Why does society need increasingly more psychologists? And is this purely a good thing?' comes across as downright inappropriate. And that is understandable: if one is wanted, and happy to be wanted, it seems reactionary to question it. On the basis of the profession's dominant ethos, it seems therefore very unlikely that they will ask 'the big questions' when the biggest question appears to be how to reproduce more quickly and grow even larger.

Nobody is happy all the time

On 26 September 2009 the newspaper *Altaposten* printed a typical article about how more and more local residents are seeking out psychological services: 'Nobody is happy all the time.' The adult psychiatric outpatient clinic (VPP) in Alta had three staff members in 1996, while today there are 16 on staff there. The professionals interviewed, Eirin Nilsen and Kristin Dahn, emphasise in particular the positive sides of going to a psychologist and normalise the considerable growth that has taken place in the past 15 years. Although many more people in the municipality seek out psychological treatment today than previously, it is not certain that more people are sick than previously, Nilsen and Dahn argue. One explanation they offer is that there is now more openness: 'Regardless, we think it's positive that more people seek out the health care services with their concerns about psychological ailments. That means that we are taking better care of ourselves' (Altaposten, 2009, p. n.a.).

The explanation of these professionals seems in principle both sober-minded and sensible, and is wholly usual for the psychology profession. The explanation fits in well with a larger picture in which the underlying perception of the psychology profession's ethos is connected to explanations stating: 'We are better off now than before.' Psychology and the increase in the incidence of psychological ailments are thereby written into a narrative in which development is moving in the right direction: we live in a society that is more open than before, and we have better methods for diagnosis and treatment and we have the resources to implement them. The overall social development, the technological and scientific development and greater openness all pull together towards a common goal. However, the profession's tendency to assure those in its surroundings that 'everything is getting better' results in the failure to have fundamental discussions about the high incidence of psychological ailments. The degree to which increased prevalence has a connection with a social development that promotes illness is only to a limited extent the subject of a broader discussion. The article mentions briefly increased immigration to Alta and a lack of networks among new residents, greater uncertainty in relation to school and work, increased use of drugs and alcohol, and unrealistic expectations for happiness as possible causes, but these intimations of large-scale social analyses disappear under the pressure of the positive development of people coming to the outpatient clinic to do something about the problem.

The positive assessment made by professionals at Alta VPP of the increased influx of clients is far from being unique, as we will see, but rather appears to be a part of what I have elected to call 'the ethos of profession-based thinking'. Here the use of psychologists is presented and defended as a desirable and good development, while this help in itself is seldom addressed and made the subject of a critical analysis. The result becomes a profession that risks carrying out a form of academic and professional imperialism where the answer is always more psychology and more psychologists and where the politicians and social planners who are responsible and dare to ask the question of whether everything is really getting better and if we are really becoming more healthy, are thwarted. In this manner the profession also fails in compliance with its own established ethical guidelines which stipulate that it must take its social responsibility seriously by openly discussing the society it is a part of.

Psychological ailments are extremely widespread. The Norwegian Institute of Public Health in 2010 released a report that established that one-third of the Norwegian population will suffer with a psychological ailment in the course of one year. Every second Norwegian will in the course of their lifetime be afflicted by one or more psychological ailment (Norwegian Institute of Public Health, 2010). The most common ailments are anxiety and depression. There are several models that can explain the high incidence of psychological ailments in the population. One hypothesis is that we are actually becoming more and more ill. Another hypothesis is that the boundaries for what is considered pathological and abnormal are being expanded all the time to include more cases. A third hypothesis is that nowadays we have new treatment methods and techniques, a better developed welfare system and support services, not to mention greater openness – as was mentioned in the example – so that far more people can receive help than previously. The perspective we employ is of great significance. The first hypothesis – we are getting sicker and sicker – is based on an actual increase in the incidence of psychological ailments in the population while the next two hypotheses are based on the idea of a relative stability in the incidence viewed across time periods. Here it is only the statistics that increase. The first two hypotheses speak of an unwanted development that can be due to aspects of the social development which produce illness, or of an anti-liberal attitude or treatment zeal on the part of professionals which produces illness. The last hypothesis on the other hand speaks of a welcome development; there are quite simply more people who receive help than before. On the basis of sheer common sense we can perhaps imagine that all of the hypotheses have a bit of truth to them. We have perhaps become more psychologically ill than before, but elements of the increase are perhaps due to redefined boundaries for what is considered abnormal, and we also have greater openness and more treatment methods, which means that more people receive help today. My intention in this context is, however, not to try and find a definitive answer to why we are seeing an apparent increase in the incidence of some psychological ailments in the population. It is moreover a question that is far too complex to permit my making any statement about at this juncture. What is of interest on the other hand is to look at the models and arguments used by key stakeholders in the psychology profession in defending the profession's positive contribution to the development of society.

Therapy for children – a problem?

A commentary made by Hofgaard, the president of NPF, in 2007 touches upon this issue. The background for his remarks was a statement made by the then Minister of Health Sylvia Brustad, who reacted with concern to new figures from one hospital, Sykehuset Buskerud, indicating that 300 toddlers were attending therapy, which represented a tripling in the course of one year. In a response, Hofgaard (2007, n.p.) wrote a blog commentary entitled 'Therapy for toddlers – good news or bad?' which I will here quote in its entirety:

> 300 toddlers in therapy. A tripling in one year, the newspaper *Drammens Tidende* reports. Local politicians and health personnel are shaken. But perhaps they should instead express joy. It can be that the figures speak of an appropriate and welcome development.
>
> Minister Sylvia Brustad paid Sykehuset Buskerud a visit last year and even then called the figures extreme and disturbing. The question however is a matter of the perspective one uses.

Philosophically speaking it is naturally deplorable that problems even exist for the youngest among us. But it is of course not negative that the children are receiving help, or that more children receive help today than was the case one year ago. There were feasibly a large number of children and families who, even 10 or 20 years ago, should have received an offer of treatment or the support of a psychologist.

At the time, the need or struggle had not been detected. The children were therefore not seen by the support services until perhaps they reached adolescence, if they were at all intercepted and offered assistance. Perhaps they were not seen again until substance abuse and behavioural problems had become so extensive that the children's quality of life had been permanently impaired.

Early intervention to help families with infants and young children means stepping in before a disturbance takes hold, says the team leader of the infant team at Buskerud Hospital, Sidsel Haug. And here we are at the heart of the matter: we know a great deal today about how early intervention provides significantly better prognoses. That is why the Norwegian Psychological Association, together with user organisations, has for a long time highlighted the need to expand the psychological assistance services to reach people where they live, with an open door policy and few impediments for those who wish to seek help.

The example from the Drammen region should serve as a good image of a public healthcare service that is doing its job and of regional health politicians who are prioritising correctly.

Hofgaard constructs here a counter example where he starts by speculating about how formerly there were very many who also should have received help, but did not. The result of this was that the problems flourished freely until such time when they were so extensive that it was too late. It is therefore not only good treatment practice to intervene as early as possible before the problems take root, it is also the only right thing to do. The alternative is paralysis, or philosophical sentimentality about the fact that the ailment and problems even exist. Freidson (1988) called this 'the clinical mind' – the practitioner has another view of the world than the theorist. The goal is action rather than knowledge. There is a tendency on the part of practitioners to initiate treatment on the basis of an unsound premonition that doing *something* is better than doing *nothing*. There are further signs that the practitioners have taken control of the psychology profession in recent years and imposed a stronger clinical character on the profession's ethos. According to Parker (2007) a power shift has taken place in the APA where the practitioners are taking over more and more as the driving force of the profession to the detriment of scientific activity, by among other things seeking support for the right to write prescriptions for medication for psychological ailments and in general by selling psychology in a way that makes more people take it seriously. The editor of *The Journal of the Norwegian Psychological Association*, Bjørnar Olsen (2010), recently wrote a critical commentary of how professional psychology studies are to an increasing extent targeting individual clinical treatment to satisfy the public health care service's need for more clinicians, while work and organisational psychology, health and social psychology, cultural psychology and psychosocial science are phased out and converted into master's degree programmes for those with a special interest. Olsen (2010) asks whether the 'intoxicating success' that psychology has had within the health care sectors in recent years, with a high demand for its services, is in the process of reducing the psychology profession to a health profession focused on the individual, while more systematic perspectives are left out.

If we return to the analyses of Hofgaard's commentary another striking feature is that it is first and foremost clinical thought which dictates the ethical-moral reasoning and not the other way around. He starts with the premise 'We know a great deal today about how early intervention provides significantly better prognoses' and concludes with 'a public healthcare service that is doing its job and regional health politicians who are prioritising correctly'. Here it is the research on clinical interventions that makes references to better prognoses with earlier intervention, which becomes then the authoritative principle. This is, admittedly, correct and is relevant information. But it is possible to imagine that somebody will say: 'We know today that if we focus on problems in young children too early on, we risk including in treatment a number of problems that are simply a normal variation,' which also would be correct and relevant. Arguments such as 'Research shows . . . ' are in other words seldom unambiguous; in many cases it is possible to find relevant research supporting the opposite view. One is therefore always dependent on a discussion at the level of principles – the policy as such is about prioritising different values and groups where one should take into account relevant research but where this alone cannot dictate the prerequisites for the policy.

In the next round, Hofgaard brushes off these concerns with the reassurance that the development is welcome because people today receive help with problems for which there was no help available previously. Here one suspects that it is first and foremost Hofgaard the political spokesperson for the psychology profession who is speaking. Everything is moving in the right direction, if only politicians would listen to the professional expertise of NPF which together with user organisations has long emphasised the unmet need for local psychological health care services. Hofgaard manages to create a virtually hermetically sealed, coherent argument that legitimises the increase in psychological treatment of young children and which in turn expresses a positive development which can be even more positive if only psychological health care services received more funding and more psychologist positions were created. In the manner of any skilled lawyer, Hofgaard is here perhaps just doing his job, which is to protect and promote the interests of his profession in the best possible manner. It is the clinical gaze or psychology's special view of the world – the therapeutic spectacles – which is dictating the rhetoric at all times. Hofgaard also chooses hypothesis three (in accordance with my breakdown) – the increase in therapy for toddlers is purely statistical and therefore good news, because we are now treating far more children than previously. But he does so apparently through a purely ad hoc assumption – he writes among other things: 'There were feasibly a large number of children and families who, also 10 or 20 years ago, should have received an offer of treatment or the support of a psychologist.' Nonetheless, he is peremptory when he concludes, in the same paragraph: 'But it is of course not negative that the children receive help, or that more children receive help than was the case one year ago.' The explanation for this logical leap from belief to certain knowledge is presumably that Hofgaard and probably most psychologists are certain that they are acting in the service of the good in their right to treat and intervene in the event of any suspicion. And the sooner, the better – in this way the odds are better for bringing about change.

This is the clinical self-perception. Simultaneously, society-based explanations for why there is an increase in the statistics do not allow for such certainty, but the profession's self-perception or bias, depending on the context, implies choosing the explanation most in harmony with psychology's given and unshakeable position in the ethical equation. In this way society-based explanatory models and also political concern about the development receive a subordinate status. Politics enter the equation only at the very end and are reduced to 'making the right priorities' (economic), questioning the professional expertise as little as possible and letting them do their job.

The minister Brustad's concern was presumably rooted in what I have called hypothesis one or two, or a combination of these. Is of today organised in such a way that increasingly more young children are diagnosed with psychological ailments, she may have wondered. Here we can envisage many possible forms of causation, such as that young children become victims of the hectic speed of modern life, which does not give children and adults many hours together per day. This then finds expression as an increase in psychological ailments such as anxiety, depression, phobias and compulsive traits in young children. The second hypothesis can be understood in the sense that the boundaries for normality among young children have become narrower – an unhealthy diagnostic and treatment zeal has been established whereby we are treating far more people than previously. This represents a constriction of normality, or simply that the requirements imposed on parents and the young are becoming increasingly extensive and are imposed earlier than previously, and so forth. It can of course be that Hofgaard is right and Brustad is wrong. The point I am seeking to demonstrate is that the psychology profession's ethos dictates that one find explanatory models that give legitimacy to its increased presence through a combination of the developed clinical gaze, professional policy and professional imperialism, plus the lack of arenas, ability and will to think critically about the diffuse area of the psychology profession and politics.

The example from the hospital also illustrates the poor state of the critical thinking used. As we have already seen, the psychology profession cherishes a fundamental optimism about the future, provided that psychology succeeds in taking the central role in solving the problems of society. However, any group from outside the profession that challenges its ambition, and in so doing threatens its optimism, is dismissed out of hand. Philosophy is rejected by Hofgaard in this case as being a sentimental, passive contemplation of evil in the world which a responsible psychologist cannot permit him/herself. It is a matter of action: as early as possible, as quickly as possible and as locally as possible. And politicians receive a stamp of approval and are reminded of their rightful place and their sole duty: to prioritise how much money is to be spent on psychological healthcare, by listening to professional expertise. This same tendency to give politicians a slap on the wrist is to be found on the part of other important stakeholders in the profession.

On 27 December 2009 five years had passed since the tsunami catastrophe in Southeast Asia which took some 284,000 human lives, among them 84 Norwegians. In this context psychiatric nurse and member of the Norwegian Parliament Kari Henriksen received media attention over a blog post where she asked whether people can become sicker from talking about grief. Henriksen writes the following: 'Is it the case that talking about grief and feelings always helps? I don't know, we are certainly quite different, but I think that we have never talked more about how we are feeling, but never have we been more afflicted with loneliness and psychological ailments' (Moi, 2009, p. 7). Henriksen highlights here a phenomenon which elsewhere has been called 'health's paradox' (Barsky, 1988). The more that attention is dedicated to health, the more ill the population seems to become. This incitement to a potentially interesting debate about this paradox was however quickly smothered by a representative for the psychology profession. Atle Dyregrov from the Center for Crisis Psychology rejected

Henriksen's view point blank. Those with afflictions benefit from health care, he maintains. In addition to this he states: 'This illustrates how little knowledge members of parliament have about grief' (Moi, 2009, p. 7). As with the example involving Hofgaard, Dyregrov as a representative for the psychology profession first expresses his disagreement on academic grounds and then takes advantage of the opportunity to attack the politician who dared to question the development with an accusation of being irresponsible and having an inadequate understanding of psychological problems. It is not difficult to imagine that, when trusted professional experts behave in such a protectionist manner, it leads to politicians and others being reluctant to take part in a difficult debate. To question psychological treatment in a manner that in any sense can be perceived as threatening to psychology's legitimacy becomes taboo.

It is naturally possible to object that this rhetoric is not shared by all Norwegian psychologists, but in the case of Hofgaard he is a democratically elected president. The political strategy he adheres to is supposed to reflect NPF and the interests of its 7,000 members. Hofgaard and Dyregrov are not alone in their attitude either; the same mentality can be found with perhaps even greater clarity in one of the great founders of Norwegian psychology, Bjørn Christiansen (1927–1987). Christiansen was the architect behind professional psychology studies and managed virtually single-handedly to establish what today is still the only separate Faculty of Psychology in Norway (University of Bergen, 1996). In the mid-1980s Christiansen (1984, p. 16) also took part in a debate about the increase in the incidence of psychological ailments in the population:

> Despite statements from individual prophets of doom there is little evidence indicating that the situation has undergone any significant change – neither for the better nor for the worse, over the past 25 years. There is perhaps greater recognition for the prevalence of emotional ailments and functional disorders, it has become easier to get professional help and it has become more accepted to express problems and a need for psychological help. But this can just as easily be interpreted as an expression of an increased accountability for [one's] own life situation, as for the opposite. [. . .] We have no certain evidence for maintaining that the prevalence of emotional ailments was greater or less in times past than in our times.

Christiansen's observations were in response to a discussion he was having against claims put forward by critics from the psychology profession itself of how an increased professionalisation of psychology will result in clientification, as the use of ever more psychologists entails a risk of greater dependency on professional expertise, whereby people become less self-sufficient and less able to make their own decisions and consequently, less free. One can detect an underlying perception in Christiansen which also arose with Hofgaard and in the article from Alta, namely on the question of taking responsibility. Hofgaard argues that the increase in treatment of young children is due to health care personnel and politicians who took responsibility. Christiansen weaves a narrative here in which psychology helps people to assume greater responsibility for their lives and their own psychological health. This idea that people should take more responsibility for themselves is one we can recognise from the ideal for the consumer society's autonomous consumers and the neoliberal strategy of governance. Here we find again the same strange logical leap from our having no 'certain evidence' for stating that the prevalence of emotional ailments has changed, to presumptuously listing the reasons why it is not the case and then arguing that the development of society is moving in the right direction.

The underlying message of the profession's mentality that can be identified in the representatives mentioned here is actually reminiscent of the old idea of enlightenment – whereby man becomes more and more autonomous through rationality and throws off all bonds that hold him back. This optimism about the future becomes particularly evident when Christiansen puts the professionalisation of psychologists into the debate about other rationalising tendencies in society. He can hardly be accused of being humble: 'The industrial revolution in the last century was also accused of undermining human beings' freedom and independence' (Christiansen, 1984, p. 15). As did the industrial revolution in its day, psychology today represents the future. And as the industrial revolution had its critics, psychology also has its reactionary Luddites.

Déformation professionnelle

Weber was one of the first to examine the characteristic feature of all professions of seeking to give legitimacy to the value of their own profession. Weber uses among other things a concept of social closure to describe this: professions exclude and limit the access of others to the resources in order to maximise own interest (Dæhlen and Svensson, 2008). The psychology profession as led by the NPF is no exception to this rule. Freidson (1988) describes in his extensive study of the medical profession how the critical weakness of professional autonomy is that it encourages the segregation of autonomous institutions which then develop and uphold the profession's self-deceptive view of its own neutrality, the reliability of its knowledge and the excellence of its members. The constant requirements and attempts at control from external forces result in the profession having to protect its virtues. When a profession acquires a special status, the profession forms quite as a matter of course a separate perspective, a perspective that becomes increasingly more quaint and narrow-minded given the autonomous status it has gradually developed. Professions are not self-interested organisations grasping for funding to the detriment of public interests, Freidson warns us against believing. They are to the contrary well-meaning groups that believe they know best what humanity needs, with a protected title from society which in many cases results in being protected from sincere self-scrutiny. While the profession's autonomy seems to have led to an improvement in the scientific knowledge about different illnesses and treatment, it appears that the same autonomy has obstructed the most sensible application of this knowledge (Freidson, 1988).

Ideology entails that the dominant group with an interest in upholding a biased view of the world is de facto unaware of its ideology (Sampson, 1983). Ideology as a linguistic superstructure does not only direct the attention away from actual social conditions, but in a structural fashion excludes areas of reality from thought itself (Barrett, 1991). *Déformation profession-nelle* is a French expression for the propensity to explore phenomena from the perspective of one's own profession and to forget other approaches. This plays upon the expression *formation professionnelle*, which means professional training. The implication is that almost all professional training to some degree will lead to the formation of the profession's view of the world. The well-known expression 'When the only tool you have is a hammer, every problem looks like a nail' provides a pointed summary of this phenomenon. For the psychology profession it means that if the only tool you have is a clinical therapeutic view of the world, then all problems will appear to be psychological. The question asked is therefore always 'How can psychologists . . . ' or 'How can psychology contribute to . . . ' This is a poor basis for ethical and critical thought. Why? Because psychology is automatically taken for granted as an external, positive contribution. 'To make a negative contribution' seems almost semantically impossible.

Psychology is a relatively young science and has an even younger professional history and historical legitimacy for the practice of that profession. This certainly entails some uncertainty, both as a science and a profession, as a result of which self-critical questions are little developed and little desired. This can be compared with the medical profession, where one finds for example a longer and more developed tradition of criticism within the discipline, such as in the journal of the Norwegian Medical Association. The discipline of psychology is located between the soft and hard sciences. Without the natural sciences' secure epistemological grounding perhaps the fundamental philosophical questions become more threatening and less welcome. 'What is the difference between a true science and pseudo-science?'

asks Foucault rhetorically. Well, a true science recognises and is aware of its own history without feeling attacked (Martin, 1988).

The underlying values

Psychology as a separate field arose around the study of the individual human being, and today is predominantly about this as well. More or less all of the discipline's practitioners will be able to accept this premise (Sampson, 1983). On the basis of this general consensus, 'the great debate in psychology' is therefore about what it is about the individual human being that should be studied. The answers range from behaviour, the cognitive processes, the neuropsychological processes, attachment patterns, the entire human being, and so on. Although there is indeed social psychology which aims to venture beyond the purely individual perspective, it is also here often a matter of studying the effects other people have on the individual, which is after all the original focus of the investigation (Sampson, 1983). For example, the most famous debate over fundamental principles in the field of psychology in the last decade – the evidence debate – is about which criteria should be valid for therapy, and it is as such a debate that is constructed around the individual. Although this is a very important debate about fundamental principles which includes the role of research, standardisation, unarticulated knowledge, different traditions of psychotherapy, it is equally so a debate that relates exclusively to the psychology profession, even though it is also found in affiliated disciplines such as medicine and nursing science.

Psychologist Edward Sampson (1983) presents three types of approaches to the relation between psychology and society which he holds to be dominant in psychology: (1) the impotent, (2) the purist and (3) the liberalist. (1) The impotent position is based on the perception that psychology has little impact on human life and therefore need not worry about the type of knowledge it is communicating and what it has to say about human life and behaviour. (2) The purists on the other hand, are scientists who research in accordance with the idea that they gain access to the facts through certain methods that are without bias and therefore neutral in terms of values. For the purist, there are therefore two independent worlds which have nothing to do with each other – the everyday world that is made up of interests and values, a world of *should*, and the scientific world that is made up of things and facts and is a world that *is*. (3) The third position for the relation between psychology and society Sampson calls the liberal. Here one accepts that what one is researching is in principle not neutral but determined by values, but when they are brought under the microscope of research, we can nonetheless achieve neutral knowledge about the world as long as the researcher is careful. This attitude accepts that *is* and *should* are not in fact strictly speaking separated, but when it really comes down to it, values and science go their separate ways. As long as those who apply this distinction make their value standpoint known, value-free research can be carried out.

Sampson (1983) maintains that all three of these dominant positions are inadequate, even the last, because among other things it presupposes that any prejudices and ideologies can be identified and weeded out, which is often not the case. Sampson's preferred perspective on the relation between psychology and society is therefore that *is* and *should* are always inexorably connected.

Parallel to this Sampson criticises what he calls the voluntaristic model in which it is assumed that social reality is constructed out of the sum of the intentional actions of free individuals. It is this model of the individual and society that we have found throughout the entire book, from Freud to the self-help culture to neoliberalism. The assumption here is that the individual is free to create society in his/her image more or less as God created the universe. The true image for the relation between the individual and society is instead the sculptor and the block of stone, Sampson claims. We inherit the tool and the material we can work with. Man is not fully free to create – but can reproduce society or transform society through his actions.

Sampson holds that the relation between the individual and society, and psychology and society, respectively, have clear parallels. He presents this analogue relation by reference to the American sociologist and psychologist George Herbert Mead (1863–1931) who is known for his symbolic interactionism and theory about the Me. Consciousness is not an independent, self-reliant entity that exists independent of society, Mead holds, since we must use the pre-existent social forms of understanding to acquire self-awareness and knowledge about the world around us. The Me can then later interact and influence the social reality by confirming the existing structures or by changing them. For many reasons the latter is more difficult, but nonetheless a possibility. Psychology's relation to society is equivalent to the individual's relation to society. The social sciences such as psychology can therefore never be neutral because they must contribute to either social reproduction or social transformation.

Sampson gives two examples: by getting married, we reproduce the nuclear family and by working we reproduce the underlying structures of working life. Without pre-existing forms of understanding and values to guide these behaviours, it would not be possible to reproduce the underlying structures. Any reversal of the existing structures through human action is thus contingent upon the individual's self-perception. The most important contribution of the humanities is to organise and develop social self-perception. They are not alone in this – the media and religion are other examples that Sampson mentions. His point is therefore that psychology is internally bound to society – it comes from the same structures and mechanisms as the rest of society – and is causally bound to society – the self-perception it develops and organises has a causal connection to the underlying structures in reproducing them.

This is actually just the old lesson that the sciences about humans participate in forming the subjects they study. Psychology organises the self-perception that reproduces the pre-existing structures, which in turn generate these self-perceptions. Psychology is therefore causally bound to society. Psychology can never be neutral, indifferent or impartial because its epistemological horizon about human life will either contribute to social reproduction or potentially social change. Sampson (1983) uses capitalism as an example and argues that since psychology is a result of specific underlying social formations (capitalism), it has an internal and causal relation to the society and individuals it studies. The forms of self-perception it develops and organises are causally related to these underlying structures and psychology therefore participates causally in the reproduction of the capitalistic structures. The clinical treatment of Tove the cleaning assistant with burn-out (in Chapter 2) provided in both form and content a biographical and individual solution that strengthened Tove's self-perception in a specific direction. It could potentially have contributed to another self-perception, although it is less likely and more difficult to imagine, but like individual stakeholders, psychology has a choice and is therefore also morally responsible for either confirming the status quo or producing resistance to it. Being unaware of this moral responsibility implies the inevitability that one will blindly follow and reinforce the existing structures and frames.

Grimen (2008) points out that today there are constantly new requirements and challenges for the professions which entail that one cannot discuss the ethics of a profession without discussing the politics behind them. He mentions neoliberalism in particular and the affiliated modernisation process and market management of the public sector, New Public Management, as an example. It is tempting to speculate about whether it is precisely these tendencies that have led him to understand that traditional professional ethics in a profession such as psychology is at risk of becoming an apolitical ethics. We can imagine an extremely well-qualified clinical psychologist with the highest level of ethical awareness about the client, but who all the same is part of a system in which political questions to an increasing extent are stripped down and presented in a psychological form. Even the brilliant psychologist will probably not be able to reflect upon this, other than that she notices that the flow of patients to her office seems to increase. If she should all the same have any concerns about this, these concerns will be as shown here efficiently handled by the dominant mentality in the profession: the more psychological ailments that become evident in the population, and the more we bring out the underlying afflictions in society, the better. This mentality is in turn supported by the cultural perception that people today assume greater responsibility and take better care of themselves and their problems.

An objection that may be worth addressing here is whether I am essentially asking too much of psychology. Should not the psychologist be allowed to carry out therapy or research in peace, without having to address questions of a philosophical, sociological or political nature, and instead do what he or she does best? This is an important question with great implications for the realm of responsibility of psychology. If we look at the *Ethical Principles for Nordic Psychologists*, these are predominantly ethical principles which provide guidelines for the therapist's relation with his/her clients. But the guidelines also contain two items (§§II.2 and III.3) in which responsibility towards society is emphasised (Norwegian Psychological Association, 1998). It is explicitly established that the psychologist in carrying out his or her role shall be attentive to how external social conditions can inhibit the expedient use of psychological knowledge and to be aware of the relation of responsibility to the society in which he/she lives and works. The problem is that social development serves psychology in such a way that it becomes in great demand. The neoliberal project provides social and work-related conditions that promote the use of psychology's expertise and methods. Without a school of thought within the profession enabling reflection in a critical fashion about 'expedient use' beyond the scope of purely individual and clinical criteria, and the problematising of a unilateral individual-society model as has been described in several chapters of this book, psychology will only be expansive, as is precisely the situation today.

Around the turn of the new millennium a debate was taking place in the journal of the Norwegian Medical Association about the contradictions between individual ethics and social ethics – to what extent a doctor in his/her assessments was also obliged to accept and take into consideration political assessments in making life and death decisions. In other words, whether the physician is also to practise a form of social ethics, or if the Hippocratic Oath – to do one's best to heal and alleviate the suffering of one's patients – is the only value and norm she shall follow. The physician Edvin Schei and colleagues (2000) warn against what they call an individualistic Samaritan ethics, wherein the physician's calling is to blindly follow this model and leave important value-related choices to politics. Their argument is that since the physician's role constantly touches upon social-ethical dilemmas, the individual treatment specialist must also include this in his/her ethical awareness, in addition to the Hippocratic oath: 'Physicians do not serve the cause of their individual patients if they make choices that in the long term lead to an emaciated community of human beings' (Schei *et al.*, 2000, n.p.). Nor do psychologists help their clients if their activities are slowly undermining society. We find a supporting argument from Beck (1992) who emphasises precisely the profession's ability for self-reflection and critical awareness of its own role as completely decisive in terms of meeting the challenges of the risk society, where the sciences have become so differentiated that it is becoming increasingly more difficult for politicians and social planners to have the insight required in order to make ethical assessments. Psychology must strengthen its ability and commitment to profession-related ethical and critical reflection. But psychology is characterised by what I would call an intellectual and critical vacuum. The clinicians for their part are busily engaged in applied psychology and clinical interventions, while the researchers as a rule carry out research in a narrowly defined field, which seldom stimulates critical perspectives, and particularly not about psychology's own blind spots. Unless the proper structural accommodations are made through professional studies, continuing education, the policy of the psychology profession and professional ethics, it is unlikely that much will occur on its own.

Conclusion

From the entrepreneurs of psychology such as Christiansen and Hofgaard there appears to be a line of thought in accordance with which the argument is made claiming that the number of psychological ailments is constant over time. The high incidence of psychological ailments in the population is expressive of a positive development with a greater focus and more use of resources on psychological health than ever before. In previous times everything was worse. Many went around with untreated ailments due to prejudices and stigma, less adequate knowledge and a health service system that was more poorly developed. The psychology profession appears to unconsciously prefer in good faith an explanatory model that to the greatest possible extent gives legitimacy to psychology as something for which there will be even greater need in the future.

The ideological thinking at the professional level: *déformation professionnelle* – the tendency to investigate phenomena in accordance with the perspective of one's own profession – implies that there are perspectives that are simply not seen. It can appear as if only arguments and opinions that are suitable to strengthen psychology's position in society are automatically included in the profession's self-perception and professional policy activities. I believe that this in turn has an impact on the interest in social-psychological ways of thought, in that one can find features in social development that psychology underpins that are illness-engendering, whether it's a matter of working life, schools, local communities, political solutions, values or ideologies. The professional bias of psychology dictates the basis of its existence, which in turn provides the basis for the way psychology perceives itself: psychology is exclusively a scarcity that we cannot get enough of.

The magical element of which psychology is the secular and internally governed carrier lies in its nature without principles, and it therefore meddles with everything it might have a reasonable hope of subjugating. The opinion of anthropologist Tian Sørhaug (1996) about psychotherapy is that, as a whole, it constitutes a project with an enormous lack of respect for boundaries. Indeed, Sørhaug (1996, p. fn. 251) was writing with specific reference to the therapeutic virtue of sometimes remaining silent: ' . . . it [is] more important for psychologists than for almost all other professions to know exactly when to keep their mouths shut – when they should leave things alone.' In this context it is not about a therapeutic flair for knowing when one should speak or hold one's tongue, but about socio-ethical awareness. Unfortunately, the ability to set boundaries is wanting and the result becomes instead a boundless expansion of a therapeutic logic because the professional ethos entails a lack of understanding for other values, systems of meaning and principles besides the purely therapeutic, attributable to the belief that one serves only the cause of the good, in that everything is actually psychology. 'One waits in vain for psychologists to state the limits of their knowledge,' linguist Noam Chomsky said (as cited in Dineen, 1998, p. 11). The story of the psychology profession and its ethos is therefore the classical story about how the road to hell is paved with good intentions.

9   Conclusion

The time has come for summing up and a conclusion. The review of the thera-peutic culture has been critical at times, challenging the perception of psych-ology as 'the good knowledge', something which will certainly produce a certain resistance on the part of some readers to a number of the premises of this book. I have therefore sought to gather some objections that I have run into previously in discussions about the same themes. Some of these misgiv-ings are clearly qualified objections while at the same time I would hold they do not alter the validity and relevancy of the book's perspective.

Tale of woe?

In the introduction I warned the reader about reading this as the full and final story of psychology; I could just as easily have written of our times. In that the focus is often on problem areas that psychology runs into, the description of the contemporary age is perhaps particularly disheartening. It has not been my intention to act as the prophet of doom in relation to late modern life. I will here enlist the support of Foucault's semi-famous statement: 'My point is not that everything is bad, but that everything is dangerous' (Foucault and Rabinow, 1997, p. 256). The task of the social critic is to address the dangerous aspects of the current age – those which generally evade debate. At all times and in different eras what this means will change and it is therefore the social critic's task to attempt to highlight it. Well-evolved democracies and professions that are genuinely concerned about how best to manage society's resources should at all times be open to and understand the value of this.

What is the alternative?

If one criticises any type of subject matter it is common to hear the objec-tion: 'What is the (your) alternative?' Presenting critical perspectives of psychology is in this sense no exception from this rule. The claim is understandable. Unilateral critique can easily deteriorate into pure destructiveness. But at the same time, there is critique that is worth listening to even though the critic might not necessarily have any concrete alternatives in hand. The Danish artist Palle Nielsen described his project as follows:

> I can't give anything positive to our times. The only thing I can give is a presentation of that which pulls the times down, so that I at least know that this is not the path to follow. I have shown the negative and that is positive enough.
>
> (Hagen and Lindgren, 2009, n.p.)

Cushman (1995) has aptly explained that to criticise psychology today is like criticising the weather. We can complain but nobody believes that the complaint will lead to any changes. From this one can draw the conclusion that critique of psychology is futile, but my perspective is rather the opposite – because no alternative to the therapeutic framework as outlined by Cushman and others appears to exist, we need more than ever to develop a critical awareness in order to understand what this hegemony entails. This lack of alternatives appears otherwise to be a general theme that is connected to the postmodern era as a whole and to late capitalism in particular, which has neither a clear exterior nor a clear alternative, according to influential contemporary theorists such as Fredric Jameson (1994) and Slavoj Žižek (Konner and Taylor, 2006).

Totalitarian longing?

In problematising the psychology of today and highlighting ancient religion it is probably unavoidable that one will be accused of a certain totalitarian longing. So be it. My intention is to investigate this as a historically new situation with a set of unfamiliar consequences. My ambition has not been to reinstate authority or the patriarchy, as the neoconservatives might hope to do. Here I am more comfortable seeking support from the strategies of Nietzsche, Foucault or Munk Rösing which seek beyond the existing axis towards a new ethical horizon – towards establishment of a new truth policy. But the therapeutic truth regime is for the time being too boundless for it to be meaningful to speak about.

Psychology is older than 'psychology'

Psychology, understood as the subjective dimension of being a separate, unique human being, extends naturally further back than to the formation of psychology as an independent science and profession at the end of the nineteenth century. Psychology has probably always been an essential part of human cultures as long as human beings have existed, but then in a form different from what we are familiar with today, rather as a part of society's religious, spiritual or magical dimensions. Ekeland (1999) demonstrates convincingly that 'the role of the psychologist' has always been filled by an important person in primitive cultures. This historical background entails that the book that begins with 'psychology' as a science and profession risks exaggerating what is unique and worthy of concern about psychology in the modern age. Have not human beings always been concerned about physical and spiritual health? Probably, but there are a number of features of our age that support the theory that this focus has become more important today than ever before and in a wholly different manner than previously. It also goes without saying that the book's limited perspective – about the challenges related to psychology in our age – does not rule out the fact that there have been similar types of problems before, such as abuse of power and oppression of people in alliance with the society's spiritual or religious elites.

Are not the critical objections to psychology 'psychological' in their own right?

In his review of Jensen's *The Fatherless Society* Lykkeberg (2007) criticises the author for employing a talking and therapeutic gaze. A paradox about this book is certainly as well that the analysis and critique of psychology at times is based on both a psychological mentality and psychological language use. For example, the concern that psychology and the development of society can give rise to more psychological ailments is in itself a psychological motif. Symptomatically, the critique has been psychologised, if only tendentiously. There also need be no contradiction here. Social critics such as Adorno and Marcuse both used Freud and psychoanalysis critically, while they were also critical of aspects of the outcome of this school of thought in culture.

Can I not see the society for the therapists?

Everyone who has attempted to write about a large topic will perhaps have discovered that at times one can enter a special type of state in which one becomes like a sponge that absorbs impressions which immediately seem to be of the greatest relevance to one's own project. Sometimes one can become uncritical and take in too much. This perhaps sounds anything but scientific; research should, as is well known, be refutable and the ideal is to find counter examples for one's own hypothesis rather than confirmations. At the same time I believe that by focusing on something one will as an indirect consequence simultaneously overlook contradictory phenomena at times. The literature about the therapeutic culture has for example been criticised for having overlooked other spheres such as the religious (Loss, 2002). Although in this case I have demonstrated how religion in first and foremost the West still appears to have a therapeutic function today, there are undoubtedly coexisting systems of values and meaning today – such as non-Western European religiosity – that deviate from an individualistic therapeutic world view. Similarly there are other perspectives on social development that will potentially disclose aspects other than the influence of psychology itself, such as a social economic or political science approach.

Could you have not just as well criticised other professions?

Indeed. This is also done. A profession such as medicine can again serve as a comparison. Here there is a separate field and over time a lot of research has been carried out on both the history of medicine and the ethics of medicine that discuss cultural, ethical and critical features of medicine as a science and profession. It is not thereby the case that these critical traditions necessarily exercise great influence on the practice and formation of medicine. But these critical traditions at the very least exist. They do not exist to the same degree in psychology. Possibly this is because it is a much younger profession without the same tradition and position. I could thus have written critically about other disciplines but I have chosen to do so about psychology, in part because it is the discipline that I know and in part because I feel that there is a need for it.

Conspiracy theory?

I emphasised by way of introduction that I wanted to distance myself from critique that bases itself on a hidden conspiracy in which psychology and psychologists are included in an overt alliance with important elements of society. Nonetheless, my critique may perhaps look this way – such as in the discussion about neoliberal formulas for governance and its need for psychological expertise. The difference in my eyes is just that these power relations arise as unfortunate alloys. As Foucault would have put it: power has become anonymous. This appears difficult for some to understand. For something to be credible it is preferable that there are human agents behind it who are responsible. It is worth pointing out that this requirement in itself represents a psychologising or rather an anthropomorphisation of the critique.

What should be the task of psychology?

A question that has arisen during the work on this book concerns what should be the task and area of responsibility of psychology and psychologists. Does problematising psychology as a whole in light of the general development of society and the contradictions of modernity entail writing one's way out of psychology? My answer is an unequivocal no; others have claimed the answer is yes (cf. Hillestad, 2009). Since psychology is both influenced by and influences the culture and our times, it is in my opinion reasonable to demand that the profession be able to reflect upon what this mutual influence involves. This can even be interpreted as part of the profession's own ethical guidelines about being attentive and accountable to the society in which one lives and works. In terms of policy, the psychology profession also has a concrete objective of becoming a more prominent contributor to social design and debate. At the same time, I do understand that not all of the stakeholders in the discipline can at all times concern themselves with questions of this nature in their daily practice. But it is unacceptable that none of the stakeholders of the discipline concern themselves with these questions or, even worse, that they have not heard of these problem areas and ethical challenges. This is regrettably the case to a large extent today, given the profession's unilaterally positive self-perception with respect to its influence on society. It is ethically untenable that it is possible as a student to go through the entire psychology education to become a clinician without knowing what individualisation is and which ideological role such mechanisms can potentially play for one's own practice of the profession, in the same manner as if one had not heard of the judicial and moral restrictions that regulated the relation between client and therapist.

I stated by way of introduction that the question of the psyche today is about the most important moral and political issues of our times, in that all of human existence has been dressed in a therapeutic manner of speaking and thinking worldwide. Giddens (1991) calls *life politics* questions of a political nature that arise in the post-traditional society where globalisation processes acquire an intimate significance for the self's reflective project, which in turn gains significance for political processes. If we look at the time period for the triumph of therapy in the West from the 1960s up to the present day, this time period coincides with the youth revolution, liberation movements and the great breakthrough to the consumer society. Today's generations of young adults live in a society less defined by tradition and authority than previously, where the opportunities for free choice and self-actualisation are greater. When society changes, the challenges change along with it. New problems arise in this individualised and therapeutic culture of rights. Has the new radical freedom become a form of choice under coercion? Does the requirement for self-actualisation imply a greater burden on the individual than before? Does the incidence of psychological ailments increase in the population as a result? Does oppression still exist, but in new, more covert forms? Is 'the external revolution' – which sought to change society – permanently called off to make way for 'the internal revolution'? Is politics synonymous with life politics? The therapeutic culture encompasses in a sense all of these important questions and as I have attempted to argue, professional expertise comes into contact with them every day through the practice of the profession. In the attempt to shed a critical light on socio-ethical dilemmas related to psychology and psychotherapy, I have simultaneously struggled against what many critics of the therapeutic culture fear, such as Lasch (1991), who wrote regarding the psychology movement in the USA as early as the 1970s that after having thrown religion out of the public domain it now threatened to undermine politics as the final bastion of ideology.

The death of ideology?

One of the most influential and famous works on the possibilities of social criticism and revolt in our time is the German philosopher Herbert Marcuse's (1969) essay 'Repressive Tolerance'. Marcuse addresses here the difficulties of carrying out social criticism and revolt in that the status quo – the establishment – is not only the lord of property (as before the French Revolution) or of the means of production (as before the Russian Revolution) but now of language and consciousness as well. The consumer society encourages young people to actualise themselves, which in Marcuse's opinion thereby sets them apart from the only dimension that can bring about a better society – the political. The rebellious norms of the countercultures encouraged nonconformity and a fuck-everything attitude which allowed the actual foundation of the society to remain intact: the more 'personal' the revolt, the more authentic it was, tragically enough, perceived as being.

In order for people to truly become free and autonomous, they must first have been liberated from this existing indoctrination of the modern democracy, he claimed. The death of ideology means for Marcuse the seemingly final breakthrough of the false consciousness as the only consciousness. The psychological talk about 'being yourself' is a conceptual product which a priori determines the direction in which the thought processes move. The same holds for alienation understood exclusively as a subjective illness and psychological condition. Marcuse sought instead to call attention to alienation as the objective feature of the subjective condition of all human beings, the solution of which was therefore collective and political and not individual and psychological. Today it is obvious that Marcuse has not been heard: self-actualisation has long since been made manifest as 'self-esteem' – where this psychological condition is no longer a future goal for young, searching people but something that everyone experiences and Scandinavians along with people all over the rest of the world are hunting for more of in lonely herds.

The fate of revolution in the modern consumer society is reminiscent of the Orwellian, where the basic vocabulary serves as a priori categories for our understanding, which will therefore never touch the framework, according to Marcuse. The possibility for a revolt against the system lay therefore in stopping the words and images that feed consciousness. It is there the false consciousness takes shape. Only a potential break with the false consciousness can be the Archimedean point for a large-scale emancipation. The job of the intellectual was therefore to indicate such potential ruptures:

> It is the task and duty of the intellectual to recall and preserve historical possibilities which seem to have become utopian possibilities – that it is his task to break the concreteness of oppression in order to open the mental space in which society can be recognized as what it is and does.
>
> (Marcuse, 1969, p. 95)

Had Marcuse lived today, I believe that he would have been even less optimistic about finding an Archimedean point for the liberation of human beings. The conditions for critical thought appear eroded. The concept of ideology is today considered out of date because it invites thought about a clear distinction between true and false which no longer seems possible to uphold. At the same time, consumerism and the therapeutic ethics tell us all the time that we are liberated and free to do what we want. Foucault (1998) writes in *The History of Sexuality, Volume 1*, about how the late-modern Western idea of liberation from oppressed sexuality must be understood as a form of pseudo-liberation, in that in reality it is a new form of oppression in line with the Freudian ethics whereby everything should come into the open. A programme from the abundant flora of therapeutic reality shows that illustrate this reality is the British series *Embarrassing Illnesses* (2007–) in which participants voluntarily display intimate parts of their bodies to a team of doctors while on camera. The ethos of self-disclosure is assisted by an onslaught of experts on intimacy. With the scientification of sexuality and the psyche the control of them increases as well. According to the Slovenian philosopher Slavoj Žižek, it is a complete misunderstanding to read Foucault and

The History of Sexuality as a general recipe for the individual about how to 'open up' the power mechanisms in which he or she is caught. Foucault's entire point, according to Žižek, is to demonstrate how resistance to power is generated by the same matrix that one believes one is opposing. Foucault's conception of 'biopower' is precisely about showing how the disciplinary power mechanisms can constitute individuals directly and bypass the level of politics and ideology and thereby any resistance. There is therefore no visible external element against which to exercise resistance (Žižek, 1999).

The post-political

There are no opportunities given today for achieving a new subjectivity, according to the Italian philosopher Giorgio Agamben (2009), in an essay about Foucault's concept the 'dispostif' or 'apparatus'. Apparatuses are formations or governing forces that give subjectivation processes a specific direction. The more the apparatuses permeate and spread their power within every area of life, the more governance is carried out by way of an intangible element. The political sphere of action becomes therefore smaller in the therapeutic culture. When everything becomes political nothing is political. Agamben (2009) makes the argument that we are bombarded under late capitalism with new apparatuses which are no longer subject to the possibility of human control. The result is a quasi-democracy where the actual governance is out of our control, while *realpolitik* blindly pantomimes its insistence that the choices between the right and the left wing in politics are of huge significance. The political theorists Ernst Laclau and Chantal Mouffe (2001) have stated that true politics today is not primarily about counting the number of votes for and against an issue. The real political struggle is about how the political subjects are formed.

> Psychology can be understood as an apparatus that steers one of our times' most widespread subjectification mechanisms in a specific direction. 'The harmless citizen' is how Agamben describes the individual of the post-industrial democracies who readily does everything that he is asked to do, inasmuch as he leaves his everyday gestures and his health, his amusements and his occupations, his diet and his desires, to be commanded and controlled in the smallest detail by apparatuses.
>
> (2009, p. 23)

We can recognise the type of control behind these apparatuses as the governing rationality of neoliberalism – you shall govern yourself – with a ludicrous focus on bodily and spiritual health and well-being. All areas are made available for individual control, while at the same time, none of these areas are recognised as being controlled by the state and oppressive towards the subject. Meanwhile the apparatuses become increasingly more pervasive and spread their power into all areas of life.

Žižek (1999) claims that our age – five decades after Marcuse and the revolt of 1968 which was inspired by him – must be described as *post-political*, in that the development of history and society is wandering about blindly. When nobody stands at the wheel there is no traditional authority to criticise, attack and rebel against. The term post-politics implies that expert systems and scientific knowledge and techniques are more important political contributors than politics itself, by way of their formation of the current structural, social and political conditions.

This transfer of power creates an even greater need than previously for the sciences and the professions, such as psychology and psychotherapy, to develop and conduct themselves with a large degree of socio-political awareness regarding their social impact. Important political, moral, social and structural dimensions disappear in the undertow of the scientific or clinical expertise in 'democracy's black hole'. Beck writes about *the reflexive modernity* that it is crucial for the specialised knowledge systems and different forms of expertise to begin reflecting upon the direction the development is taking. This self-critique and self-restraint is perhaps the only means of discovering errors in advance which can sooner or later destroy our world. Reality has become so complicated that politics no longer has the requisite qualifications for critical thought at the same level as the technological and scientific development and, therefore, in many cases will not discover the risk in time. In the case of psychology this is perhaps particularly true of individualisation processes – where structural, social and political problems are transformed into problems of a private and psychological nature. The challenge for psychology today is both to understand its role in the individualisation processes, and, in addition, to continuing to treat psychological ailments in the population. The problem that I have illustrated is, however, that psychology does not recognise the problems' origin in the social dimension and is blind to its own contribution in individualisation: consequently it has a vested interest in the situation remaining unchanged.

The immediate ideological reward is that the individual is treated as an asocial and ahistorical being, artificially removed from a larger socio-political context (Prilleltensky, 1989). In the therapeutic culture, society's conflicts and contradictions therefore tend to an increasing extent to be located in the self, while the social order remains undisturbed. A tendency in our times is therefore to evaluate all human subject matter in accordance with psychological and individual categories, with *The Secret* being the extreme case here. The greatest ethical challenge for psychology is not psychologists' potentially unconscious exploitation of their power, Prilleltensky (1989) has claimed, but rather the efficient socialisation psychologists go through whereby they learn not to question the social system. In *The German Ideology* Marx and Engels (1998) established that it is the social and economic conditions that determine conscious-ness and not the opposite. This can serve as a type of entryway for radical thought in both philosophy and politics, without implying the necessity to embrace Marxism. Psychology's starting point as a science – the study of human beings – is in many ways diametrically opposed to this radical point of departure. Psychology has therefore in its conception a conserva-tive bias in favour of the status quo. This should then entail a particular alertness for this type of problem.

Prilleltensky (1989) does not hesitate to characterise as uncritical psychology's current thought about the individual and society and the management of its social responsibility. He presents two possible models for psychology's relation to and influence on society: (1) a *conservative* which both confirms and reinforces the status quo, or (2) a *radical* which criticises the social situation and contributes to change. Unfortunately, the psychology profession's self-perception at the moment is based on a strong belief in ideological immunity, which has an inhibiting effect on a potential exploration of the mutual interaction of social forces and psychology. The result is that predominant ideologies permeate psychological knowledge (Prilleltensky, 1989). Parker (2007) writes with humour that psychologists are not consciously dedicated to the survival of capitalism, but their insuf-ficient ability to reflect upon what they in fact are contributing to is just as widespread as the cognitive inadequacies they claim to find in their patients. Psychologists do not play the heroic or innocent role they believe they are playing. Psychologists often believe that they are standing on the barricades of social justice and change, but in reality they are only decorating the facade, he states categorically.

There are, however, forces in psychology that are working to make psych-ology a radical, ethical profession that recognises its influence on social development. So-called critical psychology is often critical of mainstream psychology for unilaterally emphasising the individual psyche and neglect-ing surrounding factors and structures, while it seeks to apply psychology progressively with an eye towards social change to reduce the incidence of psychopathology in society. Critical psychology's most important task today is to explore the individualisation of the late capitalistic system, as Parker (2003) and others have claimed. This challenge demonstrates well critical psychology's advantages and limitations.

An anthology on critical psychology edited by the renowned critical psychologist Valerie Walkerdine (2002) is entitled *Challenging Subjects: Critical Psychology for a New Millennium*, and one of the chapters concerns, in particular, individualisation processes in working life. Social scientists Mary Walsh and Mark Bahnisch (2002, p. 25) write: 'Individualisation at the workplace demonstrates that the political realm is undergoing transformation and critical psychology as a discipline can assist in understanding the complexities involved here'. Their message is that psychology can contribute by offering its expertise in the study of individualisation in working life. But the point is that psychology is already contributing, in a negative sense, by strengthening individualisation processes. Much of critical psychology, even though it has merit beyond mainstream psychology in its explicit ambition to change the status quo, appears to share general psychology's perception of psychology as a positive contributor external to the problem complex that one is seeking to change. Prominent critical psychologists such as Prilleltensky and Parker therefore warn against the use of psychology in many situations: 'Psychological explanation is always poisonous, and no less so when it is incorporated into a bigger picture to complete it' (Parker, 2007, p. 211). Critical psychology should therefore put its own house in order before it starts on the houses of others.

There are however a number of features in general psychology that indicate that it is highly unlikely that a critical psychology will achieve penetration with its perspectives. An obvious strategy is to have it exist as a separate sub-discipline of psychology for psychologists with a special interest who call themselves 'critical'. And that is how it has already been for several decades. It would seem natural to think that psychology is by definition critical and that a part of being a conscientious science and profession is self-critique. Psychology's recent history shows, however, its desire to remove itself from lofty theory, meta-reflection and criticism.

About psychology as a science it is often said that it was founded as an attempt to provide scientific explanations to philosophical questions (cf. Leahey, 2012). Psychology as a science is in a special position among the sciences, caught as it is between 'the hard sciences' such as the natural sciences and medicine, and 'the softer sciences' such as the social sciences and humanities. Psychology has always been characterised by an internal friction between these two extremes – where a central conflict exists between those who hold that psychology should first and foremost be a science dedicated to a life in the laboratory and experiments, and those who hold that psychology should be an interpretive and reflective activity. The latter are often referred to as armchair psychologists (Freeman and Harriman, 1946). The term comes from

E.W. Scripture who was a teacher at Yale University and who expressed great optimism on behalf of the new science's – psychology's – ability to precisely map out the mind and its laws, in the same way that physics mapped out the laws of the universe. The hope was that it was in the process of leaving behind philosophy and the armchair psychologist once and for all. This was in 1895. The armchair psychologist thereby acquired a stain of taboo early on, in the childhood of psychology, while laboratory research was the totem it was hoped that psychologists would dance around in the twentieth century (Freeman and Harriman, 1946). Philosophical speculation was something considered to be a historical and primitive artefact which had to be left behind if psychology were to reap recognition as a separate scientific discipline along the same lines as medicine and biology. True scientific psychology could only come about when the armchair was abandoned for good, making way for the scientific research in the laboratory (Robinson, 1985). This urge to make armchair psychology taboo was something one of the founders of psychology – William James (1842–1910) – was enough of a visionary to warn against. He held that, to the contrary, psychology as a natural science would come to need armchair psychology more than ever, in that a growing psychology field would need critical reflection for its burgeoning field of knowledge and responsibility.

Psychology's internal division between the armchair researcher and laboratory research appears, however, to have been resolved today, though perhaps not in the way one might have hoped. The profession's old internal strife between natural science and the humanities is today 'solved' by allowing the market to decide (Kvale, 2003). A worldwide study published in *The International Handbook of Psychology* showed how, whether or not psychological research units were institutionally connected to the humanities, social sciences or natural sciences had significance for recognition of the scientific status and financing of the institute (Pawlik and Rosenzweig, 2000). The conclusion of the study is therefore that future psychological institutes should affiliate themselves with natural science communities. Kvale (2003) writes that researchers' support of psychology as a natural science was not done on the basis of a theoretical consideration of psychology's field of knowledge and status, but simply left up to the market to decide. Where the funding is, is also where psychology is in the postmodern age, he therefore concludes. There is in other words little to indicate that a change in the direction of a more critically and ethically aware psychology will come about any time soon, viewed from the perspective of the profession. The status quo only looks set to continue if one considers psychology in society in accordance with the notion of the therapeutic culture. There are individual characteristics in the therapeutic ethos that dictate that it is a system of meaning that has come to stay and that contains mechanisms making it extremely resistant.

The therapeutic turn

The critique in the literature on the therapeutic culture that is perhaps the most worrying highlights the potentially irreversible element of what I have called *the therapeutic turn*. Eva Illouz (2008) discloses the potentially irreversible feature of the therapeutic culture through her treatment of the question of theodicy – Why do the innocent suffer while the evil succeed?– which has had a wholly central position in Western culture, the religions of the world and modern social utopias up to this day. The therapeutic world view represents therefore a watershed. Cultures up until now have all sought to explain the gap between merit and luck. Clinical psychology is the first cultural system that seeks to do away with the problem of theodicy by making the ailment into the result of a damaged or faulty psyche (Illouz, 2008). Psychology perfects one of religion's objectives: to explain, rationalise and in the end always justify suffering. Religion served as an explanation of the status quo by legitimising a good or bad destiny through hidden virtue or vice. Psychology resuscitates such forms of theodicy with full force, Illouz claims. The successful penetration of the therapeutic ethos entails that there is no longer anything that can be called meaningless suffering and chaos; everything has received a name and a diagnosis, for which something can potentially be done. This should worry us, Illouz maintains, because it is the meaningless suffering – which in the religious or political systems of meaning of former times could not be explained – which has served as the driving force for people to challenge and change the society.

Does the therapeutic system of meaning contain the moral basis for opposing the practices we take for granted if its form of freedom should come to inhibit our freedom?, asks James Nolan Jr (1998) with corresponding concern in *The Therapeutic State*. In the work he compares the therapeutic ethos with previous state systems of legitimation such as religion and republicanism. The comments of Nolan Jr and Illouz highlight a shared concern: does the therapeutic culture have an exterior? Does it contain the possibilities to terminate itself – does it have an auto-trigger mechanism if it should prove to function at cross purposes with its own intention – to lead to oppression rather than liberation, or coercion rather than freedom? Nolan Jr makes a comparison with republicanism where there was in the end a revolt against slavery as an institution because it was in violation of the system's own values about freedom. But it is difficult to imagine that the therapeutic framework will terminate itself if the psychological ailments should increase or self-esteem become worse; this will instead only strengthen the system in the manner of requirements for more self-sustenance and self-esteem and more psychologists. This is possibly connected to the fact that the therapeutic ethos is the first moral system in which authority is no longer founded in an external, transcendent principle but in the self.

Freudian, orthodox psychoanalysis is sometimes portrayed (often with a humorous undertone) as if a patient's reactions to the analyst's conjectures, regardless of whether these express verification or denial, serve to confirm the therapist's presentiments. Two diametrically different logical outcomes are therefore held as grounds for the same thing. Regardless of whether the answer is a 'yes' of confirmation or a 'no' of denial, the analysis nonetheless captures the phenomenon and the treatment is on the right track. Sir Karl Popper's (1963) critique of Freud's psychoanalysis and Adler's individual psychology was that both theories were able to explain phenomena regardless of what had taken place. All human behaviour can thereby be explained. These are examples of how psychological theory contains certain common characteristics that can turn them into hegemonic myths that cannot be challenged. It is no longer possible to test them and neither is it any longer legitimate to do so. The same type of pseudologic can be found in the therapeutic project's self-perpetuating and potentially irreversible character: regardless of whether the incidence of psychological ailments increases or decreases in the culture, this will confirm psychology's validity and importance. In the case of a possible increase, this proves that we need psychologists. In the case of a possible decline, this proves that psychology works. The psychological metaphors are so applicable that they can be employed regardless of success or failure, as demonstrated in the chapter about sports and psychology.

In the therapeutic culture what is missing is quite simply the outcome in which one would question its given framing and organisation of the modern Western society. We may see a connection here with the absence of meaningless signs or chaos absence, which Illouz touches upon. These meaningless signs are essential because they are the source from which to question the value of the existing social reality. They provide an incitement to think alternatively or think in utopias.

The term 'the therapeutic culture' is misleading, according to Rieff, the man responsible for much of the existing research on the therapeutic culture. Why? Because what is characteristic about the therapeutic culture is precisely that it does not contain the right features, specifically, a sacred order or authoritative core, to enable its characterisation as a culture. The late-modern era we are living in is therefore a radical deviation from history, in that it is history's first horizontal social structure and accordingly an anti-culture. This means that there is little hope of change being forthcoming. It is the case that the potential for social change depends upon the sacred order being understood as a social order that is open to revision and revolutions (Rieff, 2006). The irreversibility of the therapeutic project points toward the self-perpetuating logic of the therapeutic ethos. The self becomes on an increasing larger scale the only reference point. 'The cultural emotivism', whereby everything is assessed in accordance with how it feels for me, becomes given and self-sufficient. Parallel to this, the idea that we live in the best of all possible worlds is securely reinforced: the social imagination and fantasy are weakened – the Western consumer society's economy of desire and psychological system becomes the only conceivable world. Psychology rules and exists within a priori established linguistic frames of interpretation and relations of power (Marcuse, 1969).

The Enlightenment project was revitalised with Freud and saw an upswing – the idea of science that defined the human being as the final frontier to be conquered. The colonisation of the external reality has been a disappointment and one therefore turns to the internal, endless borderline. It has become an inexhaustible source. As in football, you can always improve on 'the mental aspect'. Individual self-creation is boundless and unlimited in its possibilities. This is the only great story today – one which, indeed, exists as an atomised grand narrative. The facticity is instead standardisation – the freedom to choose the same – and social pathologies, with a high incidence of psychological ailments when people become worn out from the work of governing themselves and pulling themselves up by their bootstraps so as to make better choices and fully exploit their possibilities. The poet Theodore Roethke described this paradox as follows: 'Self-contemplation is a curse/That makes an old confusion worse' (as cited in Illouz, 2008, p. 244).

Society will in all likelihood always have a certain level of psychological ailments in the population but the number and pressure of such ailments depends upon society's capacity for normative integration of individuals (Willig, 2005). If our needs are not regulated by external limits, we are tossed into an unceasing struggle to satisfy our needs which will be experienced as agonising (Durkheim, 2010). If we are to avoid this, the individual needs external limits in the manner of social norms that limit him or her, Durkheim claimed. It is not a matter of simply providing for 'the social dimension' but of viewing the social dimension as something that constitutes the personal aspect, but simultaneously without losing 'the authentic' of the personal sphere (Frosh, 2003, p. 1564). Psychology is, however, stuck in its view of the individual as primary, among other things because there are such good reasons of a professional policy, moral and scientific nature for viewing it in this way that to think innovatively about the relation between the individual and society is unfamiliar and not very appealing.

Although it perhaps does not look that way, we have actually just as many decrees today as did people of previous generations, Ehrenberg (2010) claims, but the decrees have changed. They create fewer neurotic conflicts based on dependent pathological relations to others. It is futile to long for a return to this interdiction or to continue to insist on the limitations these entailed for the young people of today who never experienced it. But we must recognise that the unknown inside of us is changing and try to understand the costs associated with this. Liberation has perhaps taken us away from guilt and subjugation but confronts us simultaneously with requirements imposed on the self for accountability and action. Depression has become the new epidemic because people must live out the illusion that everything is potentially possible (Ehrenberg, 2010). The enduring fatigue of depression has replaced the anxiety of neurosis. We have gone from longing and the *compulsion* to be oneself to the *obligation* to be oneself.

Conclusion

'Nowadays men often feel that their private lives are a series of traps. They sense that within their everyday worlds, they cannot overcome their troubles, and in the feeling, they are often quite correct.' This is how the American sociologist C. Wright Mills (2000, p. 3) opens his classical work *The Sociological Imagination* which was written at the end of the 1950s at the entrance to a new age – the consumer society's total penetration and the start of the psychological age, which, combined, would prove to strengthen the very development he warned against. Here Wright Mills shows that the great paradox of modern democracy after a few centuries of capitalism is that the individual's ability to see connections between his/her own personal destiny and biography and large-scale historical events is debilitated. He defines *the sociological imagination* as the disposition of being able to understand the connection between larger social changes and one's own life. The sociological imagination is in short the ability to shift perspectives back and forth between the political and the psychological (Mills, 2000). Part of the reason why this disposition is in a bad way is due to what Wright Mills refers to as 'the psychiatric', about which a public interest was dawning in his time, and which Wright Mills already then saw as a chilling attempt to sweep the problems of modern society under the rug.

In investigating the entrance of psychology into the many spheres of society, this book has shown that modern society today views psychological science as one of its more beloved instruments (Prilleltensky, 1989; Rose, 1999; Sampson, 1983). The love for psychology in modern society is due among other things to psychology's convincing dichotomy between the individual and society. Instead of the social dimension being thought of as something that constitutes the individual consciousness, psyche, and as taking part in determining every single individual's destiny, in our times society has become something secondary and external to the individual, which the latter would preferably avoid. Regardless of how well-intentioned psychologists are in doing research on the psyche and in helping individuals in an individualised society, the result is that this enterprise undermines the sociological imagination, which is a prerequisite for people to be able to understand how their own destiny is connected to changes in society and the fates of thousands of others. And worst of all: the will of individuals to change their own situation (status quo) is also thereby undermined, beyond becoming (slightly) improved versions of themselves. That does not mean that it is futile for every single individual: how you are feeling is, of course, important (life politics) but it is a futile strategy if one wants to influence or change the external structures that create the life conditions for each individual (the politics). It is nonetheless difficult to convince the profession's own actors and others that psychology contains an ideological bias. Because what is paradoxical and tragicomic about this is that, just as psychologists and other therapeutic experts will experience even greater legitimacy in society and even greater demand, so the state of the sociological imagination will worsen and the incidence of psychological ailments in the population will increase, and vice versa.

Psychology is political. One must therefore also begin to treat it as a political phenomenon. A radical solution, which Parker (2007) has recently proposed, is therefore to turn the focus away from psychology as a universally valid study of the psyche, towards critical studies of the effects of psychology – *psychologisation* – whereby increasingly more non-psychological phenomena are understood as something that arises from and thereby has its natural solution in the psyche of the individual or, even better, in the brain. This book has, despite much of its tendency towards negativity, been an attempt to *contribute* to that.

References

Adorno, T. W. (2002). *The stars down to earth: And other essays on the irrational in culture.* London: Routledge.

Agamben, G. (2009). *What is an apparatus? And other essays.* Stanford, CA: Stanford University Press.

Akerlof, G. A., and Shiller, R. J. (2009). *Animal spirits: How human psychology drives the economy and why it matters for global capitalism.* Princeton, NJ: Princeton University Press.

Albright, J. (2007). Impossible bodies: TV viewing habits, body image, and plastic surgery attitudes among college students in Los Angeles and Buffalo, New York. *Configurations,* 15(2), 103–123.

Altaposten. (2009, 26 September). Ingen er lykkelig hele tiden [Nobody's happy all of the time]. *Altaposten,* p. n.a.

Altman, I. (1987). Centripetal and centrifugal trends in psychology. *American Psychologist,* 42(12), 1058–1069.

American Psychiatric Association. (2013). *DSM-5: Diagnostic and statistical manual of mental disorders* (2nd ed.). Washington, DC: American Psychiatric Association.

American Society for Aesthetic Plastic Surgery. (2010, n.d.). Statistics. *The American Society for Aesthetic Plastic Surgery.* Retrieved from http://www.surgery.org/media/statistics

Andersen, M. K. (2010, 7 July). Villdyret har våknet [The beast within awakens], *Adressaavisa,* p. 5.

Andrejevic, M. (2004). *Reality TV: The work of being watched.* Lanham, MD: Rowman & Littlefield.

Anrell, L. (2010, 8 February). Norrmännen är rädda – det är bara losergäng som anlitar psykologer [The Norwegians are afraid. Only losers seek out psychologists]. *Aftonbladet.* Retrieved from http://www.aftonbladet.se/sportbladet/kronikorer/anrell/article6562528.ab

Apotek 1. (2009, n. d.). ADHD [ADHD]. *Apotek 1.* Retrieved from http://www.apotek1.no/raadogtjenester/raad/hjerne-og-nerver/adhd

174   *The Therapeutic Turn*

Arnet, E. (2009). *Terapi. Hva passer for meg?* [Therapy: What is right for me?].
Oslo: Gyldendal Akademisk.

Askeland, Ø. (2010, 8 February). Norske eksperter om svensk kritikk: Bjørndalen
er ingen taper [Norwegian experts on Swedish critique: Bjørndalen is no loser].
VG. Retrieved from http://www.vg.no/sport/ol/2010/artikkel.php?artid=589194

Askheim, O. P. (2007). Empowerment. Ulike tilnærminger [Empowerment:
Different approaches]. In O. P. Askheim and B. Starrin (Eds), *Empowerment. I
teori og praksis* (pp. 21–33). Oslo: Gyldendal Akademisk.

Bakke Foss, A., and Sødal, H. (2009, 11 May). Gudstro daler ned i skjul [Belief in
God withers]. *Aftenposten*. Retrieved from http://www.aftenposten.no/nyheter/
iriks/article3069011.ece

Barrett, M. (1991). *The politics of truth: From Marx to Foucault*. Stanford, CA:
Stanford University Press.

Barry, A., Rose, N., and Osborne, T. (Eds). (1996). *Foucault and political reason:
Liberalism, neo-liberalism and rationalities of government*. London: UCL Press.

Barsky, A. J. (1988). The paradox of health. *New England Journal of Medicine*,
318, 414–418.

Baudrillard, J. (2003). *The consumer society: Myths and structures*. London: Sage.

Bauman, Z. (1998). Postmodern religion? In P. Heelas (Ed.), *Religion, modernity
and postmodernity* (pp. 55–78). Oxford: Blackwell.

Bauman, Z. (2001). *The individualized society*. Cambridge: Polity Press.

Beasley, R. (2010, 19 June). Capello reveals his Cape Fear. *The Sun*. Retrieved from
http://www.thesun.co.uk/sol/homepage/sport/football/worldcup2010/3021022/
Fabio-Capello-says-England-cracking-under-World-Cup-pressure.html

Beck, A. T. (1988). *Love is never enough: How couples can overcome misunderstandings, resolve conflicts, and solve relationship problems through cognitive
therapy*. New York: Harper & Row.

Beck, U. (1992). *Risk society: Towards a new modernity*. London: Sage.

Beck, U., and Beck-Gernsheim, E. (2002). *Individualization: Institutionalized individualism and its social and political consequences*. London: Sage.

Becker, D. (2005). *The myth of empowerment: Women and the therapeutic culture
in America*. New York: New York University Press.

Becker, D. (2013). *One nation under stress. The trouble with stress as an idea*.
Oxford: Oxford University Press.

Bellah, R. N. (2008). *Habits of the heart: Individualism and commitment in American
life* (with a new preface). Berkeley, CA: University of California Press.

Bergsli, B. (2010, 9 July). Blomstrer på hesteryggen [Thrives on horseback],
Telemarksavisa, pp. 30–31.

Biressi, A., and Nunn, H. (2005). *Reality TV: Realism and revelation*. London:
Wallflower Press.

Bloom, A. (1987). *The closing of the American mind*. London: Penguin Books.

Borud, E. (2010, 13 February). Jacobsen: Ammann er sterkere enn meg psykisk
[Jacobsen: Ammann is mentally stronger than me]. *VG*. Retrieved from http://
www.vg.no/sport/ol/2010/artikkel.php?artid=587121

Botvar, P. K., and Schmidt, U. (Eds). (2010). *Religion i dagens Norge* [Religion in
contemporary Norway]. Oslo: Universitetsforlaget.

Bourdieu, P. (1998a). *Acts of resistance: Against the new myths of our time.* Cambridge: Polity Press.

Bourdieu, P. (1998b, December). The essence of neoliberalism. *Le Monde diplomatique*, English edition. Retrieved from http://mondediplo.com/1998/12/08bourdieu

Brenna, T. (2008, 8 August). Fotballjentenes psykiske overtak [Women footballers' mental advantage], *Dagbladet*, p. 27.

Brinkmann, S. (2008). Identity as self-interpretation. *Theory and Psychology*, 18(3), 404–422.

Bruland, K.-M. (2008). *Tidsskrift for Norsk Psykologforening: ideologiske og normative endringer 1974–2007* [Journal of the Norwegian Psychological Association: Ideological and normative changes 1974–2007]. (Masters thesis). Bergen: University of Bergen.

Bråtebrekken, C., and Emanuelsen, B. (2010, 24 July). Gamlisungdommen [The old youth], *Dagens Næringsliv*, pp. 25–33.

Burckhardt, J. (1990). *The civilization of the Renaissance in Italy.* London: Penguin.

Byrne, R. (2006). *The secret.* New York: Simon and Schuster.

Byrne, R. (Producer), and Heriot, D. (Director). (2006). *The secret* [Motion picture]. Australia: Prime Time Productions.

Carroll, J. (1985). *Guilt: The grey eminence behind character, history, and culture.* London: Routledge and Kegan Paul.

Casey, M. A. (2002). *Meaninglessness: The solutions of Nietzsche, Freud and Rorty.* Lanham: Lexington Books.

Chase, D. (Producer). (1999–2007). *The Sopranos* [Television series]. New York: HBO.

Christiansen, A. K. (2010, 8 February). Se, en svensk idrettspsykolog! [Look, a Swedish sport psychologist!]. *VG.* Retrieved from http://www.vg.no/sport/artikkel.php?artid=589250

Christiansen, B. (1984). Om psykologprofesjonens røtter [On the origin of the psychology profession]. In P. A. Holter, S. Magnussen and S. Sandsberg (Eds), *Norsk psykologi 150 år* (pp. 13–49). Oslo: Universitetsforlaget.

Clarke, J. (2005). New Labour's citizens: Activated, empowered, responsibilized, abandoned? *Critical Social Policy*, 25(4), 447–463.

Coppola, F. F. (Producer and Director). (1974). *The godfather part II.* USA: Paramount Pictures.

Coppola, F. F. (Producer and Director). (1990). *The godfather part III.* USA: Paramount Pictures.

Couldry, N. (2003). *Media rituals: A critical approach.* London: Routledge.

Couldry, N., and Littler, J. (2008). The work of work: Reality TV and negotiation of neo-liberal labour in *The Apprentice.* In T. Austin and W. De Jong (Eds), *Rethinking documentary. New perspectives, new practices* (pp. 258–267). Maidenhead: McGraw-Hill.

Cruikshank, B. (1996). Revolutions within: Self-government and self-esteem. In A. Barry, T. Osborne and N. Rose (Eds), *Foucault and political reason. Liberalism, neo-liberalism and rationalities of government* (pp. 231–251). Chicago, IL: University of Chicago Press.

Cruikshank, B. (1999). *The will to empower: Democratic citizens and other subjects.* Ithaca, NY: Cornell University Press.

Cushman, P. (1990). Why the self is empty: Toward a historically situated psychology. *American Psychologist*, 45(5), 599–611.

Cushman, P. (1995). *Constructing the self, constructing America: A cultural history of psychotherapy.* Reading, MA: Addison-Wesley.

Dale, R. S. (2010, 12 July). Har ingenting i Europa å gjøre [We are not ready for Europe], *Budstikka*, pp. 16–17.

Davis, K. (1986). The process of problem (re)formulation in psychotherapy. *Sociology of Health and Illness*, 8, 44–74.

Dean, M. (2009). *Governmentality: Power and rule in modern society* (2nd ed.). London: Sage.

Dineen, T. (1998). *Manufacturing victims. What the psychology industry is doing to people* (2nd ed.). Westmount, QC: Robert Davies Multimedia Publishing.

Dovey, J. (2008). Simulating the public sphere. In T. Austin and W. De Jong (Eds), *Rethinking documentary. New perspectives, new practices* (pp. 246–257). Maidenhead: McGraw-Hill.

Dubrofsky, R. E. (2007). Therapeutics of the self: Surveillance in the service of the therapeutic. *Television New Media*, 8(4), 263–284.

Dufour, D.-R. (2008). *The art of shrinking heads: On the new servitude of the liberated in the age of total capitalism.* Cambridge: Polity Press.

Durkheim, É. (1971). *The elementary forms of the religious life.* London: Allen and Unwin.

Durkheim, É. (2010). *Suicide: A study in sociology.* New York: The Free Press.

Dæhlen, M., and Svensson, L. G. (2008). Profesjon, klasse og kjønn [Profession, class and gender]. In A. Molander and L. I. Terum (Eds), *Profesjonsstudier* (pp. 119–129). Oslo: Universitetsforlaget.

Døving, R. (2009, 9 February). Hva er galt med forbruk? [What is wrong with consumerism?] *Minerva*. Retrieved from http://www.minervanett.no/ hva-er-galt-med-forbruk/

Dåstøl, A. (2010, 21 June). Dobbelt så mange på ADHD-medisin [Twice as many on ADHD medicine], *Vårt land*, pp. 6–7.

Ehrenberg, A. (2007). Trasformazioni della societa e trasformazioni della psichiatria [Transformations of society and changes in psychiatry]. *Rivista Sperimentale di Freniatria: La Rivista della Salute Mentale*, 131(3), 29–38.

Ehrenberg, A. (2010). *The weariness of the self: Diagnosing the history of depression in the contemporary age.* Montreal: McGill-Queen's University Press.

Ehrenreich, B. (2009). *Bright-sided. How the relentless promotion of positive thinking has undermined America.* New York: Metropolitan Books.

Ekeland, T.-J. (1999). *Meining som medisin: ein analyse av placebofenomenet og implikasjonar for terapi og terapeutiske teoriar* [Meaning as medicine: An analyis of the placebo phenomenon and implications for therapy and theory]. (PhD). Bergen: University of Bergen.

Ekeland, T.-J. (2006). Biologi som ideolog [Biology as ideology]. *Vardøger*, (30), 65–84.

Ekeland, T.-J. (2007). Psykoterapi – ein kulturkritikk [Psychotherapy – a cultural critique]. *Matrix. Nordisk tidsskrift for psykoterapi*, 24, 101–122.

References 177

Ellis, A., and Harper, R. A. (1975). *A new guide to rational living*. Hollywood, CA: Melvin Powers Wilshire Book Company.

Epictetus. (2004). *Enchiridion*. Mineola, NY: Dover.

Eriksen, E. O. (2001). *Demokratiets sorte hull: om spenningen mellom fag og politikk i velferdsstaten* [Democracy's black hole: On the tension between science and politics in the welfare state]. Oslo: Abstrakt forlag.

Eriksen, P.-K. (2010, 31 October). Viste at jeg er den største [I proved that I am the greatest]. *BT*, p. 24.

Eriksen, T. B. (2000). *Freuds retorikk: en kritikk av naturalismens kulturlære* (2. utg.) [Freud's rhetoric: A criticism of naturalism's teaching of culture (2nd ed.]. Oslo: Universitetsforlaget.

Ferdinand, R. (2009, 1 February). Prime Minister's questions. *The Observer*. Retrieved from http://www.guardian.co.uk/politics/2009/feb/01/gordonbrown-rio-ferdinand

Flinck, J., and Thorén, P. (2010, 8 February). Nya hånet mot Norge [The new ridicule against Norway]. *Aftonbladet*. Retrieved from http://www.aftonbladet.se/sportbladet/vintersport/skidor/article12142514.ab

Foucault, M. (1991). *Discipline and punishment: The birth of the prison*. London: Penguin.

Foucault, M. (1998). *The history of sexuality volume I: The will to knowledge*. London: Penguin.

Foucault, M. (2007). *Security, territory, population: Lectures at the Collège de France, 1977–78*. Basingstoke: Palgrave Macmillan.

Foucault, M. and Rabinow, P. (Eds) (1997). *Michel Foucault: Ethics, subjectivity, and truth*. New York: The New Press.

Franco, J. (2008). Extreme makeover: The politics of gender, class, and cultural identity. *Television and New Media*, 9(6), 471–486.

Freeman, G. L., and Harriman, P. L. (1946). *Twentieth century psychology: Recent developments in psychology*. New York: The Philosophical Library.

Freidson, E. (1988). *Profession of medicine: A study of the sociology of applied knowledge*. Chicago, IL: University of Chicago Press.

Freud, S. (1927). *The future of an illusion* (Vol. 21). London: Hogarth.

Freud, S. (1939). *Moses and monotheism* (Vol. 22). London Hogarth.

Freud, S. (1998). *Totem and taboo*. New York: Dover.

Freud, S. (2002). *Civilization and its discontents*. London: Penguin.

Frosh, S. (2003). Psychosocial studies and psychology: Is a critical approach emerging? *Human Relations*, 56, 1545–1567.

Fukuyama, F. (1992). *The end of history and the last man*. London: Penguin.

Furedi, F. (2004). *Therapy culture: Cultivating vulnerability in an uncertain age*. London: Routledge.

Førsund, S. K. (2010, 16 July). Trening vs. kirurgi [Working out vs. cosmetic surgery]. *Kvinner and Klær*, 11–18.

Gabbard, G. O. (2002). *The psychology of the Sopranos: Love, death, desire and betrayal in America's favorite gangster family*. New York: Basic Books.

Garcia, R. (Producer). (2008–2010). *In treatment* [Television series]. New York: HBO.

Gauchet, M. (1985). *The disenchantment of the world. A political history of religion.* Princeton, NJ: Princeton University Press.

Geertz, C. (2000). *The interpretation of cultures: Selected essay.* New York: Basic Books.

Genter, R. (2007). 'With great power comes great responsibility': Cold War culture and the birth of Marvel Comics. *Journal of Popular Culture,* 40(6), 953–978.

Gibbon, J. (Producer). (2002, 23 May). *The England patient* [Television broadcast]. London: BBC.

Gibbs, N. (2001, 24 June). The EQ factor. *Time.* Retrieved from http://content.time.com/time/magazine/article/0,9171,133181,00.html

Giddens, A. (1990). *The consequences of modernity.* Stanford, CA: Stanford University Press.

Giddens, A. (1991). *Modernity and self-identity: Self and society in the late modern age.* Cambridge: Polity Press.

Giddens, A. (1998). *The third way: The renewal of social democracy.* London: Polity Press.

Gjerstad, T. (2009, 29 August). Mellom linjene [Between the lines], *Dagbladet Magasinet,* pp. 23–27.

Goleman, D. (1996). *Emotional intelligence: Why it can matter more than IQ.* London: Bloomsbury.

Gray, P. (1993, 29 November). The assault on Freud. *Time.* Retrieved from http://www.time.com/time/magazine/article/0,9171,979704,00.html

Grimen, H. (2008). Profesjon og profesjonsmoral [Professions and professional ethics]. In A. Molander and L. I. Terum (Eds), *Profesjonsstudier* (pp. 144–160). Oslo: Universitetsforlaget.

Gross, M. L. (1978). *The psychological society: A critical analysis of psychiatry, psychotherapy, psychoanalysis and the psychological revolution.* New York: Random House.

Grønlund, O. J. (Producer). (2008, 5 December). *Grosvold* [Television broadcast]. Oslo: NRK.

Guardian, The. (2009, 23 October). Fabio Capello says fear led to England's Euro 2008 failure. *The Guardian.* Retrieved from http://www.guardian.co.uk/football/2009/oct/23/fabio-capello-england-fear-euro2008

Habermas, J. (2006). Religion in the public sphere. *European Journal of Philosophy,* 14(1), 1–25.

Hacking, I. (1995). *Rewriting the soul: Multiple personality and the sciences of memory.* Princeton, NJ: Princeton University Press.

Hacking, I. (1998). *Mad travelers: Reflections on the reality of transient mental illnesses.* Cambridge, MA: Harvard University Press.

Hagen, A. v. d. (2009, 27 March). Samfunnstjeneste som plikt [Community service as duty], *Morgenbladet.* Retrieved from http://www.morgenbladet.no/apps/pbcs.dll/article?AID=/20090327/OLEDER/172553519

Hagen, A. v. d., and Lindgren, L. (2009, 15 July). Kullsvart Bleken [Coal-black Bleken]. *Morgenbladet.* Retrieved from http://www.morgenbladet.no/apps/pbcs.dll/article?AID=/20090109/OKULTUR/742211942

References 179

Hall, G. S. (1923). *Life and confessions of a psychologist*. New York: D. Appleton and Company.

Halvorsen, S. (2010, 13 July). Skal jekke ned pappa [Aims to put dad in his place]. *Budstikka*, p. 11.

Hankiss, E. (2006). *The toothpaste of immortality: Self-construction in the consumer age*. Washington, DC: Woodrow Wilson Center Press.

Harvey, D. (2005). *A brief history of neoliberalism*. Oxford: Oxford University Press.

Havemann, E. (1957). *The age of psychology*. New York: Simon and Schuster.

Heelas, P. (1991). Reforming the self. Enterprise and the character of Thatcherism. In R. Keat and N. Abercrombie (Eds), *Enterprise culture* (pp. 72–92). London: Routledge.

Heelas, P. (1996a). Introduction: Detraditionalization and its rivals. In P. Heelas, S. Lash and P. Morris (Eds), *Detraditionalization. Critical reflections on authority and identity* (pp. 1–20). Cambridge, MA: Blackwell.

Heelas, P. (1996b). *The New Age movement: The celebration of the self and the sacralization of modernity*. Oxford: Blackwell.

Heller, J. (1994). *Catch-22*. London: Vintage.

Havemann, E. (1957). *The age of psychology*. New York: Simon and Schuster.

Helstrup, T. (2009). Psykologi og erkjennelse. Forsøker psykologien som vitenskap å løfte seg selv etter håret? [Psychology and epistemology: Does psychology as science attempt to pull itself by the hair?]. In B. R. Hansen and S. Magnussen (Eds), *Psykologiens yttergrenser* (pp. 13–30). Oslo: Abstrakt forlag.

Henriksen, A.-L. (2010, 16 July). 'Jeg måtte selv ta tak i livet mitt'. *Kvinner and Klær*, 44–46.

Hillestad, T. M. (2009). Forfeilet psykologikritikk [Mistaken critique of psychology]. *Tidsskrift for Norsk Psykologforening*, 46(5), 494–495.

Hinshaw, S. P., Scheffler, R. M., Fulton, B. D., Aase, H., Banaschewski, T., Cheng, W., Mattos, P., Holte, A., Levy, F., Sadeh, A., Sergeant, J. Taylor, E. and Weiss, M. D. (2011). International variation in treatment procedures for ADHD: Social context and recent trends. *Psychiatric Services*, 62(5), 459–464.

Hofgaard, T. L. (2007, 10 January). Småbarnterapi – god eller dårlig nyhet? [Therapy for small children – good or bad news?] *The Norwegian Psychological Association*. Retrieved from www.psykol.no?/did=9139172

Hofgaard, T. L. (2010, 24 February). Psykologi tar gull i OL [Psychology strikes gold in the Olympics]. *The Norwegian Psychological Association*. Retrieved from http://www.psykologforeningen.no/pf/Foreningen/Nyheter-og-aktuelt/Blogg-Merk-verden/Psykologi-tar-gull-i-OL

Holte, M. A. (2009, 13 May). TIL får mental hjelp [TIL gets mental assistance]. *Aftenposten*. Retrieved from http://fotball.aftenposten.no/eliteserien/article138521.ece

Horkheimer, M., and Adorno, T. W. (2002). *Dialectic of enlightenment: Philosophical fragments*. Stanford, CA: Stanford University Press.

Huxley, A. (1932). *Brave new world: A novel*. London: Chatto & Windus.

Hytner, D. (2008, 26 January). How professor Ramos became king of the cups. *The Guardian*. Retrieved from http://www.theguardian.com/football/2008/jan/26/newsstory.tottenhamhotspur

180 *The Therapeutic Turn*

Hytner, D. (2008, 3 November). Stupid dances, delirium and dreams of Europe as Redknapp's miracles enliven new-look Spurs. *The Guardian*. Retrieved from http://www.theguardian.com/football/2008/nov/03/premierleague-tottenham hotspur

Ingvaldsen, R. P. (2009, n. d.). Drillo-effekten? Om treningslære og psykologisering av prestasjoner [The Drillo effect? On the art of training and psychologisation of performances]. *Fotballtreneren*. Retrieved from http://www.trenerforeningen. no/printfriendly.asp?id=720

Illich, I. (1976). *Medical nemesis: The expropriation of health*. New York: Pantheon Books.

Illouz, E. (2003). *Oprah Winfrey and the glamour of misery: An essay on popular culture*. New York: Columbia University Press.

Illouz, E. (2007). *Cold intimacies: The making of emotional capitalism*. Cambridge: Polity Press.

Illouz, E. (2008). *Saving the modern soul: Therapy, emotions, and the culture of self-help*. Berkeley, CA: University of California Press.

Imber, J. B. (Ed.). (2004). *Therapeutic culture: Triumph and defeat*. New Brunswick, NJ: Transaction Publishers.

Jameson, F. (1984). Postmodernism, or the cultural logic of late capitalism. *New Left Review*, I/146, 53–92.

Jameson, F. (2003). *Postmodernism, or, the cultural logic of late capitalism*. Durham, NC: Duke University Press.

Jameson, F. (1994). *The seeds of time*. New York: Columbia University Press.

Jansz, J., and van Drunen, P. (Eds). (2004). *A social history of psychology*. Oxford: Blackwell.

Jarvis, M. (1999). *Sport psychology*. New York: Routledge.

Jensen, H. (2006). *Det faderløse samfund* [The fatherless society]. København: People's Press.

Jensen, T. Ø. (2010). Passivisert stat og politisert marked: utviklingstrekk i marked og styring [Passive state and politicised market: Trends in market and govern-ment]. In O. J. Madsen and S. A. Øyen (Eds), *Markedets fremtid. Kapitalismen i krise?* (pp. 81–113). Oslo: Cappelen Akademisk Forlag.

Johannessen, T. (2010, 3 July). For en oddsbombe! [What a bombshell!], *VG*, pp. 2–3.

Johansson, T. (2006). *Makeovermani: om dr Phil, plastikkirurgi och illusionen om det perfekta jaget* [Makeovermania: On Dr. Phil, cosmetic surgery and the illu-sion of the perfect self]. Stockholm: Natur och Kultur.

Johansson, T. (2007). *Experthysteri: kompetenta barn, curlingföräldrar och super-nannies* [Expert hysteria: Competent children, curling parents and supernan-nies]. Stockholm: Bokförlaget Atlas.

Johnston, D., and Saad-Filho, A. (Eds) (2005). *Neoliberalism: A critical reader*. London: Pluto Press.

Jung, C. G. (1972). *Two essays in analytical psychology* (Vol. 7). Princeton, NJ: Princeton University Press.

Jung, C. G., and Jaffe, A. (1963). *Memories, dreams, reflections*. London: Collins and Routledge and Kegan Paul.

Jørgensen, C. R. (2002). *Psykologien i senmoderniteten* [Psychology in late modernity]. København: H. Reitzel.

Kaye, H. L. (2003). Rieff's Freud and the tyranny of psychology. *Journal of Classical Sociology*, 3(3), 263–277.

Keat, R., Whiteley, N., and Abercrombie, N. (Eds) (1994). *The authority of the consumer*. London: Routledge.

King, J. and Gill, A. (1980). Natural's not in it [Recorded by Gang of Four]. On *Entertainment!* [CD]. London: EMI.

Koldtoft, G. (2010, 16 July). Coach deg selv! [Coach yourself!]. *Kvinner and Klær*, 42–44.

Konner, L. (Producer) and Taylor, A. (Director). (2006). *Zizek!* [Motion picture]. USA/Canada: Zeitgeist Films.

Kornspan, A. S. (2007). The early years of sport psychology: The work and influence of Pierre de Coubertin. *Journal of Sport Behavior*, 30, 77–93. Retrieved from http://www.thefreelibrary.com/The+early+years+of+sport+psychology%3A +the+work+and+influence+of+Pierre...-a0159644779

Kristiansen, I. (2013, 19 September). Hold maratonfarten oppe – og tenk på noe gøy [Keep up the marathon pace and think of something fun]. *Osloby*, p. 33.

Kristoffersen, A. (2009, 30 April). Skål for lærarane [A toast for the teachers], *Bergens Tidende*, p. 3.

Krogseth, O. (2001). Identitet og religion [Identity and religion]. In O. Krogseth and J.-O. Henriksen (Eds), *Pluralisme og identitet: kulturanalytiske perspektiver på nordiske nasjonalkirker i møte med religiøs og moralsk pluralisme* (pp. 155–184). Oslo: Gyldendal Akademisk.

Krogseth, O. (2003). Identitet i en pluralistisk kultur [Identity in a pluralistic culture]. In I. Markussen (Ed.), *'Å bli det du er' oppvekst – identitet – kontekst* (pp. 96–128). Oslo: Institutt for kulturstudier.

Kuper, S., and Szymanski, S. (2009). *Soccernomics: Why England lose, why Germany and Brazil win, and why the U.S., Japan, Australia, Turkey and even India are destined to become the new kings of the world's most popular sport.* London: Da Capo Press.

Kvale, S. (1992). Postmodern psychology: A contradiction in terms? In S. Kvale (Ed.), *Psychology and postmodernism* (pp. 31–57). London: Sage.

Kvale, S. (2003). The church, the factory and the market: Scenarios for psychology in a postmodern age. *Theory and Psychology*, 13(5), 579–603.

Kvam, L. H. (2008, 5 February). Landslaget trenger psykolog [The national side in need of a psychologist], *Dagbladet*, pp. 22–23.

Laclau, E., and Mouffe, C. (2001). *Hegemony and socialist strategy: Towards a radical democratic politics* (2nd ed.). London: Verso.

Lasch, C. (1991). *The culture of narcissism: American life in an age of diminishing expectations*. New York: Norton.

Leahey, T. H. (2012). *A history of psychology: From antiquity to modernity* (7th ed.). Boston, MA: Pearson.

Lears, T. J. J. (1983). From salvation to self-realization. Advertising and the therapeutic roots of the consumer culture, 1880–1930. In R. W. Fox and T. J. J. Lears (Eds), *The culture of consumption: Critical essays in American history 1880–1980* (pp. 1–38). New York: Pantheon Books.

Lears, T. J. J. (1985). The concept of cultural hegemony: Problems and possibilities. *The American Historical Review*, 90(3), 567–593.

Lears, T. J. J. (1994). *No place of grace: Antimodernism and the transformation of American culture, 1880–1920*. Chicago, IL: University of Chicago Press.

Lemke, T. (2001). The birth of bio-politics: Michel Foucault's lecture at the Collège de France on neo-liberal governmentality. *Economy and Society*, 30(2), 190–207.

Loss, C. P. (2002). Religion and the therapeutic ethos in twentieth-century American history. *American Studies International*, 40(3), 61–76.

Lykkeberg, R. (2007, 25 July). Midt i en føle- og famletid [In the middle of a feel and fumble period], *Information*. Retrieved from http://www.information. dk/130967

McGee, M. (2005). *Self-help, inc.: Makeover culture in American life*. Oxford: Oxford University Press.

Marciniak, B. (2004). *Path of empowerment. Pleiadian wisdom for a world in chaos*. Makawao, HI: Inner Ocean.

Marcuse, H. (1969). Repressive tolerance. In R. P. Wolff, B. Moore Jr and H. Marcuse (Eds), *A critique of pure tolerance* (pp. 95–137). Boston, MA: Beacon Press.

Marsdal, M. E., and Wold, B. (2005, 28 January). Den store lemenmarsjen [The great lemming march]. *Samtiden*. Retrieved from www.samtiden.no/marsdal-wold.html

Martin, R. (1988). Truth, power, self: An interview with Michel Foucault. In L. H. Martin, H. Guttman and P. H. Hutton (Eds), *Technologies of the self* (pp. 9–15). London: Tavistock.

Marx, K., and Engels, F. (1998). *The German ideology*. New York: Prometheus Books.

Maslow, A. H. (1943). A theory of human motivation. *Psychological Review*, 50(4), 370–396.

Maslow, A. H. (1968). *Toward a psychology of being* (2nd ed.). New York: D. Van Nostrand.

Maslow, A. H. (1993). *The farther reaches of human nature*. New York: Arkana.

Melucci, A. (1996). *The playing self: Person and meaning in the planetary society*. Cambridge: Cambridge University Press.

Meyer, J. W., Boli, J., Thomas, G. M., and Ramirez, F. O. (1997). World society and the nation-state. *The American Journal of Sociology*, 103(1), 144–181.

Mills, C. W. (2000). *The sociological imagination* (40th anniversary ed.). Oxford: Oxford University Press.

Mischel, W., Ebbesen, E. B., and Raskoff Zeiss, A. (1972). Cognitive and attentional mechanisms in delay of gratification. *Journal of Personality and Social Psychology*, 21(2), 204–218.

Moi, H. (2009, 27 December). Syke av prat om sorg? [Sick from talking about sorrow?], *Aftenposten*, p. 7.

Monbiot, G. (2010). *The age of consent*. London: Harper Perennial.

Moskowitz, E. S. (2001). *In therapy we trust*. Baltimore, MD: Johns Hopkins University Press.

Murphy, R. (Producer). (2003–2010). *Nip/tuck* [Television broadcast]. Dallas: FX.

Mydske, P. K., Claes, D. H., and Lie, A. (Eds) (2007). *Nyliberalisme: ideer og politisk virkelighet* [Neoliberalism: Ideas and political reality]. Oslo: Universitetsforlaget.

Nafstad, H. E. (2008). Assumptions and values about human suffering in research and practice: Towards an area ethics of psychology. In S. Robinson and J. Strain (Eds), *Ethics for living and working* (pp. 52–63). Leicester: Troubador Publishing.

Nafstad, H. E., Blakar, R. M., Carlquist, E., Phelps, J. M., and Rand Hendriksen, K. (2009). Globalization, neo-liberalism and community psychology. *American Journal of Community Psychology*, 43, 162–175.

Neumann, I. B., and Sending, O. J. (2003). Du skal regjere deg selv [Thou shalt govern thyself], *Le Monde Diplomatique*, Nordisk utgave, (5), pp. 1–2.

Nietzsche, F. (2001). *The gay science*. New York: Cambridge University Press.

Nilsen, H., and Østerberg, D. (1998). *Statskvinnen: Gro Harlem Brundtland og nyliberalismen* [The stateswoman: Gro Harlem Brundtland and neoliberalism]. Oslo: Forum Aschehoug.

Nolan, J. L. (1998). *The therapeutic state: Justifying government at century's end*. New York: New York University Press.

Norwegian Institute of Public Health. (2010). *Folkehelserapport 2010: helsetilstanden i Norge* [Public health report 2010: The health condition in Norway]. Oslo: The Norwgian Insitute of Publich Health.

Norwegian Institute of Publich Health. (2013, 4 March). ADHD – faktaark [ADHD – fact sheet]. *Norwegian Institute of Publich Health*. Retrieved from http://www.fhi.no/eway/default.aspx?pid=233andtrg=MainArea_5661andMainArea_5661=5631:0:15,4430:1:0:0:::0:0

Norwegian Psychological Association. (1998). *Etiske prinsipper for nordiske psykologer* [Ethical principles for Nordic psychologists]. Oslo: The Norwegian Psychological Association.

Norwegian Psychological Association. (2007, n. d.). *Norsk Psykologforening* [The Norwegian Psychological Association]. Retrieved from http://www.psykol.no/

NRK (Producer). (2010, 20 January). *Aktuelt* [Television broadcast]. Retrieved from http://www.nrk.no/nett-tv/klipp/600858/

NRK teletext. (2010, 5 February). Kan få psykologhjelp døgnet rundt [Psychology aid 24/7] [TV]. Oslo: NRK.

NTB. (2010, 8 July). Hopperne på barneski [Ski-jumpers on children's skis], *Adressaavisa*, p. 6.

Olsen, B. (2010). Norsk klinisk psykologforening [Norwegian clinical psychological association]. *Tidsskrift for Norsk Psykologforening*, 47(1), 65–67.

Overvik, J. (2013, 7 October). Den største forskjellen på Høgmo og Drillo [The greatest difference between Høgmo and Drillo]. *VG*. Retrieved from http://vgsporten.vg.no/2013/10/07/den-storste-forskjellen-pa-hogmo-og-drillo/

Parker, I. (2003, 12 October). Psychology is so critical, only Marxism can save us now . . . *psychminded.co.uk*. Retrieved from http://www.psychminded.co.uk/news/news2003/oct03/psychologysocritical.htm

Parker, I. (2007). *Revolution in psychology. Alienation to emancipation*. London: Pluto Press.

Parker-Pope, T. (2008, 24 November). Michael Phelps and the potential of A.D.H.D. *The New York Times*. Retrieved from http://well.blogs.nytimes.com/2008/11/24/michael-phelps-and-the-potential-of-adhd/?_r=0

Pawlik, K., and Rosenzweig, M. R. (2000). Psychological science: Content, methodology, history and profession. In K. Pawlik and M. R. Rosenzweig (Eds), *International handbook of psychology* (pp. 3–19). Thousand Oaks, CA: Sage.

Perkin, H. (1996). *The third revolution: Professional elites in the modern world*. New York: Routledge.

Petersen, A. (2005). Depression – selvets utilstrækkelighedspatologi [Depression: The pathology of the incomplete self]. In R. Willig and M. Østergaard (Eds), *Sociale patologier* (pp. 61–78). København: Hans Reitzel.

Polsky, A. J. (1991). *The rise of the therapeutic state*. Princeton, NJ: Princeton University Press.

Popper, K. (1963). *Conjectures and refutations: The growth of scientific knowledge*. New York: Harper and Row.

Prilleltensky, I. (1989). Psychology and the status quo. *American Psychologist*, 44(5), 795–802.

Princess Märtha Louise of Norway and Nordeng, E. (2009). *Møt din skytsengel* [The spiritual password: Enter your new world of bliss]. Oslo: Cappelen Damm.

Railo, W., Eriksson, S.-G., and Matson, H. (2001). *Inside football – the mental game*. London: Carlton.

Revell, L. (1996). The return of the sacred. In S. Wolton (Ed.), *Marxism, mythicism and modern theory* (pp. 111–134). Basingstoke: Macmillan.

Rieff, P. (1979). *Freud, the mind of the moralist* (3rd ed.). Chicago, IL: University of Chicago Press.

Rieff, P. (1987). *The triumph of the therapeutic: Uses of faith after Freud*. Chicago, IL: University of Chicago Press.

Rieff, P. (2006). *Sacred order/social order: My life among the deathworks. Illustrations of the aesthetics of authority* (Vol. 1). Charlottesville, VA: University of Virginia Press.

Ringheim, T. (2011, 8 December). Fra dop og svik til suksess [From drugs and betrayal to success]. *Dagbladet*. Retrieved from: http://www.dagbladet.no/2011/12/08/magasinet/god_torsdag/coaching/selvutvikling/dop/19338401/

Robinson, D. N. (1985). *Philosophy of psychology*. New York: Columbia University Press.

Rogers, C. R. (1961). *On becoming a person: A therapist's view of psychotherapy*. Boston, MA: Houghton Mifflin.

Rose, N. (1987). Beyond the public/private division: Law, power and family. *Journal of Law and Society*, 14(1), 61–76.

Rose, N. (1992). Governing the enterprising self. In P. Heelas and P. Morris (Eds), *The values of the enterprise culture* (pp. 141–163). London: Routledge.

Rose, N. (1996). *Inventing our selves: Psychology, power and personhood*. Cambridge: Cambridge University Press.

Rose, N. (1999). *Governing the soul: The shaping of the private self* (2nd ed.). London: Free Association Books.

Rose, N. (2007). *The politics of life itself.* Oxford: Princeton University Press.

Rösing, L. M. (2007). *Autoritetens genkomst* [The return of authority]. København: Tiderne Skifter.

Rozema, P. (Producer). (2007). *Tell me you love me* [Television series]. New York: HBO.

Ruddy, A. S. (Producer) and Coppola, F. F. (Director). (1972). *The godfather* [Motion picture]. USA: Paramount Pictures.

Sakshaug, S., Strøm, H., Berg, C., Blix, H. S., Litleskare, I., and Granum, T. (2013). *Drug consumption in Norway 2008–2012.* Oslo: Norwegian Institute of Public Health.

Sampson, E. E. (1983). *Justice and the critique of pure psychology.* New York: Plenum Press.

Sandvig, J. (2010a, 29 July). Fagfolk advarer mot gale ADHD-diagnoser [Specialists warn against wrong ADHD diagnosis], *Aftenposten,* pp. 4–5.

Schei, E., Norheim, O., Rørtveit, G., Lysebo, D., and Hjörleifsson, S. (2000). Legen – den enøyde samaritan? [The doctor – the one-eyed samaritan?]. *Tidsskrift for Den norske legeforrening,* 120(10), 1207–1209. Retrieved from http://tidsskriftet.no/article/4229/

Science Daily. (2009, 25 January). Makeover shows correspond with increased body anxiety. *Science Daily.* Retrieved from http://www.sciencedaily.com/releases/2009/01/090122163319.htm

Sel, T. (2010, 9 July). André i Europatoppen [André among the best in Europe], *Jærbladet,* p. 17.

Sennett, R. (1992). *The fall of public man.* New York: Norton.

Shoda, Y., Mischel, W., and Peake, P. K. (1990). Predicting adolescent cognitive and self-regulatory competencies from preschool delay of gratification: Identifying diagnostic conditions. *Developmental Psychology,* 26(6), 978–986.

Skjerdingstad, A. (2009, 16 November). Jeg har noen mentale arr [I have a few mental scars]. *TV2 Nettavisen.* Retrieved from http://www.nettavisen.no/sport/vinter/article2758204.ece

Skogstrøm, L. (2004, 8 November). Skepsis til grønn resept [Scepticism towards green prescriptions], *Bergens Tidende,* p. 5.

Skuterud, A. (2009, 4 September). PR-ekspert uten kontroll? [PR expert with no control?], *Dagbladet,* p. 58.

Smith, C., and Denton, M. L. (2005). *Soul searching: The religious and spiritual lives of American teenagers.* New York: Oxford University Press.

Solbrekke, T., and Karseth, B. (2006). Professional responsibility – an issue for higher education? *Higher Education,* 52(1), 95–119.

Strong, T. B. (1984). Psychoanalysis as a vocation: Freud, politics, and the heroic. *Political Theory,* 12(1), 51–79.

Sundbye, B. (2010, 23 March). Botox-salget til himmels [Sales of Botox rocketing]. *VG.* Retrieved from http://minmote.no/index.php/2010/03/botox-salget-til-himmels/

Sæther, E. O. (2010, 18 February). Bare gledestårer nå [Only happy tears now]. *Dagbladet.* Retrieved from http://www.dagbladet.no/2010/02/18/sport/tora_berger/ol_i_vancouver/skiskyting/esten_kommenterer/10474944/

Sæther, N. Ø. (2006). Kosmetiske inngrep som terapi [Cosmetic surgery as therapy]. *Samtiden* (2), 107–113.

Sætre, N.-J. (2010, 5 July). Andersen vurderer formasjonsendring [Andersen considers tactical change]. *Bladet Tromsø*, p. 23.

Sørhaug, H. C. (1996). *Fornuftens fantasier: antropologiske essays om moderne livsformer* [The fantasy of reason: Anthropological essays on modern life forms]. Oslo: Universitetsforlaget.

Taylor, C. (1999). Foreword. In C. Taylor (Ed.), *The disenchantment of the world. A political history of religion* (pp. ix–xv). Princeton, NJ: Princeton University Press.

Taylor, C. (2004). *Modern social imaginaries*. Durham, NC: Duke University Press.

Taylor, D., and Hunter, A. (2009, 13 March). Benítez denies outburst cost Liverpool title. *The Guardian*. Retrieved from http://www.guardian.co.uk/football/2009/mar/13/rafael-benitez-sir-alex-ferguson-liverpool-manchester-united

Törnblom, M. (2007). *Mer selvfølelse!: i kjærlighet og forhold, i foreldreskap og arbeidsliv* [More self-esteem! In the love life, parenthood and work life]. Oslo: Pantagruel.

Törnblom, M. (2010). *Selvfølelse nå!* [Self-esteem now!]. Oslo: Pantagruel.

University of Bergen. (1996). *Universitetet i Bergens historie. Bind I* [The history of the University of Bergen. Vol. I]. Oslo: Universitetsforlaget.

Vetlesen, A. J. (2007). Når valgfrihet blir valgtvang [When freedom to choose becomes duty to choose]. In T. Hylland Eriksen and A. J. Vetlesen (Eds), *Frihet* (pp. 49–78). Oslo: Universitetsforlaget.

Vetlesen, A. J. (2009a). Fellesskap i individualismens tidsalder [Community in the age of individualism]. In H. E. Nafstad and R. M. Blakar (Eds), *Fellesskap og individualisme* (pp. 19–55). Oslo: Gyldendal Akademisk.

Vetlesen, A. J. (2009b). *Frihetens forvandling: essays og artikler 2002–2008* [The transformation of freedom: Essays and articles 2002–2008]. Oslo: Universitetsforlaget.

Vetlesen, A. J. (2009c, 1 December). Total kapitalisme [Total capitalism], *Klassekampen*, p. 3.

Vetlesen, A. J. (2010, 17 April). Sannhet og individ [Truth and individual], *Klassekampen*, pp. 24–25.

Vitz, P. C. (1991). *Psychology as religion: The cult of self-worship*. Grand Rapids, MI: W. B. Eerdmans.

Walkerdine, V. (Ed.) (2002). *Challenging subjects: Critical psychology for a new millennium*. New York: Palgrave.

Walsh, M., and Bahnisch, M. (2002). Political subjects, workplaces and subjectivities. In V. Walkerdine (Ed.), *Challenging subjects: Critical psychology for a new millennium* (pp. 23–38). New York: Palgrave.

Weber, M. (2001). *The Protestant ethic and the spirit of capitalism*. London: Routledge.

Weiner, M. (Producer). (2007–). *Mad men* [Television broadcast]. New York: AMC.

Weissmann, M. M. (1992). The changing rate of major depression. *Journal of the American Medical Association*, 268, 3098–3105.

White, M., and Epston, D. (1990). *Narrative means to therapeutic ends*. New York: Norton.

Willig, R. (2005). Selvrealiseringsoptioner – vor tids fordring om anerkendelse [Self-realizations options: Contemporary demands on recongition]. In R. Willig and M. Østergaard (Eds), *Sociale patologier* (pp. 13–40). København: Hanz Reitzel.

Wolton, S. (Ed.). (1996). *Marxism, mysticism and modern theory*. London: Macmillan.

Women and Clothes. (2010, 16 July). Ny kk-ekspert! [New KK expert!]. *Kvinner and Klær*, 71.

Woolfolk, A. (2003). The therapeutic ideology of moral freedom. *Journal of Classical Sociology*, 3(3), 247–262.

World Federation for Mental Health. (2012, n. d.). *Depression: A global crisis*. Retrieved from http://www.wfmh.org/2012DOCS/WMHDay%202012%20SMALL%20FILE%20FINAL.pdf

World Health Organization. (2006, n. d.). *Constitution of the World Health Organization – basic documents, forty-fifth edition, supplement*. Retrieved from http://www.who.int/governance/eb/who_constitution_en.pdf

Žižek, S. (1999). *The ticklish subject: The absent centre of political ontology*. London: Verso.

Zondervan, A. A. W. (2005). *Sociology and the sacred: An introduction to Philip Rieff's theory of culture*. Toronto: University of Toronto Press.

Øgar, S. (2009, 8 February). Jakten på Drillo-magien [The hunt for the Drillo magic]. *VG*, pp. 8–10.

Øiestad, G. (2009). *Selvfølelsen* [Self-esteem]. Oslo: Gyldendal.

Øiestad, G. (2011). *Selvfølesen hos barn og unge* [Self-esteem among children and youths]. Oslo: Gyldendal.

Østerberg, D. (1974). *Emile Durkheims samfunnslære* [The sociology of Émile Durkheim]. Oslo: Pax.

Østli, K. S. (2008, 27 June). Jan Thomas-evangeliet [The gospel of Jan Thomas]. *A-magasinet*, 6–12.

Åbyholm, F. E. (2003). Plastikkirurgi i et kosmetisk marked [Plastic surgery in a cosmetic market]. *Tidsskrift for Den norske legeforening*, 123(18), 2554.

Index

Aambø, J. 101
Aamodt, I. A. 102
accountability 16, 123
ADHD (Attention-Deficit/Hyperactive Disorder) 123–8
Adler, A. 79, 168
Adorno, T. W. 60, 86–7, 88–9, 107, 118
advertising 18–19, 26–7
Aftenposten 127
Aftonbladet 101
Agamben, G. 162
Aguiluz, A. F. 93
alienation 19, 30, 83, 160–1
Altaposten 139
Altman, I. 8
American Psychological Association (APA) 1, 142–3
Ammann, S. 102
analytical psychology 20
Andersen, L. 102
Andersen, M. K. 93, 94
Andersen, T. L. 94
Andrejevic, M. 77, 78
Anrell, L. 101–2, 103
Apotek 1 125
Aristotle 17–18, 115
Arnet, E. 8
Askeland, Ø. 102, 105
Askheim, O. P. 120
astrology 88–9
authority: crisis of 6, 29–44; ethics of self-disclosure 39–43; Freud's view 30, 31, 32–3, 34–9, 40–3, 56, 63; morality 13, 25, 34, 36, 40, 116; Nietzsche's view 30–1, 34–5; parental authority 126; psychology 116; Rieff's critique 29, 31–2, 33–5, 36–8, 39–41, 42–4
autonomy 115

Bacon, F. 87
Bahnisch, M. 165
Bakke Foss, A. 52
Barsky, A. J. 145
Baudrillard, J. 26
Bauman, Z. 12, 52, 53
Beasley, R. 101
Beck, A. T. 70
Beck, U. 5, 11, 12, 13–15, 153, 163
Becker, D. 121–2
Beckham, D. 99
Bellah, R. N. 46
Benitez, R. 95
Bent, D. 95
Berbatov, D. 95
Berger, T. 103
Berggren, A. 81
Bergsli, B. 93
Big Brother 77, 78
Bjørgen, M. 102–3, 105
Bjørndalen, O. E. 104
Blair, T. 106, 117
Bloom, A. 65–6
Bourdieu, P. 112, 122
Brinkmann, S. 2
Brown, D. 75
Brown, G. 94
Bruland, K.-M. 131
Brundtland, G. H. 110

Brustad, S. 141, 144–5
Burckhardt, J. 38
Byrne, R. 12, 75–6

California Task Force to Promote
  Self-Esteem and Personal and Social
  Responsibility 119, 120
Capello, F. 101, 104, 105
capitalism 22–4, 26, 151
Carroll, J. 57–8, 62
Casey, M. 33
Center for Crisis Psychology 145–6
children, therapy for 141–7
Chomsky, N. 154
Christiansen, B. 146–7, 153
climate change 63–4
clinical psychology 13–14,
  17, 151, 167
cognitive psychology 70
collective thought and action 63–4
consciousness 41, 42, 150, 161, 164
consumer power 122
consumer society 6, 11–27; capitalism
  and Protestantism 22–4, 25; the
  enterprise self and the therapeutic
  ethos 24–5; individualisation 11–17;
  self-actualisation 17–22, 23, 25, 27
cosmetic surgery 78–81
Coubertin, P. de 105
critical psychology 129, 164–5
Cruikshank, B. 118–20, 132, 133, 134
cultural critics 86–8
culture 43
Cushman, P. 17, 18–19, 20, 22, 129,
  156

Dagbladet 95–6
Dahlmann, C. H. 10 25
Dahn, K. 139
Dale Oen, A. 4, 93, 94, 106
Dale, R. S. 93
Davis, K. 16–17
De Tocqueville, A. 120
Denton, M. L. 47–8, 50
depression 21, 25, 132, 140, 170
Dineen, T. 154
Dubrofsky, R. E. 78
Dufour, D.-R. 61
Durkheim, É. 21, 55, 169
duties 41, 49, 59, 60, 62, 63
Dylan, B. 60

Dyregrov, A. 145–6
Døving, R. 26

Ehrenberg, A. 1, 20, 21, 61, 170
Ehrenreich, B. 76
Eisenstadt, S. N. 70
Ekeland,T.-J. 125, 126, 157
Ellis, A. 70
empowerment 24–5, 75, 77, 81, 111,
  117, 119–23
the empty self 18–19, 26, 130
Engels, F. 41, 113, 164
The England Patient (BBC
  documentary) 98–9
English Football Association 98
Enlightenment 24, 34, 40, 54, 58, 65,
  75–6, 86–7, 147, 169
the enterprise self 24–5
Epictetus 75
Eriksen, E. O. 5
Eriksen, T. B. 33
Eriksson, S.-G. 98–100
eros 35, 43
*Ethical Principles for Nordic
  Psychologists* 152
Evensen, J. R. 103
Extreme Makeover 78, 79

the fatherless society 59–61, 157
fatigue effect 60
feminism 62, 86
Ferdinand, R. 94
Ferguson, A. 95
finance 4
Fjørtoft, J. Å 97
football 93, 94–101, 106–7
Foucault, M. 111, 114, 131, 133, 149,
  155, 158, 161–2
Franklin, B. 23
freedom 27, 29, 30, 38–9, 40, 133
Freidson, E. 131, 142, 147–8
Freud, S.: on authority 30, 31, 32–3,
  34–9, 40–3, 56, 63; on guilt 57,
  58–9; psychoanalysis 2, 3, 58, 61,
  66, 105, 169
Frosh, S. 9, 169
Furedi, F. 1, 106, 117, 118
Førsund, S. K. 80

Garcia, R. 89
Gauchet, M. 46, 62

Geertz, C. 22, 85
gender roles 16–17, 82, 86, 121–2, 126
Giddens, A. 111, 159
Gill, R. 53
Gjerstad, T. 81, 82
globalised media 83–4
Gnosticism 27, 50, 51, 74
The Godfather 90–1
Goethe, J. W. von 42
governance 113–17, 132
governmentality 118, 132
Gray, P. 66
green prescription scheme 121
Grimen, H. 136–7, 151
Gross, M. L. 1, 136
Grosvold, A. 81
The Guardian 95
guilt 30, 57–9, 60, 61

Habermas, J. 45
Hacking, I. 127
Hagen, A. v. d. 60, 156
Hall, G. S. 1
Halvorsen, S. 107
Hammer, Ø. 104, 105
Hankiss, E. 26
Hansen, M. B. 93
happiness 64, 139–41
Hareide, Å. 96–7, 104
Harvey, D. 110
Haug, S. 142
Havemann, E. 1, 136
health 3, 62, 83–4, 117, 139, 145–6
Heelas, P. 25, 50, 51, 132
Heller, J. 105
Hellner, M. 101, 103
Helstrup, T. 9
Henriksen, K. 145–6
Heseltine, M. 132
Hobbes, T. 38
Hodgson, R. 101
Hofgaard, T. L. 4, 103, 104, 138, 141–2, 143–4, 145, 146, 147, 153
Holmen, A. 138
Holte, M. A. 96, 107
Horkheimer, M. 86–7, 88
humanistic psychology 18–22, 51, 69, 129
Huxley, A. 8–9
Hytner, D. 95
Høgmo, P.-M. 98
Høybråten, D. 121

identity 52–3, 73
ideology 7, 26, 38, 148, 153–4, 160–2; *see also* neoliberalism
Illich, I. 10
Illouz, E. 2, 54, 67, 69–70, 84, 85–6, 87–8, 167, 168
Imber, J. B. 1
In Treatment 89
individualisation 11–17, 62; consequences of 12–13; and neoliberalism 112, 131; and psychology 13–15, 17, 163–4, 165; and psychotherapy 15–17; *see also* self-actualisation
individualism 12, 19, 60, 63–4, 110, 111; and religion 46, 47–8; therapeutic individualism 48–9
inferiority complex 79
Ingvaldsen, R. P. 97–8, 106
International Handbook of Psychology, The 166
International Society of Sports Psychology 104

Jacobsen, A. 102, 103, 105
James, W. 166
Jameson, F. 84
Jansz, J. 9
Jensen, H. 59–60, 62, 63, 157
Johannessen, T. 95
Johansson, T. 73
Jönsson, J. 93
Journal of the Norwegian Psychological Association, The 143
Jung, C. G. 2, 20, 61
Juul, J. 72
Jørgensen, C. R. 17, 19, 129, 130–1

Karseth, B. 137, 138
Keegan, K. 98
Kojonkoski, M. 93
Koldtoft, G. 21
Koppinen, M. 96, 107
Kornspan, A. S. 105
Kristiansen, I. 93
Krogseth, O. 51, 52, 53, 130
Kuper, S. 106, 107
Kvale, S. 47, 53–4, 65, 71, 113, 128–9, 166
Kvam, L. H. 96, 97

Laclau, R. 162
Larsen, T. 4
Lasch, C. 24, 76, 160
Lears, T. J. J. 3, 42
Lee, S. 5
Lemke, T. 112
liberalism 38, 59–60, 118, 133
liberation 26, 39, 120
Lindgren, L. 156
Loss, C. P. 46
Luther, M. 46–7
Lykkeberg, R. 63, 157

McClaren, S. 100–1
McGraw, P. 73
Mad Men 89
Mandelstam, N. 57
Marciniak, B. 74–5
Marcuse, H. 86, 160–1
Märtha Louise, Princess of Norway
    49–50, 51
Marx, K. 40, 41, 113, 164
Maslow, A. H. 18, 20
Mead, G. H. 150
Melucci, A. 83, 84
Mills, C. W. 11, 170
Mischel, W. 109
misery 84–6
modernity 5, 29, 30, 33–4, 40, 43, 52,
    65, 163
Moi, H. 145, 146
morality: and authority 13, 25, 34, 36,
    40, 116; and guilt 57–8; therapeutic
    individualism 48–9
Moskowitz, E. S. 46, 85
mother rule 59
Mouffe, C. 162
Murphy, R. 79
Mydske, P. K. et al. 110
Mørch, W.-T. 127

Nafstad, H. E. et al. 110, 137
narrative therapy 129–30
neo-fundamentalism 45, 52, 53
neo-religiosity 45, 46, 49–54
neo-spiritualism 45, 46, 52
neoconservatism 62–3
neoliberalism 7, 109–34; ADHD
    epidemic 123–8; the art of governing
    113–17; birds of a feather 131–2;
    defined 40, 110–11; empowerment

120–2; and individualisation 112,
    131; new social glue 117–18; the
    postmodern subject 128–31; and
    professional ethics 151, 158–9; and
    self-actualisation 112–13, 115, 132;
    self-esteem movement 73, 118–20;
    self-government 77, 119–20, 123–4,
    138, 162–3; social psychology 111–13,
    149; transfer of power? 122–3
Neumann, I. B. 109, 116–17
New Age 46, 50–1, 55
Nielsen, P. 156
Nietzsche, F. 20, 23, 30–1, 34–5, 62
nihilism 30, 40
Nilsen, E. 139
Nolan, J. L. 1, 24–5, 167
nomos 29
Nordeng, E. 49–50
Norwegian Football Association 98
Norwegian Institute of Public Health
    125, 140
Norwegian Medical Association 148,
    152
Norwegian Psychological Association
    (NPF) 4, 5, 82, 103, 135–6, 138, 142,
    143–4, 146, 147, 152
NRK 71, 101

Oedipus complex 42, 59
Olsen, B. 143
Olsen, E. 'Drillo' 97–8
Olympic Games 4, 101–3, 104, 105
Oprah Winfrey Show, The 84–6, 87–8,
    121
Owen, M. 99

Parker, I. 37, 142–3, 164, 165, 171
Pawlik, K. 166
Pensgaard, A. M. 96, 116
Perkin, H. 135
Phelps, M. 4
Plätzer, K. T. 4
Polsky, A. J. 1
Popper, K. 105, 168
post-politics 162–7
postmodernism/postmodernity 52–3,
    61, 65, 67, 74, 84, 128–31
poverty 106
power 122–3, 132–3, 158–9, 162–3;
    see also empowerment
Prilleltensky, I. 16, 164, 165

professional ethics 7, 135–54, 158;
déformation professionelle 147–9,
153; the future of psychology 138–9;
health and happiness 139–41; social
responsibility 136–8, 159–60,
164; therapy for children 141–7;
underlying values 149–53
Protestantism 22–4, 25, 46–7, 54
psychiatry 1–2, 127, 139
psychoanalysis 2, 30, 33, 35, 37,
39–42, 61, 105; and morality 58;
scepticism 66, 168
psychologists 7–8
psychology 1–2; analytical psychology
20; authority 116; clinical
psychology 13–14, 17, 151, 167;
cognitive psychology 70; in crisis?
65–7, 155–7; critical psychology
129, 164–5; development of 2–6,
9–10, 114–16, 156–7; the future
of 138–9; humanistic psychology
18–22, 51, 69, 129;
and individualisation 13–15, 17,
163–4, 165; as a science 1, 2, 5,
7, 31, 113, 148–9, 165–7; social
psychology 111–13, 149; as a
social science 35, 66; techniques
115–16; terminology 7–8; *see also*
professional ethics
Psychology Today 3
psychotherapy 5–6, 15–17, 40–1
public health 83–4

Rabinow, P. 155
Railo, W. et al. 98–100
Ramos, J. 95
reality TV 76–8, 81–4, 161; *see
also The England Patient* (BBC
documentary)
Redknapp, H. 95
reflexive modernity 163
reframing 16
religion 6, 29, 45–64, 158; all or
nothing 61–4; the fatherless society
59–61, 157; Freud's view 32–3;
function of 54–7; God as cosmic
therapist 47–9; guilt 30, 57–9,
60, 61; individualism 46, 47–8;
neo-fundamentalism 45, 52, 53;
neo-religiosity 45, 46, 49–54; neo-
spiritualism 45, 46, 52; Protestantism

22–4, 25, 46–7, 54; and psychology
46–7, 53–4, 167–8; return of religion
45, 46; therapeutic individualism
48–9; universal codes 83–4
religiosity 46, 47–8, 51, 52, 53
repression 35–6
Revell, L. 51, 56
Rieff, P. 1, 29, 31–2, 33–5, 36–8,
39–41, 42–4, 46, 56–7, 59, 63
rights 41, 48, 59–60, 63
Ringdal, K. T. 81–2, 83
Robben, A. 94–5
Roethke, T. 169
Rogers, C. R. 20, 69
Rose, N. 66, 114, 115, 116, 132–3
Rosenzweig, M. R. 166
Rösing, L. M. 62
Rozema, P. 89

the sacred 29, 46, 51, 55–6, 58
Sampson, E. E. 149–51
Sandvig, J. 127
Schei, E. et al. 152–3
Scripture, E. W. 166
secularisation 45
Sel, T. 93
Selden, C. 78
self-actualisation 17–22, 23, 25,
27, 56, 60–1, 62–3, 64, 160; and
neoliberalism 112–13, 115, 132
self-awareness 41
self-confidence 72
self-control 41, 109, 125; *see
also* ADHD (Attention-Deficit/
Hyperactive Disorder)
self-disclosure 39–43
self-esteem 64, 71–3, 84–6, 113, 117,
118–20, 132; *see also* cosmetic
surgery
self-government 77, 119–20, 123–4,
138, 162–3
self-help culture 6, 20, 69–91;
astrology 88–9; cultural critics 86–8;
the glamour of misery 84–6; gnostic
surgery 78–81; the inner universe
12–13, 74–6; reality and therapy
76–8; reality television/reality policy
81–3; self-help literature 21, 71–4;
strong women 86; television drama
89–91; universal codes 83–4
self-perception 150–1

self-realisation 80
self-reflection 5, 9, 17
Sending, O. J. 109, 116–17
Sennett, R. 82–3
shame 61–2
Simonsen, M. 81
Skogstrøm, L. 121
Skuterud, A. 82
Smelser, N. 117
Smith, C. 47–8, 50
social imaginaries 2
social psychology 111–13, 149
social responsibility 113, 119, 135–8,
    152–3, 159–60, 164
social sciences 8, 19, 35, 65–6
the sociological imagination 170–1
Socrates 58
Solberg, E. 81–2, 86
Solbrekke, T. 137, 138
The Sopranos 89–90, 91
Southgate, G. 99
sports and psychology 4, 6–7, 93–107;
    football 93, 94–101, 106–7; the 'mental
    aspect' 93–101, 102, 104, 105–7; mirror
    of society? 103–7; Olympic Games
    4, 101–3, 104, 105; psychologists on
    call 101–3; skiing 93, 101, 102–3, 105;
    swimming 4, 93, 94, 106
sports psychology 98, 100, 101, 102,
    103–5
Stanford marshmallow experiment 109,
    123
Stoltenberg, J. 110
stress 15, 121–2
Strong, T. B. 2
sublimation 36
suffering 54–5, 61, 84–6, 87–8, 167
suicide 21
super-ego 34, 57, 62
Svindal, A. L. 102
Szymanski, S. 106, 107
Sæther, E. Ø. 103
Sæther, N. Ø. 80
Sætre, N.-J. 94
Sødal, H. 52
Sørhaug, T. 154

Tajet-Foxell, B. 103
Taylor, C. 2
television drama 89–91; *see also* reality TV

thanatos 35
Thatcher, M. 132
theodicy 54–5, 85, 167
therapeutic culture 2–3, 6, 30, 32,
    42–3, 46, 55, 59, 63, 117–18, 162,
    168–9; *see also* self-help culture; the
    therapeutic turn
therapeutic ethos 2, 3, 6, 24–5, 32,
    45–6, 61, 70–1, 84, 169; *see also*
    Protestantism
therapeutic individualism 48–9
therapeutic society 2–3
the therapeutic turn 31, 167–70
therapy 7–8, 118; narrative therapy
    129–30
the third force *see* humanistic
    psychology
Thomas, J. 81
Time magazine 66, 84
Törnblom, M. 71–4, 80–1, 86
Tvedt, B. 80

universal codes 83–4
utilitarian ethic 24–5

values 33; *see also* professional ethics
Van Drunen, P. 9
Vetlesen, A. J. 38, 63–4, 73, 123, 126
VG 97
victim culture 59, 60, 85, 86
Vitz, P. 54

Walkerdine, V. 165
Walsh, M. 165
Weber, M. 22–4, 85, 147
welfare state 117
Weltzien, A. H. 107
Willig, R. 112–13
Winfrey, O. 84–6, 87–8, 121
Wolton, S. 51
Women and Clothes 21, 25, 71, 80
work ethic 63
World Federation for Mental Health 132
World Health Organization 3, 132

Žižek, S. 161–2, 163
Øgar, S. 97
Øiestad, G. 09 72, 73–4, 82, 113
Østli, K. S. 81
Øvrebø, T. H. 101–2, 103–4, 105